EXPORTING AMERICAN DREAMS

Also by Mary L. Dudziak

Cold War Civil Rights: Race and the Image of American Democracy

Legal Borderlands: Law and the Construction of American Borders
  (coedited with Leti Volpp)

September 11 in History: A Watershed Moment? (as editor)

EXPORTING AMERICAN DREAMS

THURGOOD MARSHALL'S AFRICAN JOURNEY

MARY L. DUDZIAK

OXFORD
UNIVERSITY PRESS

2008

OXFORD
UNIVERSITY PRESS

Oxford University Press, Inc., publishes works that further
Oxford University's objective of excellence
in research, scholarship, and education.

Oxford   New York
Auckland   Cape Town   Dar es Salaam   Hong Kong   Karachi
Kuala Lumpur   Madrid   Melbourne   Mexico City   Nairobi
New Delhi   Shanghai   Taipei   Toronto

With offices in
Argentina   Austria   Brazil   Chile   Czech Republic   France   Greece
Guatemala   Hungary   Italy   Japan   Poland   Portugal   Singapore
South Korea   Switzerland   Thailand   Turkey   Ukraine   Vietnam

Published by Oxford University Press, Inc.
198 Madison Avenue, New York, New York 10016

www.oup.com

Oxford is a registered trademark of Oxford University Press

Library of Congress Cataloging-in-Publication Data
Dudziak, Mary L., 1956–
Exporting American dreams : Thurgood Marshall's African journey / Mary L. Dudziak.
p.   cm.
Includes bibliographical references and index.
ISBN 978-0-19-532901-8
1. Civil rights—Kenya—History—Sources.
2. Constitutional history—Kenya—Sources.
3. Marshall, Thurgood, 1908–1993.   4. Judges—United States—Biography.
5. Kenya—Politics and government—To 1963.   I. Title.
KSK2095.D83 2008
342.676208'5—dc22   2008001587

1   3   5   7   9   8   6   4   2

Printed in the United States of America
on acid-free paper

to Bill

CONTENTS

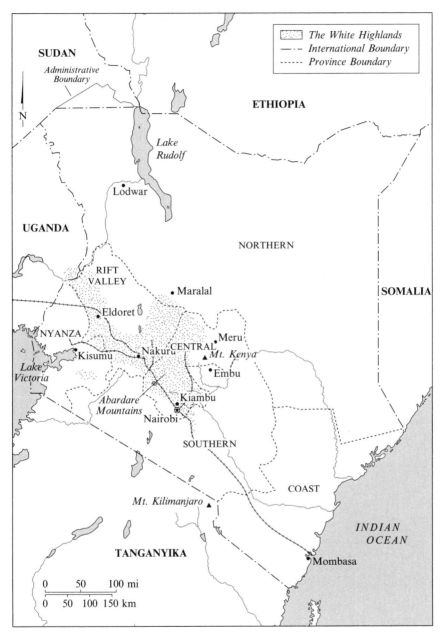

SUDAN

*Administrative
Boundary*

N

ETHIOPIA

*Lake
Rudolf*

• Lodwar

UGANDA

NORTHERN

RIFT
VALLEY

• Maralal

SOMALIA

• Eldoret

NYANZA

Meru

• Kisumu   • Nakuru   CENTRAL   ▲ *Mt. Kenya*

*Lake
Victoria*

• Embu

*Abardare
Mountains*   • Kiambu

⊗ Nairobi

SOUTHERN

COAST

Mt. Kilimanjaro ▲

INDIAN
OCEAN

TANGANYIKA

• Mombasa

0   50   100 mi

0   50   100   150 km

Map of Kenya.

ILLUSTRATIONS

EXPORTING
AMERICAN
DREAMS

INTRODUCTION

Africa is the birthplace of the blackman, but his home is in the world.

         —Tom Mboya, 1969

IT WAS JANUARY 1960, BUT IT WAS SUMMER. An American lawyer arrived in a new land, but he called it his home.

Thurgood Marshall had grown up with family legends about his strong Congo forbears, about a grandfather so ornery as to lead a frustrated slave master to release him. But the Africa his family had been stolen from was something of a mystery, until that January when Thurgood Marshall went home.[1]

Marshall was a civil rights legend in America when he began his African journey. It became one of the great adventures of his life. He followed a path well worn by others, but his journey would be different. He would not travel by riverboat into the Congo, as had American missionaries, or sail along the West African coast as did the poet Langston Hughes. Marshall flew first to Monrovia, then on to Nairobi. He was in search not of souls to save or stories to tell. Instead, Africa was on the cusp of revolution. Many hands were needed. He had come to help.[2]

"Fifty years ago it was a dark continent. Unknown," wrote Tom Mboya, a young African in 1959. "Many people from far-off lands have thought of her in terms of the jungles, the wild beasts, the 'unspoiled native people.'" But Africa was "awakening" in the 1960s. Soon, resistance leaders would become presidents, citizens would vote, and Africans would govern themselves. This awakening attracted Thurgood Marshall. But he was not just any American lawyer, with legal wares to peddle to a new nation in need of new laws.[3]

Marshall's role as an American legend complicated his African journey. In tales of other transnational crossings, Americans encounter a foreign land and along the way learn something about themselves. Another nation becomes the occasion to know one's own nation, what it is, and what it means to be a part of it. Historian James Campbell wrote that "Africa has served historically as one of the chief terrains on which African Americans have negotiated their relationship to American society.... When an African American asks, 'What is Africa to me?' he or she is also asking, 'What is America to me?'" Encountering America in a journey overseas is part of this story. But Marshall's travel intersected with others. There was Tom Mboya, a young Kenyan nationalist, whose rise to prominence in his own country was aided by his American ties. And there were other sorts of crossings. Kenya, an emerging nation, and the United States, a wary global power, engaged each other, plotting their futures. Through these intersecting stories, these multiple transnational crossings, we can unravel what Marshall did, what impact he had, what it meant for him. It is a story of a man at work in the world at a time when that work held global meaning.[4]

Marshall surely preferred not to be a symbol, but this was not his choice. He had been the lead lawyer for the plaintiffs in a case that had captivated the world. *Brown v. Board of Education* involved local struggles in American communities; it involved students and parents and teachers. But local struggles had international ramifications in the 1950s cold war world, for racial segregation in American schools troubled U.S. allies. How could American democracy be a model for other nations, many wondered, when in America itself children were sent to different schools because of their race, and when so many African Americans were disenfranchised? The U.S. government tried its best to respond to foreign critics, but by 1954 it was clear that the best way to demonstrate to the world that American democracy was a just form of government was to achieve meaningful civil rights reform. The Justice Department made this argument to the Supreme Court in *Brown*, and when the Court overturned school segregation, American diplomats used *Brown* as their prime example that democracy (not communism) would bring meaningful progress to peoples of the world.[5]

Brown became a symbol of American democracy at work, and *Brown*'s key players became more visible, at home and abroad. Chief Justice Earl Warren, author of the *Brown* decision, was derided by American segregationists, but overseas he became a household name. His role in *Brown* made him the right stand-in for President Dwight Eisenhower during a trip to India at a time when the United States hoped to counter the impact of a visit by Soviet leader Nikita Khrushchev. Warren was introduced at Delhi University as a man who needed no introduction, for he "rose to fame in 28 minutes of that Monday afternoon as he read out his momentous decision outlawing racial segregation in American public schools."[6]

And then there was Marshall, the nation's leading civil rights lawyer in the 1950s. He had worked with Charles Hamilton Houston, the legendary civil rights pioneer, in earlier years. His team in *Brown* included a brain trust of civil rights

Thurgood Marshall conferring with NAACP attorney W. J. Durham (right) in federal court in Dallas, Texas, during arguments in a Dallas school desegregation case, July 30, 1959. (© Bettmann/CORBIS)

lawyers: Robert Carter, Constance Baker Motley, Jack Greenberg, and others. The lawyers themselves exemplified a story that the United States had long told the world: that opportunity abounded for African Americans, that they worked in important fields alongside whites, and that the best and the brightest were committed to achieving a progressive vision of democracy. Marshall did not set out to fulfill an image his nation had crafted for the world, but in 1960, when he went to Africa, he did just that.[7]

The world often needed reassurance about race and American democracy. Other nations had their ethnic problems, of course. But there was a reason that race figured so prominently in cold war politics. In 1947, President Harry S Truman warned the nation that Americans faced a cold war battle against an adversary that was evil because it denied rights to its own people. There were two ways of life, two systems of government opposing each other. The Soviet Union relied on "terror and oppression...fixed elections, and the suppression of personal freedoms." American democracy embraced "free institutions, representative government, free elections, guarantees of individual liberty, freedom of speech and religion, and freedom from political oppression." A central cold war battleground, American diplomats believed, was a war of ideas. To win, the United States needed to convince others that American democracy was superior. When a black soldier in police custody was beaten in a Southern jail, when there was a lynching, the news was soon carried in newspapers worldwide. Even America's friends decried race discrimination as the nation's Achilles heel. If there was a global consensus about anything during the cold war, it was that if the United States hoped to spread democracy, it had to begin by practicing it at home. *Brown* in 1954 seemed solid evidence that racial barriers were coming down. What better representative was there of this racial progress than *Brown's* lead attorney: an African American who was raised in segregation but would play a pivotal role in putting it to rest?[8]

Symbols can serve various purposes, as Marshall's story reveals. By simply being himself, he could help recast the image of American democracy in Africa. But what role could he play for Africans themselves? At the time Marshall entered Kenyan politics, the nationalists needed more than the legal ideas he brought with him to their struggle for independence. They needed legitimacy before a world that thought of Kenyan Africans as murderous savages. White settlers in Kenya were their adversaries, and yet they needed to show that an African government would be fair to whites if Africans gained power. What better evidence that they were committed to a rule of law than to see them, the Africans, advised by Thurgood Marshall, who was committed to using law, not violent revolution, as a means of changing society? What could show more powerfully that an African government would protect rights of a white minority than to have the world's leading minority rights lawyer at their side during constitutional negotiations?[9]

Marshall's African journey was during a time when Kenyans hoped to create a democratic government for the first time. Their experiment with democracy would not last long. By the late 1960s, Kenya's government was becoming authoritarian and corrupt, and "big man" politics would dominate the country for the next two decades. In recent years, Kenyans have worked to create a more democratic government, using constitutional reform. As this book goes to press, these efforts have stalled, as Kenya plunged into a new crisis following a disputed presidential election in December 2007. The incumbent Mwai Kibaki claimed victory with a slim electoral margin amid troublesome signs of election fraud. Kenyans reacted with violence, often targeted at Kibaki's tribe, the Kikuyu. The controversy was often cast in simple terms of tribal or ethnic conflict, reinforcing a conception that "tribalism" drives politics in Kenya and other African countries. This misses the broader story of Kenya's continuing struggle for democracy and the more complex political background against which the election crisis played out. Kibaki was originally elected on a platform of constitutional reform that would have circumscribed the powers of the presidency. He not only broke that promise, but now also appeared to be rigging an election to stay in power. Much of the violence in Kenya took place in the poorest communities. While rioters often targeted Kikuyu, at stake was not simply which tribe might dominate Kenyan politics but whether Kenya's economic success should benefit all Kenyans, not just a small political and economic elite, and the failure of Kenya's leaders to realize the democratic reforms so many had hoped for.[10]

Tribalism is not the most important feature of the struggle for democracy told in these pages. Ethnic rivalries are a part of the story, of course, but it is important to avoid the reification of tribe into a natural, essential identity and instead to see ethnic politics as one feature among others in Africa. During 1960 constitutional negotiations, Kenyans came together across tribal lines out of a common interest in independence from colonial rule. The ethnic differences that principally figured in the 1960 debate over a bill of rights were among whites, Asians, and the African majority. The interests of tribes were debated more intently during 1962 constitutional negotiations, in which Thurgood Marshall did not participate. That year, minority tribes, along with some whites and Asians, supported a federal constitution that would have devolved power to regional areas. This proposal was successfully opposed by the party of Jomo Kenyatta, Kenya's first president, in favor of a more powerful central government. In the end, some smaller and less powerful tribes felt that their concerns were ignored in the political calculus. And Kenya's democratic moment in the early 1960s would collapse by the end of the decade, unleashing ethnic conflict that would affect the nation's subsequent political history. Ultimately, human rights scholar Makau Mutua has argued, transcending tribal politics is an important task in Kenya's unfinished project of nation building and democratization.[11]

Just as identity affects politics in Kenya, the question of identity is central to the history of African American engagement with Africa. Different perspectives emerge from recent works. During the heady days after Ghana's independence in 1957, historian Saidiya Hartman has written, "Not only did black Americans identify with the anticolonial struggle, they believed their futures too depended on its victory." For historian Kevin Gaines, African Americans were "strangers in their own land." African Americans working to build an independent Ghana sought a black consciousness that transcended national boundaries. Others saw Africa as a homeland, but this home illuminated not their connectedness with Africans, but their inescapable American-ness. Langston Hughes, for example, was called a "white man" and treated as a foreigner.[12]

If Thurgood Marshall was ever held at arms length by the Africans he met, he did not say so. Instead, he expressed delight in getting to know his "homeland." His bond with his African friends was not based on a common identity but on shared political commitments. It did not involve rejection of his own national identity but a determination to root out his nation's racism. Seeing his struggle as the same as that of the Africans drew upon a truth—the pervasiveness of racism—but also occluded the different character of their struggles. And there was no stepping out of Marshall's American consciousness so that, as have other Americans involved in writing constitutions for other nations, he would see problems and solutions from within the terms of an American legal model. This might limit the effectiveness of his legal proposals but not his political contribution, for in their battle with Britain, Marshall's Americanness was a strategic resource for the Kenyans.[13]

This book follows Marshall from his civil rights practice in New York to Kenya under colonial rule. This story cannot be found in traditional sources for an American biography. The Bill of Rights Marshall wrote for Kenya, for example, is not in any American archive, but in British colonial records in England. It is published here for the first time as an appendix. Other details are scattered in numerous collections, including diplomatic files, in the United States, England, and Kenya, from Thurgood Marshall's own papers at the Library of Congress to the papers of Kenyan nationalist Tom Mboya at the Hoover Institute to the records at the Kenya National Archive.

Marshall's African journey is not a triumphalist story of American law solving all problems. The legal ideas Marshall offered often were not American ones. And legal solutions did not create a legal edifice that would last for all time. Instead law could serve as a way station, giving political actors a way to talk to each other, a way to keep working together when things were hard.

It would not all be smooth sailing. Marshall loved to return to Kenya, to see how "his" bill of rights was working. But he found injustice that he thought his work should have helped to prevent, and he confronted his nationalist friends. Once his work in Africa was complete, Marshall faced the limits of his own vision for social change when he reached the apex of a legal career in 1967 with a seat on the Supreme Court, just as American cities burst into flame and American politics lost the impetus to save them. In his later years, Marshall's work in Africa informed his views about the founding of his own nation. As he became older, and as hard times came to Kenya, Marshall would remember the country only with fondness. If his friends in Kenya let him down, they had accomplished what was most important. He was there on Independence Day, when the British flag came down, and Kenya, the colony, became a nation.

– 1 –

MARSHALL AND MBOYA

You are the descendants of the tiny brave band of men who fired the shot heard round the world. Its sound has been slow to reach Africa, but now the echoes rebound from every corner of the continent. For the same freedom and right to a better life which your ancestors won we Africans now also strive.

— Tom Mboya at Carnegie Hall, 1959

[I] would like to be on the side of the natives for once.

— President Dwight D. Eisenhower, 1958

THURGOOD MARSHALL MET BERNARD TAPER in New York on a flight to Atlanta in 1956. It was a frigid and icy late February afternoon. Marshall was on the plane, in a double-breasted suit, his large frame folded into a seat, when Taper boarded. The reporter was to accompany the lawyer to a civil rights meeting. "During the takeoff, Marshall sat hunched at the window, gazing with concentration into the heavily overcast sky, as if contributing his willpower to the effort to get us off the ground." When the plane was aloft, Marshall relaxed and lit a cigarette. "One thing troubles me about this meeting ahead," he said to Taper. "We won't be able to smoke. *That's* gonna hurt."[1]

Perhaps it is a good thing that Thurgood Marshall was a large man. So outsized was the lawyer's reputation after the victory in *Brown v. Board of Education* that the reporter, coming upon a slighter person, might have been confused. Taper, writing for the *New Yorker*, cast Marshall as a living legend. "Few living individuals have had a greater effect than Marshall on the social fabric of America," he wrote that spring. In the previous fifteen years, Marshall had "attained the stature of a semi-folk hero among his people. At the same time, he has earned the deepest respect of sophisticated jurists and students of the law."[2]

The future should have looked sweet to Thurgood Marshall in 1956. The *Brown* case was won, and in the eyes of the nation his name was forever associated with that victory. His colleague Constance Baker Motley thought the case made Marshall the "undisputed spokesman for black America." *Time* magazine put him on its cover in 1955. But the years after *Brown* were difficult. "He was simultaneously exhilarated and awestruck by his leadership position in black people's struggle for equality," Motley said. "At times, he seemed immobilized by the inherent responsibility to move forward with implementation; at other times, he was literally overwhelmed by the onrush of events that the decision set in motion. It was like trying to navigate a ship in a hurricane."[3]

Marshall's problems were confounded when in 1955 the Supreme Court undercut his efforts, requiring only "all deliberate speed" in *Brown*'s implementation. The decision was widely viewed as allowing delay, and that is just what happened. It was not until 1964 that the Supreme Court changed course, announcing that "the time for mere 'deliberate speed' has run out." In 1960, over 94 percent of African American children in the South still attended all-black schools. The lack of progress was frustrating. At the same time, the National Association for the Advancement of Colored People (NAACP) and the Legal Defense Fund (LDF) lawyers were under attack in the South, targets of cold war anticommunist investigations. The war against communism was being deployed by Southern states to stymie civil rights efforts. Defending against attack drew time, attention, and resources away from enforcing *Brown*.[4]

"Where are we now?" Marshall asked Taper at some point during the flight to Atlanta, looking out the window into the darkness. "Somewhere over Virginia—North Carolina?" Going south was something Marshall had often done, but it was different now, after *Brown*. "I'm a Southerner," he said. "I know my way around. I don't go looking for trouble. I ride in the for-colored-only cabs and in the back ends of streetcars—quiet as a mouse. I eat in Negro cafés and I don't use white washrooms. I don't challenge the customs personally, because I figure I'm down South representing a client—the N.A.A.C.P.—and not myself." Marshall hadn't previously worried too much about trips south. But he did now, and his wife, Cissy, was anxious. "Those boys are playing for keeps."[5]

The flight was rough, but the conversation between the two men was easy. Marshall spoke with admiration about Southern members of the NAACP. "Some of them speak out without hesitation," he said. "I don't know how they do it. They have more courage than I would have in their place." What would happen at the meeting in Atlanta? Roy Wilkins, NAACP executive secretary, would be there, along with leaders from many Southern states. "When I get to this meeting," Marshall said, "I'll not only find out...what the situation is but also find out what *they* want to do about it, because they're the ones that are gonna have to live with any action taken." Marshall was sometimes cast as a leader "masterminding this whole campaign, somehow, against the wishes, of Southern Negroes," but he saw it differently. "Our people in the South are actually way ahead of us on this thing." Then Marshall, the storyteller, told a story about a man who saw a crowd rushing down a street. The man wanted to know what was going on, so he "grabbed a guy huffin' and puffin' along at the tail end." He asked, "'What's goin' on here?' The other guy pulled loose and cried, 'Don't hold me back, man! Don't you know I'm the leader of that crowd? And if I don't run like hell they'll get away from me altogether.'" Marshall laughed. "That's me.... The leader at the tail end."[6]

To Southern whites, Marshall was an outside agitator. To many Americans, he was moving the country too far, too fast, although it didn't seem that way to the lawyers who had worked so hard on desegregation cases. *Brown* had been greeted with much fanfare in 1954. The world celebrated the fact that basic American values embedded in the nation's constitution had finally been affirmed. But as the Supreme Court delayed *Brown's* implementation and Southern school districts devised schemes to circumvent the ruling, *Brown* became a symbol for social change that was always in the future. *Brown's* symbolism might have reassured those worried about the nation's moral fabric or its image around the world. But symbolism would not dismantle Jim Crow or begin the work of making education equal.

What if the LDF "won lawsuit after lawsuit and court decision after court decision but couldn't get the decisions put into effect?" Taper asked. "That's the sixty-four-thousand-dollar question, and I'm not even going to try for it," answered Marshall. "I don't know what we'd do. That's something I can't even contemplate. It would be anarchy. It would be the end of the country. I can't imagine it coming to that."[7]

The civil rights meeting in Atlanta the next day lasted well into the night. It was not what the white reporter had expected, venturing into this world of "Negro leaders." Taper would not have been surprised, he wrote, at "more oratory, more emotional outbursts," or "to find deep gloom at the turn of events...and demands for an agonizing reappraisal of the N.A.A.C.P.'s position, or even to hear at least some delegates, frustrated beyond endurance, call for violence or other direct action." What surprised him was "the orderliness—indeed the ordinariness—of the procedure." It was "the concreteness, the calm, the serene feeling of assurance that the law would eventually prevail." Or so it seemed to him when the meeting broke at midpoint and he took a walk through the streets of Atlanta.[8]

For all the centrality of law and order in Marshall's thoughts about strategy, he had not always chosen peaceful solutions rather than violence. Growing up in Baltimore during a bleaker time in American race relations, when lynchings were a more common means of policing the racial order, Marshall's father told him not to shrink from racial insults. "If any white boy calls you a nigger, you got to fight him." Marshall grew into a legendary fighter. But in spite of his imposing frame, he eventually traded in his fists for a different weapon. Law gave him an enduring way to get even.[9]

One of Marshall's early victories in the courtroom enabled him to right a personal wrong. In 1935, along with civil rights pioneer Charles Hamilton Houston, he represented Donald Murray, who was excluded from attending the University of Maryland Law School because of his race, just as Marshall had been five years earlier. The Maryland Supreme Court ruled in favor of Murray, finding that exclusion of African Americans from the state's only public law school violated the requirement of equality under the Fourteenth Amendment of the U.S. Constitution. *Pearson v. Murray* forever changed the university. Not only was Murray admitted, but the overt racial exclusion Marshall had suffered was now illegal. And *Murray* provided an important precedent in the effort to undermine the constitutionality of segregation.[10]

After two years of law practice in Baltimore, Marshall joined Houston at the Legal Department of the NAACP in 1936. A Harvard Law School graduate, Houston was a brilliant lawyer and teacher. As dean of Howard Law School from 1929 to 1935, he turned the African American school into a civil rights think tank, a testing ground for the ideas that would shape constitutional equality in the twentieth century. Houston's heart gave out at the age of fifty-seven, in 1950, but by then he had passed the baton to Marshall. So it was Marshall, with Robert Carter, Constance Baker Motley, and their team, who brought *Brown* to the Supreme Court. The lawyers had their differences in later years, but in the 1950s they maintained a unity of purpose. American society had to be changed. And law seemed the right tool for their purposes.[11]

In the evening, when the meeting in Atlanta resumed, NAACP Executive Secretary Roy Wilkins reflected on their efforts. He spoke of the "tremendous effect we are having on the nation. All these little decisions we worked out today are part of a social revolution that is taking place. The whole face of a third of America is changing."[12]

Thurgood Marshall interrupted him. "Never mind the philosophy, Roy! You don't know the news I've just heard." A young man had entered the meeting and whispered in his ear.

"Yes, I do, Thurgood," Wilkins responded. He was waiting for confirmation, he said. "Dr. Brewer's just had his head shot off."[13]

Dr. Thomas H. Brewer was the plaintiff in a lawsuit to desegregate the Columbus, Georgia, municipal golf course. His photograph had just been in the local paper. He had been receiving threats. Brewer's murder was not the first one tied to civil rights work. Two Mississippi NAACP leaders had been killed in the previous year.[14]

At this point, Bernard Taper's account of the meeting begins to trail off. It is as if he could not reconcile the focus on the bloodless machinery of the law with the violence that swirled around them. How could people in suits brandishing legal documents change a system that was enforced by shotguns and bombings, by a rope and a tree?

Yet it was this very violence that drove the lawyers into the courtroom. It was because there were hooded men who roamed at night that they sought refuge in the legal order. It may have been slow but it seemed more than steady. For Thurgood

Marshall, it was the only way he knew to overturn the social order without a conflagration.

There was one thing Marshall didn't know in 1956: that this struggle for justice in America would lead him many miles from home, for the story of *Brown* had special meaning on another side of the world.

FOR A BLACK NEW YORKER IN 1956, flying to Atlanta meant crossing a boundary into Jim Crow territory. But borders are relative. When Tom Mboya from Kenya flew into New York's Idlewild airport that same year, he crossed more than national boundaries. He was a colonial subject in search not of a new homeland but of a lever to employ in his revolution back home. George Houser and his friends at the American Committee on Africa cannot have known what a phenomenon Mboya would become when they first met him at the airport in 1956. A polite young man with a ready smile, Mboya told them simply, "I am very glad to be here."[15]

Mboya had much in common with the NAACP leaders he met on this trip. Like them, he believed in democracy and the rule of law. But Mboya was attracted as well to another element in American history. This democracy was governed by law, but it had been forged in revolution. In Carnegie Hall one night in 1959, he reminded Americans of their revolutionary heritage. "You are the descendants of the tiny brave band of men who fired the shot heard round the world," he said. "Its sound has been slow to reach Africa, but now the echoes rebound from every corner of the continent. For the same freedom and right to a better life which your ancestors won we Africans now also strive."[16]

Africans could see themselves in the story of America, Mboya wrote in 1956. The American War of Independence had made the United States a symbol of "the struggle and success of a people to free themselves from the yoke of colonialism." The icons of the American revolution became symbols for Africans:

"The Boston Tea Party, the Stamp Acts, and the 'No taxation without representation' slogan . . . are common knowledge among Africans." "Government of the people, by the people, for the people" from the Gettysburg Address was a common slogan in African politics. Because American history served as an inspiration to Africans, "there is a sense of remote alikeness, sometimes even of belonging, and an unspoken acceptance of America as the symbol of heroic victory over colonialism."[17]

This sense of a shared identity was reinforced by the presence of descendants of Africans in the American population. But the status of African Americans cut both ways. "The segregation of Negroes in schools in the South," said Mboya, "has done a lot of harm to American prestige. As the upholder of democracy she is expected to be blameless within her own boundaries." But progress had been noted. The *Brown* case in particular had special meaning: "the Supreme Court decision of 1954 is hailed by many Africans, particularly in British East and Central Africa and in South Africa, where Africans do not have the right to bring discriminatory practices before courts."[18]

Many Americans were inspired by Mboya. Africa was the "dark continent" and he brought news of its "political awakening." Only twenty-six years old when he first arrived in the United States, Mboya was a labor leader in Kenya, a colony in which labor politics were restricted by a state of emergency. The son of a sisal worker who had just completed a year at Oxford University, Mboya made clear the purpose of this 1956 visit in a statement released on his arrival. "The United States is not a colonial power, but the problems of Africa are a challenge to the whole of the free world." The role of the United States was important, for the "American attitude to colonialism can be a decisive factor in the struggle of the African people to gain their freedom and to raise their standards of living." Mboya hoped to engender "an enlightened American public opinion on Africa."[19]

Mboya returned for a whirlwind tour of the United States in 1959, starting with a spellbinding performance on the CBS news program *Face the Nation*. By this point, he had chaired the All-African People's Conference in Accra, Ghana, in 1958 and was widely regarded as a leader of great promise. Many in both Africa and America pinned their hopes on him. Still, the thing that was most often said about Mboya was that he was so very young. "I'd read a lot about this serious young man who sat across the luncheon table from me," wrote a reporter for *Sepia* magazine who opened his interview by asking Mboya how old he was. "Twenty-nine," the article continued. "The same age, I thought, as our own Martin Luther King."[20]

Mboya believed that Americans had much to learn about Africa. "You still see us in Hollywood terms of jungles, wild beasts and fierce, ignorant, furiously dancing tribesmen," Mboya said. "Little do you Americans, with whom we have basically so much in common, realize that Africa, too, shares in the 20th Century—that we have modern cities, roads, airfields, houses, cars and so on." One obstacle to Mboya's efforts to build bridges with Americans was the way the Western press had character-ized Kenya's recent history.[21]

The struggle to overthrow colonialism had deep roots in Kenya, and it came to a head in the 1950s. The colony's larg-est tribe, the Kikuyu, struck back in what was called the Mau Mau rebellion. Americans heard the story of the resistance, and of Britain's bloody and torturous counterinsurgency cam-paign, from the British press and a handful of sensationalistic American reporters. They did not tell of the torture, the mur-ders in the prison camps, or the detention of entire communi-ties of Kikuyu. Instead, their focus was the stories of the whites in Kenya and the Africans loyal to the colonialists. Kenya was depicted as the site of violent debauchery, and those who com-mitted the so-called Mau Mau murders could not be seen as fully human. Mboya hoped to tell "the other side of the story," about the atrocities committed by the British colonial government against Africans in Kenya.[22]

With his dazzling smile, his quick intelligence, and his pleasant manner, Mboya was a reassuring figure to many Americans. Some remained skeptical. Could anything but chaos follow if self-governance were placed in the hands of Africans? But most Americans believed that were African nations to govern themselves, power should be vested in people like Mboya.

Mboya's travels in the United States won him financial support, which would aid his rise to political prominence in Kenya, and ultimately would be his Achilles heel, limiting his influence. But in 1959, his future seemed bright. Many Americans saw their own history reflected in events in Africa. Robert L. Tallmon, a retired farmer from Creston, Iowa, wrote Mboya a letter after reading about him in *Time* magazine. "To your country," he wrote, "you are what George Washington was to our United States."[23]

Mboya's rise to global prominence emerged through his work as a labor leader. He became general secretary of the Kenya Federation of Labor at the age of twenty-three and represented the union in the International Confederation of Free Trade Unions (ICFTU), a labor organization composed of national noncommunist unions, which provided support for African trade union activity in Kenya. Through the ICFTU, Mboya met American AFL-CIO leaders. Walter Reuther of the United Auto Workers Union was taken with this charismatic and articulate young African and became an important supporter of Mboya's activities. A. Philip Randolph of the Brotherhood of Sleeping Car Porters also became a supporter and mentor. Randolph served as a bridge between Mboya and the labor and civil rights communities. Mboya met with Roy Wilkins and NAACP staff and with Martin Luther King Jr. among others.[24]

Tom Mboya (right) and Harry Belafonte meeting with others, including Eleanor Roosevelt (not pictured), April 1, 1959. (Photo by Joseph Scherschel/Time & Life Pictures/Getty Images)

One of Mboya's objectives in 1959 was to generate support for an airlift of Kenyan students to the United States. Mboya gained support in this effort from baseball player Jackie Robinson, entertainer Harry Belafonte, and others. With $1 million in private funds committed for scholarships in 1960, he sought U.S. government support for air transportation, and when that was not forthcoming presidential candidate John F. Kennedy provided $100,000 to the effort, boosting Kennedy's appeal among African American voters. Mboya's political rival Oginga Odinga in turn organized an airlift to communist countries. Two beneficiaries of the airlifts were Barack Obama Sr., the father of U.S. senator and 2008 presidential candidate Barack Obama, and Raila Odinga, Kenyan opposition presidential candidate in 2007.[25]

One feature that attracted Americans to Mboya was that he aligned himself with Western anticommunists. When he spoke at Carnegie Hall for the first African Freedom Day in 1959, he called for an "internationalism of democracy" to "match the internationalism of communism." His vision of democracy included a dedication to "freedom, independence and the elimination of disease, poverty and ignorance all over the world." Many were concerned that African independence would play into the hands of communists. Mboya responded by saying that if those who made this charge "spent all their efforts in practicing the democracy they preach they would have nothing to fear from communism."[26]

Mboya did not make anticommunism a part of his political platform, however. He worked effectively with nationalists from other African countries who were sympathetic to socialism, and he served as chair of the pan-Africanist All-African Peoples Conference in Ghana in 1958. Mboya argued that Kenya should be nonaligned, which attracted Americans, many of whom were coming to see Africa as a cold war battleground. Some who offered support to Mboya made it clear that they did so not because they supported African nationalism generally but because they saw in him a moderation they hoped for. Mboya's support in the United States came not only from labor and civil rights leaders, but also from Americans with vague backgrounds and lucrative offers. For example, Keith Smith, who identified himself only as an American businessman, attempted to meet with Mboya in late 1959 and early 1960, offering him $250,000 in support from unnamed foundations. Smith stressed that "by not associating yourself with the less reliable and overtly radical political elements of Africa, you will ultimately succeed in leadership of your people after these other foolish people have destroyed themselves. May you ever continue your sane, sensible, non-violent approach to freedom for your people." This came at a time when the

Central Intelligence Agency (CIA) was reaching out to moderate African leaders. Whether "Keith Smith's" offer was part of those efforts was not disclosed.[27]

Mboya would later face criticism in Kenya for his American ties, including persistent rumors that he had CIA connections. It is entirely possible that some of Mboya's American financial support came from the CIA. His biographer, David Goldsworthy, noted that "Mboya's attitude was basically just as expedient as the Americans'. Quite simply, he wanted the money for domestic political purposes and had no qualms about its sources." And once communist sources became available, his opponents readily turned to them. "Neither Mboya nor his opponents ever regarded themselves for a moment as the 'agents' of their international suppliers," Goldsworthy argued. "To the Kenyans, the great powers were essentially peripheral allies in their struggles for local power."[28]

Mboya won admiration from Americans who hoped one day to see a free Africa. At Howard University, he was given an honorary degree. For many who praised him at Howard, or who gathered at Carnegie Hall to celebrate with him on African Freedom Day, Mboya embodied hope for an entire continent.[29]

After his triumphant tour of the United States, Mboya received a very different greeting when he returned to Kenya. Colonial police searched his luggage for two and a half hours at the Nairobi airport, looking for seditious literature and prohibited documents. They found nothing. Africans at the airport to greet Mboya were dispersed by police. "I have never been so treated and humiliated in my life," Mboya wrote to an American friend, Ralph Helstein. "But I guess under Colonial rule we have learned to take this sort of thing without any hard feelings. This is what keeps us going." The *New York Times* reported that whites in the Kenya government "contend that Mr. Mboya's speeches are provocative and that to give him a free hand politically would lead to revolution. They scoff at his appeal for 'undiluted democracy' with an African majority in the Government and say 98 percent of the Africans do not know what he means." There was no parallel media coverage in Kenya. Nairobi's principal paper, the *East African Standard*, did not cover Mboya's most recent speech, attended by more than 3,000 Africans.[30]

THE POLITICAL CONFLICT THAT TOM MBOYA RETURNED to in 1959 had its origins decades earlier, when Europeans laid claim to African territory. One early Scottish adventurer to Kenya, Joseph Thompson, helped spread the news of the beautiful land at the equator. On the evening of November 3, 1884, Thomson appeared before a crowd at the Royal Geographic Society in London and enthralled his audience with stories of his trek across the treacherous Maasai Land in search of a shorter route from the ports of East Africa to Lake Victoria. The land he traversed would soon become the British colony of Kenya. In the early 1880s, it was thought by Europeans to be an uncharted land ruled by a feared warrior tribe. As with any good adventure, Thomson's tale included close brushes with death, when calamity was avoided only through his own ingenuity. Western technology, of course, could trick the Maasai, whose amazement in the face of innovation fell into a predictable nineteenth-century script of white superiority and the ignorance of the darker races. Kenyan writer Nicholas Best reinforced these conceptions:

> Surrounded by a Masai war party intent on cutting him to pieces, the Scots explorer Joseph Thomson did the only thing possible to save his life. He took out his false teeth and flashed them at the advancing warriors.
>
> The Masai drew the obvious conclusion. Clearly the twenty-five-year-old white man, the first they had ever seen, was a sorcerer and caster of spells. Abandoning all thoughts of murder, they turned to run and were only persuaded to creep back after

Thomson had discreetly replaced his teeth and tapped them with his knuckles to show how firm they were.

Thomson's journey led to the bestseller *Through Masai Land*, which helped construct the image of Kenya in the mind of the British as a land of beauty, adventure, and danger.[31]

The hope of fame and the allure of exoticism were not the only things that had attracted Thomson to Kenya. "A more charming region is probably not to be found in all Africa," he wrote. Gazing on the peaks of Mount Kenya for the first time "roused stirring memories of home scenes, so distinctly European-like was the aspect of the crags." In the decades after Thomson's adventures, thousands of British citizens would make Kenya their home. Michael Blundell, a settler and important Kenyan political figure, would write, "That the region was largely populated already with Africans seems to have been lost in the general enthusiasm for the creation of a new white country in these territories."[32]

For all the romance of the stories the British would tell about themselves in Kenya, however, what drove their expansion in that region of the world was trade. As Germany began to lay claim to parts of East Africa in the 1880s, the British moved to protect their access to African territory. Soon a scramble for Africa was on, until the European powers had divided much of the continent up among themselves. The boundaries of European domains would become the boundaries of their colonies, and later, by and large, the boundaries of independent African nations. "In the ten years between 1895 and 1905, 'Kenya'...was transformed from a footpath 1000 km (600 miles) long into a colonial administration," historian John Lonsdale wrote. To achieve this, "the British employed violence on a locally unprecedented scale, and with unprecedented singleness of mind."[33]

British troops first took control of the Kenya coast, then moved into the interior, first along the route of a railway constructed from the coast to mineral-rich Uganda. But how would the country, without great expense, gain sovereignty over the interior, in a territory about the size of France? To accomplish this, Lonsdale explains, the British needed to turn the force of conquest "into internal, negotiable and productive power." To do this, they emulated "their own Roman governor, Agricola, of whom the admiring Tacitus said that 'when he had done enough to inspire fear, he returned to mercy and proffered the allurements of peace.'" Kenya's first British commissioner said, "These people must learn submission by bullets—it's the only school; after that you may begin more modern and humane methods of education."[34]

The British then applied themselves to capitalizing on the politics of conquest. Having claimed this part of the earth, the next step was to make it pay for itself. In contrast to Uganda and Tanganyika, which did not attract large white settler populations, the more temperate Kenya highlands, Blundell wrote, "were euphemistically and flatly called 'White Man's Country', as if the bracing air of the Yorkshire Moors was consonantly sweeping through the African plains." The British government encouraged settlement with promises of land. After World Wars I and II, Kenyan land was given to British soldiers as a reward for their wartime service. Veterans received a thousand acres to settle and till. Though the settlers would say it was empty, some land in the highlands had been temporarily vacated by the Kikuyu tribe due to disease and drought.[35]

The white-owned farms needed laborers. Taxing Africans offered a way to generate a labor pool and to raise money for colonial government expenses at the same time, since the Africans needed the wages to pay the taxes. The growing colony attracted immigrants from East Asia. Some came temporarily to work on the railroad. Others came as traders and stayed. In time they would become the racial and economic middle class in a strictly stratified colonial society.[36]

A Kenyan farmer on his horse, supervising workers on his farm picking pyrethrum flowers, including women with small children, circa 1960. (© POPPERFOTO/Alamy)

SIR EVELYN BARING, GOVERNOR OF KENYA, insisted in 1954 that British support for the settlers would be enduring: "Her Majesty's Government are not likely to lend themselves to encouraging people to come if they intend to betray them. They will be entitled to feel confidence in the possession of the homes they have built for themselves and for their children." Though nationalist tensions were growing in the early 1950s, Blundell claimed that the settlers were unaware of them, having "little conception of the stirrings of nationalism which were all around" them.[37]

The Kenyan highlands seemed a paradise to the white settlers. Best described trout fishing, hunting dogs, and outdoor sport. There were "luxurious log fires at night and endless wild parties in each other's homes." The 1920s were the "daffodil days" of the settlers, the "days of opulent manor houses, flowing green lawns, and picnick[ing] on the grass.... The altitude was high, the air was clean and it was a life of laziness and laughter and long, lingering looks between fit men and their best friends' wives, leading invariably to strange beds and a reputation for casual promiscuity that ultimately gave the place and the people the enduring nickname of Happy Valley." While Thomson saw in Kenya an essence of the Britain he had left behind, these white settlers found an escape from the more rigid sensibilities of their native land.[38]

British rule in Kenya was not a happy experience for the Africans, of course. By the time of the Mau Mau rebellion, the colony had been divided into regions based on race, class, power, and privilege. The best land was the domain of the whites, while the Africans were divided and assigned to "reserves." Colonial government efforts to divide and rule the Africans reinforced tensions and divisions between tribes. By the late 1950s, many white settler families were in their third generation, on land that Africans worked but could not claim title to.[39]

We can see this experience reflected in the characters of *Weep Not, Child,* by Kenyan novelist Ngũgĩ wa Thiong'o. There is Mr. Howlands, a "typical settler," who had escaped his memories of World War I England by turning to Africa, "a big trace of wild country to conquer." When he lost his son in World War II, he "lost all faith.... He would again have destroyed himself, but again his god, land, came to the rescue. He turned all his efforts and energy into it. He seemed to worship the soil." But Ngotho, who worked the land, watched over the same soil. "Ngotho felt responsibility for whatever happened to this land. He owed it to the dead, the living and the unborn of his line, to keep guard over this *shamba*." When Howlands confessed to Ngotho one day that he didn't know who would cultivate the land when he was gone, Ngotho asked if he was thinking of going home. "My home is here!" Howland retorted. "Ngotho was puzzled," wrote Ngũgĩ. "Would these people never go?"[40]

THE DIFFERENCES THAT TEAR AT AFRICAN COMMUNITIES can
be lost to American eyes. When Americans have turned to Africa,
they have embraced it, often, as a monolith, with little awareness
of the differences of regions or the diversity of African peoples.
Most Americans in Africa in the eighteenth and nineteenth centuries were more interested in what they could take from the
continent—first African slaves, later natural resources—than in
establishing a foothold there. The U.S. role in Africa changed
after Winston Churchill and Franklin Delano Roosevelt met
aboard ships in the Atlantic during World War II and hammered out the Atlantic Charter. They pledged that the British
and U.S. governments would "respect the right of all peoples to
choose the form of government under which they will live; and
they wish to see sovereign rights and self-government restored
to those who have been forcibly deprived of them." Although
Churchill insisted that he meant the nations then under the
yoke of Nazism, not colonies like those in Africa, the cat was
out of the bag. All across Africa, historian Elizabeth Borgwardt
writes, "letters and articles appeared in local newspapers insisting that the Atlantic Charter should indeed apply to Africa." *Life*
magazine editors wrote in an open letter to the English people
in 1942: "One thing we are sure we are *not* fighting for is to hold
the British empire together."[41]

In 1945, after the war had ended, the fifth Pan-African Congress convened in Manchester, England. For the first time, the
meeting consisted principally of young leaders from Africa,
including Kwame Nkrumah of Ghana and Jomo Kenyatta of
Kenya. They demanded "autonomy and independence...sub-
ject to inevitable world unity and federation," and they declared
that "if the Western world is still determined to rule man-
kind by force," then Africans seeking freedom, might, as a last
resort, need to use force, "even if force destroys them and the
world."[42]

Independence was coming, but it would play out in a global cold war arena. Africa became a pawn in the cold war, with each superpower determined to ensure that more dominoes did not fall into the camp of the other. Under the old colonial order, the principal foreign affairs dynamic in Africa involved the way relations between European powers affected the peaceful coexistence of their colonies. This was replaced by a world in which two nations that had not colonized Africa—the United States and the Soviet Union—vied for the allegiance of independent African states. As the cold war intensified, the United States became more conservative about decolonization, historian Thomas Noer has argued. Self-determination was secondary to the containment of communism. Concerned about communist involvement in independence movements, the United States tried to dampen the nationalism it had fostered. Still, Africa was a low priority during the 1950s. The CIA warned that U.S. policy left African resistance forces open to communist influence and urged that more be done "to court 'moderate' members of the African opposition." But American leaders had conflicting sympathies. President Eisenhower, criticized for his lukewarm support for African independence, expressed his frustration. "[I] would like to be on the side of the natives for once," he said in 1958. "We must believe in the right of colonial peoples to achieve independence," but if this was emphasized too strongly, it would create "a crisis in the relations with the mother countries."[43]

Cold war concerns led the U.S. government to support the white South African government, but Kenya would be different. By 1960, the United States was supporting nationalists thought to be pro-Western and multiracial. Kenyan politics were driven by tribe, race, and class, but American diplomats viewed Kenya's politicians through a simpler lens: their likely East-West sympathies. Western-style multiracialism became a proxy for pro-Western anticommunist values. Before his release from detention, nationalist leader Jomo Kenyatta's influence was feared, but diplomats were reduced to finding communistic qualities not in his policies, but in his dress and demeanor. Politics within Kenya then reinforced this distorting echo chamber. Once Mboya found support from Americans, his rival, Oginga Odinga, turned to the East for support and advice. Mboya's relationship with Americans drew Odinga and his communist supporters together.[44]

There was a racial politics of the cold war that affected U.S. relations with emerging African nations, having an impact on the transition from the European colonial order to the cold war order. Blundell explained the problem in 1959 by drawing a lesson for Kenya from an unexpected place: Little Rock, Arkansas.[45]

What did Little Rock have to do with ethnic politics in Kenya? Race in America was a well-established international news story by September 1957 when the governor of Arkansas, supported by white mobs, blocked the integration of nine African American students into Central High School. The Little Rock crisis, with dramatic images of federal troops with bayonets escorting neatly clad students with books into a school surrounded by angry mobs, became a signal event, covered extensively in the world press over a period of weeks. Secretary of State John Foster Dulles and others urged the president to act in part because the crisis damaged the nation's international standing. President Eisenhower was concerned as well that the rule of law at home was under siege.[46] He had sworn off using troops to enforce a desegregation order, but did an about face, explaining to the nation:

At a time when we face grave situations abroad because of the hatred that Communism bears toward a system of government based on human rights, it would be difficult to exaggerate the harm that is being done to the prestige and influence, and indeed to the safety, of our nation and the world.

Our enemies are gloating over this incident and using it everywhere to misrepresent our whole nation. We are portrayed as a violator of those standards of conduct which the peoples of the world united to proclaim in the Charter of the United Nations.

Much of the world lauded the president's efforts, but Little Rock remained a symbol that all was not well with American democracy, that the system of government heralded as a model for all was failing some of its own citizens.[47]

Blundell invoked Little Rock to explain why there was no hope for white minority rule in Kenya by 1959, and whites in Kenya would have to support multiracial governance. "The plain truth," he argued, was that "with the heady wine of race and colour sweeping the world, the menace of communism to the north, and the anxiety of the United States of America to demonstrate to Africa that Little Rock never happened, the European in Kenya [was] not in a position to stand alone in glorious isolation." Once African independence became a reality, the United States could not count on these new nations to line up in the same cold war columns as their former colonizers. Winning them over would require two things: The United States must do its best to keep its own racial house in order and, when possible, align itself with noncommunist leaders for independence in Africa. Whites in South Africa might have found an ally in the United States of America; for whites in Kenya, however, a crisis in Arkansas helped seal their very different fate.[48]

AFRICAN AMERICANS DID NOT NEED THE COLD WAR to take an interest in Africa. During the nineteenth century, many had traveled there as missionaries, hoping to "Christianize and civilize" the continent. Others moved to Liberia seeking a refuge from

American racism. Later generations saw in Africa not a primitivism in need of redemption, but a source of their history. W. E. B. Du Bois organized pan-African conferences hoping to unite peoples of African descent and to aid African liberation. Ralph Bunche played a leadership role at the United Nations, helping move the colonies of the losing powers toward eventual independence after World War II. But as the cold war closed in, anticolonial organizations found themselves on the wrong side of American cold war politics. The internationalism of African Americans during the 1950s and early 1960s was constrained by the cold war even as its politics also created opportunities, as when African American cultural figures were sent overseas on government-sponsored trips. The status of these prominent African Americans turned them into ambassadors of the multiracial character of American society, living rebuttals to Soviet propaganda that portrayed American democracy as ravaged by racial segregation and discrimination. But African Americans, along with other activists, sometimes lost their passports because of their politics, especially if they criticized American racism while overseas. Paul Robeson, W. E. B. Du Bois, and others were barred from travel during the early cold war years because it was thought to undermine U.S. foreign relations. Still, travel, for those who could manage it, had an impact. James Baldwin described the paradox of the African American soldier overseas, "far freer in a strange land than he has ever been at home."[49]

The black college was an important meeting ground for Africans and African Americans. Since its founding in 1854, Lincoln University in Pennsylvania, the oldest historically black college in the United States, sought to train African Americans who would work in Africa, especially as missionaries. Many Africans attended Lincoln over the years, including Kwame Nkrumah, who became prime minister of Ghana at independence. Thurgood Marshall attended Lincoln, and Nnamdi Azikiwe, who would become president of Nigeria, was one of his undergraduate classmates.[50]

In his law practice, Marshall sometimes worked on legal problems of Africans in the United States when they turned to the NAACP for assistance. For example, Reuel Mugo Gatheru, a Lincoln student from Kenya, was threatened with deportation in 1953 and sought help from the NAACP. The organization believed that the U.S. government wanted to deport Gatheru because the British suspected that he had ties to the Mau Mau uprising, and was concerned that he would be persecuted by the Kenyan colonial government. Marshall got involved, expressing "great enthusiasm at the possibility of being able to take over this particular case." He made inquiries on the student's behalf at the Justice Department, though the case was ultimately handled by others.[51]

Marshall got to know Tom Mboya when Mboya traveled to the United States during the 1950s. Mboya's 1959 trip was shortly before Kenyan nationalists would have talks with the British government on a new constitution for Kenya. Members of the American Committee on Africa got the idea that Thurgood Marshall would be just the person Mboya needed as an advisor at the talks. Frank Montero of the Urban League and another friend of Marshall's active in ACOA approached Marshall with the idea. That it was not Mboya who needed Marshall but rather a Kenya delegation may not have occurred to these men. They were convinced Mboya was destined to be Kenya's president. Other possible advisors had been contacted, like Yale constitutional scholar Thomas Emerson, who was interested but unable to attend the talks. But what lawyer could be better for Mboya than Thurgood Marshall? In Marshall the nationalists would find a seasoned advisor and a great legal strategist attuned to the way constitutional principles affected civil rights politics on the ground. Perhaps more important, his standing as "Mr. Civil Rights" in the United States would have a utility that his friends might not have realized. As Africans sought political power, the rights of political minorities would become a central issue, a part of the bargain, even though the minorities in Kenya included privileged whites. How better for the nationalists to demonstrate their commitment to protect minorities than to have at their side the man most identified with the legal rights of minorities in America?[52]

And so began Thurgood Marshall's adventure with Kenya. It was not the adventure of new places and new experiences that most excited him. Instead, it was the chance to take a tool that he used to bring about change in America and take it to a place that sorely needed it. If law could begin to transform the American South, what might it do in Africa?

-2-

A TRICKY CONSTITUTION

A revolt might occur if the constitutional conference meeting ended with what the Kenyans considered to be an "imposed" constitution....A new uprising in Kenya that nobody can control— any more than they could control Mau Mau.
                                    —Thurgood Marshall, 1960

All of Africa will be free before the American Negro attains first class citizenship.
                                    —James Lawson, 1960

"DEAR SIRS, AFTER TEN MEETINGS 2500 of us have decided that if you give the African equal voting power as the Europeans in this country we will blow up everything in Kenya," read an anonymous letter from Kenyan settlers to British officials in January 1960. "Then the African can start from the beginning the same as we did." Another letter soon followed: "we will not leave one railway Bridge, Power Station, or any Government Building standing." There would be "nothing left in Kenya worth having." As 1960 began, Kenya was at the end of the Mau Mau era. A seven-year state of emergency was finally lifted. Although thousands remained in prison camps, and it was clear that the scars of this period would long impact Kenyan politics, the colonial government, at least, hoped for a period of calm. But now terrorist threats were coming from white settlers. The news was troubling.[1]

British colonialism had been steadily unraveling since World War II. The United Nations created a trusteeship system after the war, setting the former colonies of Germany and Italy on the road to eventual emancipation. African leaders, including Jomo Kenyatta of Kenya, demanded independence at a Pan-African Congress in 1948. Anticolonial movements achieved independence for India in 1947, Sudan in 1956, and Ghana in 1957. Motivated in part by concern that colonialism made Africa vulnerable to Soviet influence, British Prime Minister Harold Macmillan announced a change in direction in Cape Town, South Africa, in February 1960, acknowledging that "the wind of change is blowing through this continent. Whether we like it or not, this growth of national consciousness is a political fact." Ultimately, the year 1960 would be known as the Year of Africa, as seventeen African nations became independent in that year alone.[2]

The end of colonialism in Africa was not a simple, gradual process, however. It was powerfully affected by the particular conditions within each colony. Kenya differed from many other emerging African nations in that it had so many white settlers. The richest agricultural lands in Kenya, the highlands, were reserved for whites. Their agricultural produce was the colony's principal tie with global economic markets. Conflict over land would be a central issue in the anticolonial struggle.[3]

Dissent in Kenya had deep roots, but use of political channels was stymied. Africans were excluded from colonywide politics, and by the late 1940s, only a small number of representatives, hand-picked by the colonial government, participated in the Kenya legislature. In the early 1950s, Africans struck back with a guerrilla war against the colonial government. The Land and Freedom Army, also known as the Mau Mau, operated from forest hideaways in the Mt. Kenya and Aberdares ranges. The rebellion centered among the Kikuyu tribe, who sought restoration of land in the highlands they had been displaced from. Many took oaths of allegiance to the movement. The Mau Mau insurgency targeted the colonial government and white settlers, but especially focused on African loyalists. When a prominent Kikuyu chief loyal to the colonialists was murdered in October 1952, the British cracked down with a state of emergency that would last until January 1960.[4]

In the intervening years, the British government sent troops into the forests in a military campaign that wore down the insurgency, and by 1956 the military campaign was over. But military victory was not their only objective. They intended to break the spirit of the Kikuyu and did so through a system of brutal detention camps that caught up at least 150,000 people. The number of Kikuyu killed during this period is a matter of controversy. Historian David Anderson estimates it at more than 20,000. It is clear that Kikuyu deaths far exceeded the number of whites and Africans murdered by the Mau Mau. Ultimately colonial abuses embarrassed the British government, bringing an end to the state of emergency and colonial rule in Kenya. In the 1959 Hola massacre, eleven detainees were beaten to death by African guards in front of white prison wardens, acts then covered up by the colonial government. This led to a furor in England, undermining support for the colonial enterprise. The story of the Mau Mau heard by the British and American publics in the 1950s, however, was the story of brave and frightened white settlers facing horrific acts of African violence.[5]

Although the state of emergency was lifted in early 1960, Kikuyu leader Jomo Kenyatta remained in detention. Jailed in 1952 on charges that he was a leader of the Mau Mau rebellion, Kenyatta was thought to be so dangerous that he was not freed even after he had completed his sentence. New security legislation was in place that gave the colonial governor "reserve powers with which to control all public gatherings for political purposes, provide for the continuance of control over African villages and require the registration of political parties." The security regime included a Detained and Restricted Persons Bill that enabled the government "to continue to restrain and hold persons for security reasons without trial." There was a ban on colonywide political organizations, which undermined the development of a new generation of leaders. But independence in India and especially Ghana had signaled to the Africans that the colonial order was ending. Even repressive measures could not contain nationalism in Kenya or hold off the effects of a changing global order.[6]

One way the British managed colonial problems was to convene constitutional talks. These were not constitutional talks as we might ideally imagine them: representatives of free peoples meeting to chart their future. Instead they were negotiations between ruler and ruled. The way Kenyan nationalist Oginga Odinga saw it, they were designed "to forestall victorious national revolt. Former subjects were enlisted as allies, agents, and friends, were even told they were equals. A process of decolonization was set afoot that would obscure the political controls, yet guarantee the retention of economic influence." Odinga believed that the "refurbishing of the colonial image" was "necessary to blunt the edge of African independence." Political groups within Kenya battled with each other, but in this context their struggle was not over political power per se, but for the attention of Her Majesty's Government. It was through this management of colonial government that groups jockeyed with each other for position. Still, constitutional negotiations both provided a means of colonial governance and offered a path toward independence. For all the limitations, one thing seemed clear in 1960: Groups in Kenya saw this process as the one way to move forward without chaos.[7]

The stakes at the upcoming constitutional conference were high. Said one white settler woman in Kenya, "Everything here is hanging on this Conference, and whatever happens I expect it will result in strikes and riots at this end. Most people's one idea is to sell out quickly, tho' who is going to buy is quite another matter." Many thought that no constitutional protections would be strong enough to safeguard the interests of white settlers in an African-run government. Some Kenyan whites therefore developed elaborate plans for a transfer of white-owned farms to Africans and the departure of white settlers from Kenya. Meanwhile, for the Kikuyu, the aftermath of the emergency was a time of less brutality but continuing trauma.[8]

It was, in short, a tense and exciting time for Thurgood Marshall to go to Kenya. Marshall made an initial stop in Liberia, a nation settled by African Americans hoping to escape slavery and American racism. Liberia would have been familiar to any graduate of Lincoln University, like Marshall, since many of its leaders were trained there. This visit might have served as a warning. Marshall attended the inauguration of President William V. S. Tubman, who was first elected in 1943 and served twenty-seven years. Election irregularities and human rights abuses were overlooked by the United States, which considered Liberia to be a faithful cold war ally. But in Tubman, Marshall saw something that had not yet come to Kenya or America: a black man presiding over a nation. If he was troubled by anything he saw in Liberia, he did not convey it.[9]

There would be no pomp and circumstance when Marshall arrived in Kenya in early January 1960, however. As an African American activist traveling to a rigidly controlled colony with the objective of aiding the nationalists, he was fortunate to get a visa. Once in Kenya, he would face colonial government restrictions on his activities. Nonetheless, going to Kenya gave Marshall a chance to step outside of it all, to make new connections. Like many travelers before him, he found in the foreign something deeply familiar. In a letter to Marshall, Tom Mboya put it this way: "As you yourself said, you were glad to be home, and we were glad to welcome you home."[10]

It might seem strange for an American lawyer with no previous experience with African law to serve as an expert at Kenya's constitutional deliberations. But Marshall had something that an "underdeveloped" region like Kenya was thought to need: expertise in a "developed" legal system. Americans had long thought of the world as divided into developed and underdeveloped spaces. President Harry Truman argued in 1949 that promoting economic expansion was "the key to prosperity and peace" and that technical expertise would bring about development. Soon, American lawyers lent a hand in bringing law to bear to aid "underdeveloped" nations. By the 1960s, the idea of development was ubiquitous; as anthropologist Arturo Escobar put it, the world was "colonized by the development discourse," and "it seemed impossible to conceptualize social reality in other terms." According to this mind-set, Marshall's expertise in American law was all he really needed.[11]

Marshall had done legal work overseas before. In the early 1950s, during the Korean War, he responded to the pleas of African American soldiers who had received harsh sentences for misconduct. Korea was the first major U.S. military engagement after President Truman issued an executive order to desegregate the military in 1948. The war finally desegregated the army if only because it proved impractical to send needed replacement troops according to race. But reports surfaced of disparities in punishment for misconduct based on race, resulting in horrific sentences for African American soldiers. Concerned about discrimination, Marshall traveled to Japan and then to Korea to investigate, interviewing soldiers near the front lines. He was successful in reducing the sentences of thirty soldiers.[12]

When he left for Africa, Marshall had no preconceived set of constitutional plans for the colony. Legal Defense Fund (LDF) attorney Jack Greenberg recalled that he did research on British Commonwealth constitutions and gave Marshall a book on the topic that he took on the trip. James Nabritt III, a young LDF lawyer, also provided Marshall with materials, including a copy of the Universal Declaration of Human Rights. But when asked by a reporter upon his arrival whether he supported universal suffrage for Kenya, Marshall demurred. "I have got to have a look around," he replied. Although Marshall may have simply intended to be cautious, to wait and see what conditions were on the ground before committing to a position on the constitution, this comment apparently disturbed some nationalists, since they planned to push for universal adult suffrage.[13]

Marshall was quickly introduced to race relations in the colony. "The restrictions were almost unbelievable," he later said. "Africans could not hold a meeting in a building. So as a result, the only meetings they had were outside." Marshall met with a delegation that included Tom Mboya and others: "I listened to them and took their instructions, and ... I left Kenya after a week or so under great handicap."[14]

On his second day in the colony, Marshall went to the town of Kiambu for a meeting of the African Elected Members organization. The AEM were Africans elected to the few seats set aside for them in the colonial legislature. Because actual political parties were banned, their organization was a principle locus for African political organization. But even this group could not meet freely. As Marshall later recalled, "There were two thousand Africans standing out in the field, perfectly quiet, and the leaders were meeting in the building but they couldn't go in. The leaders were in one building. They were out. They were standing out in that hot sun, all day, waiting for the leaders to come out and report to them." Before Marshall could enter the building and join the meeting, a district officer intervened. He introduced himself, "very politely, like the British always are," and asked Marshall what he planned to do.[15]

> I said, "I'm going in there. That's what I came over here for, was to talk to these people."

He said, "Well, you can't go in there."

I said, "Why?"

He said, "You don't have a permit."

And Tom Mboya spoke up and he said, "Why, of course he has a permit. We got one last week."

He said, "Yes, and it was revoked yesterday."[16]

At that point, Marshall recounted,

I started to be loud and boisterous and get arrested, and suddenly it dawned on me that if I was arrested, I'd be searched. I had money and paraphernalia and stuff for Mboya and others in my pockets, and if I was caught with that, I would really spend the rest of my life in jail.

Instead, he politely said to the district officer, "Of course. I understand. But before I leave, I wonder if I could just say a word to all those people out there?" The officer said no. Marshall pressed his case: "I'm not going to make a speech. Just let me say one word of greeting." Finally, the officer relented and said, "All right, all right, just one word." At that, Marshall, a rather large man, leaped on top of Tom Mboya's station wagon. "I looked over the crowd, and they all recognized Tom Mboya, and I guess they knew who I was, I don't know," he recalled. Then he shouted one word: "Uhuru!" and "pandemonium broke out. They all crowded, cheered, and everything, and the district officer was really mad as all get out." The reason, he explained, was that "the word 'Uhuru' means 'Freedom Now.' Not tomorrow, but freedom right now." The district officer then "told me where I'd better go right quick, so I did."[17]

On January 14, Marshall's hosts showed him the White Highlands, the beautiful region outside Nairobi, with deep green vegetation set off against the rich red soil. The *white* in the highlands was a racial bar: Only whites could own land there. Marshall would have seen firsthand the way white supremacy was embedded in these hillsides: the beautiful homes of white farmers, the poverty of the Africans. The long drive from Nairobi would leave much time for conversations about the Africans who worked land that they could not own. It might have seemed like a scene transported from south of the Mason-Dixon line, like Southern plantations owned by whites but dependent on black labor. A difference between them was that Africans would soon hold political power and could change things. In the United States, many African Americans were still disenfranchised, and they remained a minority, overwhelmed in many areas by white political power. What Marshall saw in the highlands had a deep impact. He worked to protect the rights of the white minority, but they must have angered him. On a later trip to Kenya, Marshall was asked to attend a meeting with white settlers in the highlands, but he simply refused.[18]

After touring the highlands, Marshall held a press conference, announcing that he and the Africans agreed completely about the area and that "there was no reason for land to be restricted on the basis of race anywhere in the world." He added that he would "apply this principle to the African land areas of Kenya as well as the White Highlands." He and the African Elected Members were "in complete agreement" on other matters, stressing that "independence and freedom for Kenya was due now."[19]

The American press seemed unsure what to think of Marshall's role. Under the headline "Negroes' Lawyer on World Stage," the *New York Times* put it this way: "The fast-talking 51-year-old lawyer has argued for Negroes' rights in the United States for a quarter of a century. Now he is testing his talents on the larger stage of the Negro's rights in Africa." Marshall's reasons for assisting the Kenyans, according to the *Times*, were three: increased awareness of African problems in the United States;

seeking business opportunities for African Americans; and the fact that he had never been to Africa before. "I had always meant to go," he said in an interview, "but never got around to it. I was always too busy." Underneath it all was his conviction, now that he had been there, that Kenya had reached a critical juncture: "These people have had it," he wrote to his wife, "and they are not going to take any more."[20]

Marshall soon left Kenya, and then traveled to London for the Lancaster House conference on the Kenya constitution. He was the only person present who was neither British nor Kenyan. Marshall's role, as the *Cleveland Call and Post* reported it, was "to write a tricky constitution that will give the Africans in Kenya complete political power on the basis of a democratically elected government by universal franchise, while protecting the rights of the white minorities which is [sic] outnumbered about 100 to one."[21]

As Marshall described it, his delegation at Lancaster House "was made up of all native African men born in Kenya." The delegates were political leaders in the colony, having won seats in the colonial legislature during the first legislative elections that included African candidates in the late 1950s. Although the battle to overthrow colonialism brought them together, there were important divisions among these leaders. The most obvious tensions were between Mboya and Oginga Odinga. Both were members of the Luo tribe, which was concentrated in the Nyanza Province on the shores of Lake Victoria. Odinga worked to unite the Luo and would emerge as the politician with the strongest base among the tribe. He was the most persistent of the African Elected Members in working for Kenyatta's release. Mboya's political constituency was the urban Nairobi central district, and he was the only rising Kenyan political figure with a constituency that was not principally defined by tribe. This resulted both from Mboya's trajectory from labor leader to national political leader, since his labor union work placed him in contact with unions representing workers from different tribes, and from Mboya's philosophy. He believed that transcending tribalism was an essential element of nation building. The Mboya/Odinga rivalry soon took on cold war overtones. Mboya received aid from Americans, and Odinga turned for support to U.S. adversaries, including the Soviet Union, China, and East Germany. While their supporters surely influenced them, they used outside support to pursue domestic political goals. Ronald Ngala, who served as leader of the delegation, represented smaller tribes on the Kenyan coast. He would later join forces with Blundell and with minority tribes worried about losing out to the Kikuyu and Luo in an independent Kenya, ultimately backing a federal constitution that gave power to regional governments. Mboya and Odinga, in contrast, would support a stronger central government.[22]

Marshall's group was the only nationalist group at the 1960 meeting. They were united in their opposition to colonial rule despite tribal differences, which would play a more important role as political parties in Kenya developed in the years after the conference. When Kenyans convened again at Lancaster House two years later, nationalist politics had formally fractured into two competing parties (the Kenya African National Union and the Kenya African Democratic Union), and nationalists were split between two different delegations to the conference.[23]

There were three other delegations at Lancaster House. The New Kenya Group was mixed-race. This group included "moderate" white settlers, such as Michael Blundell, who had concluded that the only way to have a voice in future Kenyan politics was as part of a multiracial coalition. Another delegation consisted of Asian Indians, a major minority group in Kenya. The final delegation, representing the United Party, was all white. "The best way I can explain them is that if you compared them to the Ku Klux Klan in its heyday in this country, the Ku

Tom Mboya in London for the Lancaster House conference on the
Kenyan constitution, January 1960. (© Hulton-Deutsch Collection/
CORBIS)

Klux Klan would look like a Sunday School picnic," Marshall
said. "These were real rabid, awful."[24]

The British were not sure what to make of Marshall's presence
at Lancaster House. The British Colonial Office expressed a "tinge
of apprehension" about his appointment, expressing their hope
to the U.S. Embassy that "Marshall had Commonwealth constitutional experience." Although he was not particularly pleased,

ultimately Colonial Secretary Ian Macleod concluded that he "had no objection to Thurgood Marshall as [a] special adviser." Other British observers were less accepting. One British citizen wrote a letter of protest to Macleod, complaining that he was "surprised and astounded" to see an announcement of Marshall's role in the British press. He urged Macleod to "arrange for this to be stopped." Marshall was "leader of America's *National Association for the Advancement of Coloured People*." The writer said he was "informed on good authority that this organisation is largely run by Communists and it is known to have stirred up trouble against Britain in many parts of Africa. Surely the British Government cannot permit such an unwise and disgraceful arrangement for legal advice to be used at *our Conference on East Africa and Kenya here in London*."[25]

New York World Herald columnist Robert Ruark agreed, arguing that the conference was "none of America's interest, and...certainly...none of Mr. Marshall's business." Marshall's work was "meddling of the highest order." But Murray Kempton at the *New York Post* saw it differently. Marshall's presence at the Lancaster House conference was "one of the most extraordinary events in colonial history," he wrote. "There seems to be no record in diplomatic history of a private citizen of the United States sitting at a British government conference whose subject is Crown colonial policy." For Kempton, there was "romance in the image of Thurgood Marshall, the product of segregated schools, a child in a border city, welcomed as a distinguished American lawyer by a British Colonial Secretary. He represents the only revolutionary force that we have constructed in this century and it is suitable for export all over the world."[26]

The U.S. government was already closely following the Kenyan constitutional talks, and with an American taking a prominent role, American diplomats kept an eye on his work. On January 28, Secretary of State Christian Herter cabled the U.S. Embassy in London for information. Because Marshall was getting a lot of press, he asked the embassy in London to keep him informed. The embassy kept track of Marshall and reported back on his activities. The American position on Kenya, as the U.S. Embassy put it, was that an "orderly transition to self-government and eventual self-determination" was in everyone's interest and that "all people permanently resident in Africa have legitimate interests for which they can rightfully demand fair and just consideration." American diplomats supported the British government's position, but they also paid close attention to the nationalists, hoping to ally themselves with an independent Kenya.[27]

If the U.S. government was ambivalent about Marshall's participation at Lancaster House, Oginga Odinga, Mboya's chief rival in Kenya, had stronger feelings. He thought that Marshall's presence "gave the United States' circles a foot in the door," and he was very unhappy about it. Americans were supporting his political rival, Tom Mboya. Because of this, Odinga was concerned that an American role at Lancaster House might strengthen Mboya's hand. It didn't help that Mboya apparently acted on his own in arranging Marshall's participation. According to Mboya's biographer, Philip Goldsworthy, this was just one of Mboya's unilateral moves related to the Lancaster House conference, and his tendency to go it alone generated tension and resentment within the group.[28]

There were also broader political complications that had nothing to do with Marshall. Without Kenyatta present, the nationalists were in an awkward position. They had pledged not to work with the colonial government unless Kenyatta was released. Their very presence at Lancaster House without Kenyatta therefore raised concerns among some Kenyans at home. Because of this, the Africans announced that they sought two advisors at the meeting, Thurgood Marshall and Peter Mbui Koinange. Koinange, a nationalist in exile, could provide the group with needed legitimacy, since, like Kenyatta, the British thought of him as a Mau Mau leader and he was therefore outside what the British considered to be an acceptable political community. The British government balked, barring Koinange from the meeting, and calling him "one of the only two men outside Kenya regarded by the Government of Kenya as responsible for the unhappy events that led to the Emergency in Kenya." In response, the African Elected Members boycotted the conference.[29]

Marshall translated this turn of events for the American press in London. He explained that the Africans had already softened their position of noncooperation with the colonialists until Kenyatta was released. Having compromised on Kenyatta, the Africans thought they needed Koinange as an African elder statesman. If they gave in to objections about Koinange's participation, Marshall pointed out, "the people back home will accuse them of selling out and any agreement they make at the conference will be regarded with suspicion."[30]

The Lancaster House conference on the Kenya constitution began without the Africans, and without Thurgood Marshall. Macleod hoped that, having made their point, the Africans would join the conference, but it would take a compromise to put the meeting back on track. The controversy over Koinange led the British to change their views about Thurgood Marshall. Macleod now called Marshall "a very distinguished lawyer and one whom we will be very glad to see at our Conference." Macleod was sorry to have to proceed without the Africans. The ultimate objective of the negotiations, he stressed, was "to lead Kenya on to enjoy full self-government, or if I may use a plainer word, Independence." This word—Independence—would come as a shock to those who were counting on many more years, and many more harvests, under colonial rule.[31]

Independence, however, was not the focus of the 1960 conference. Instead, Macleod described the goal as planning "the next step in Kenya's constitutional evolution." The timing of more extensive political change would depend on the pace at which Kenya could "assume greater responsibility for the conduct of her own affairs." *Responsibility* had a particular meaning. Africans were in the majority, but for Macleod responsible government required that everyone in Kenya was entitled to contribute to governance.[32]

The central problem, as Macleod saw it, was enfranchising the majority without sacrificing minority rights, and it had to be solved before Kenya could be independent. England did not have a written constitution with a bill of rights, but he thought this American-style solution would help, and that "for the time being…the interests of minorities might have to be secured through constitutional safeguards." Macleod proposed a committee on safeguards, or a bill of rights, as one of the three working groups for the conference. While it was important to move forward with reform, that did not mean that Kenya would be independent anytime soon. At that point, some British leaders believed that Kenya might become independent in about fifteen years.[33]

Unable to attend the opening meeting due to the boycott, Marshall instead spoke to the press. He warned of serious consequences for Kenya if an agreement acceptable to the Africans on Kenya's constitution was not reached. "A revolt might occur if the constitutional conference meeting ended with what the Kenyans considered to be an 'imposed' constitution." There could be "a new uprising in Kenya that nobody can control—any more than they could control Mau Mau." He warned, "This new group throughout Africa knows exactly what they want. They want independence now—tomorrow is too late."[34]

The *East African Standard*, a paper serving the white settler community in Kenya, focused on Marshall's support for property rights. Marshall had high hopes for majority rule with "minority safeguards and an effective Bill of Rights," the paper reported.

"Most important," however, was protecting property "so that no future Government of Kenya can seize the land in the Highlands." This would have sounded good to white settlers, but their perspective was different. Marshall's own vision of rights turned more on the problem of equality than on property. He told the *Standard* that "the central fact of Kenya's political future, . . . was that there are 6,000,000 Africans as compared with 64,000 Europeans, 165,000 Asians and 35,000 Arabs." The reason to protect property rights in the Highlands was because of the minority status of the white landowners, and the reality that after independence, they simply would not be able to command the votes to prevail in the legislature. It was the vulnerability of a minority in a democratic system that worried Marshall, not any absolute preference for rights of property.[35]

While the boycott continued at Lancaster House, Marshall worked on a bill of rights. Meanwhile, "the Kenya Nationalists stood their ground," said the *Ghana Times*, the principal paper of a nation that achieved independence in 1957. They "boycotted the conference till the Colonial Secretary, perhaps, realised that a Kenya conference without the accredited leaders of Kenya was like Hamlet without the prince." Macleod's hard position on Koinange's participation had been due to pressure from white settlers. For them, "recognition of Mr. Koinange, in any form, whatsoever, is an anathema; and the very mention of the man's name, is said to cause the blood-pressure of certain people to shoot up." The *Ghana Times* was not sympathetic: "Well, these people, with all respect, will have to be told that the rising tide of nationalism in Africa is a fact which cannot be denied or ignored, and that it is more prudent to swim with the tide than against it."[36]

Ultimately, Macleod brokered a compromise. Each delegation would be entitled to one advisor in attendance at the sessions in Lancaster House. Other advisors, including Koinange, could be present in the building but could not attend sessions.

Because of this deal, the African delegation's sole advisor present at the sessions would be Thurgood Marshall. In the end, Koinange made only one appearance in Lancaster House.[37]

Macleod was now very pleased with Marshall. His presence as an alternative to Koinange made compromise possible. Marshall had no objection. He understood that the nationalists needed Koinange. He set to work but did not draw attention to himself. He received press attention, but, according to the U.S. Embassy, he did not "become [a] subject of controversy."[38]

WHILE MARSHALL WAS AT WORK AT LANCASTER HOUSE, change was brewing back home. On February 1, 1960, four African American freshmen at North Carolina Agricultural and Technical College held a sit-in at the segregated lunch counter at Woolworth's in Greensboro. The simple protest soon expanded into a widespread sit-in movement. As Jack Greenberg recalled, "It was as if a spark had been struck in an oxygen-filled atmosphere." The sit-ins quickly spread and soon blanketed the South. African Americans demanded service at segregated lunch counters and other businesses. In Northern cities, supporters demonstrated at local branches of the offending chain stores.[39]

If the United States was to offer a model of change through law that emerging nations might emulate, this new direction in the civil rights movement complicated the picture. Activists had been reading Gandhi and they were challenging the assumptions of the older generation. Not everyone thought a courtroom was the place to transform America. And the younger generation thought the lawyers' methods were too slow. "All of Africa will be free before the American Negro attains first class citizenship," James Lawson complained at a meeting of student leaders in 1960. "Most of us will be grandparents before we can live normal lives." Lawson had spent three years as a missionary in India and there had learned Mahatma Gandhi's philosophy of nonviolence. He urged members of what became the Student Nonviolent Coordinating Committee to hew to Gandhian ideas. Sit-ins would both speed social change and expose the evil of segregation. He criticized the NAACP for focusing on litigation and fund-raising. The movement's greatest resource, he argued, was an emboldened people, no longer the victims, who would "act in a disciplined manner to implement the constitution."[40]

Tension between civil rights lawyers and activists over direct action tactics had arisen before. When members of the Congress of Racial Equality (CORE) and the Fellowship of Reconciliation planned the Journey of Reconciliation, an integrated bus trip through the upper South in 1947, most African American leaders opposed it. "A disobedience movement on the part of Negroes and their white allies," Thurgood Marshall said at the time, "if employed in the South, would result in wholesale slaughter with no good achieved." Bayard Rustin retorted that Marshall was "either ill-informed on the principles and techniques of non-violence or ignorant of the processes of social change." For Rustin, discriminatory practices would not end simply "because supreme courts deliver just opinions." Progress instead came "from struggle; all freedom demands a price." That the price could be high, including the risk of injury and death, was something Rustin acknowledged. "If anyone at this date in history believes that the 'white problem,' which is one of privilege, can be settled without some violence, he is mistaken and fails to realize the ends to which man can be driven to hold on to what they consider privileges."[41]

The sit-ins inaugurated an explosive decade. The civil rights movement not only challenged the tactics of lawyers, it presented them with a potentially massive and difficult caseload. Thousands of students would end up in jail and need representation. But it was not clear that existing legal doctrine would protect them. How were civil rights lawyers to react?

Marshall has been characterized as a critic of the civil rights movement's turn to civil disobedience, but his position on the issue was complicated. After the sit-ins began in 1960, Derrick Bell, then a young lawyer at the LDF, recalled, "Thurgood stormed around the room proclaiming in a voice that could be heard across Columbus Circle that he did not care what anyone said, he was not going to represent a bunch of crazy colored students who violated the sacred property rights of white folks by going in their stores or lunch counters and refusing to leave when ordered to do so." Marshall biographer Mark Tushnet has written that Marshall and other NAACP leaders were "ambivalent" about the sit-in tactic at first. Judge Constance Baker Motley, then an LDF lawyer, recalled that "the NAACP and LDF had consciously avoided urging individuals to risk arrest by defying local Jim Crow laws and customs," because they were not confident they could successfully defend them. Under existing federal law, discrimination by private restaurants and other private businesses was not unlawful. And because the students were often prosecuted under facially valid laws prohibiting disturbing the peace or trespassing, there was real doubt about whether there was a valid legal theory to challenge the arrests. The lawyers were also concerned about their roles as leaders of the movement. Robert Carter cautioned that supporting the sit-ins "would tie us to something that some other organization has taken and run with." Tushnet suggests that Marshall's "respect for law also played a part in his reaction." It was one thing to violate a segregation law, but the students were violating laws that, on their face, were appropriate. And it would be expensive. Handling hundreds of individual cases in state court would take tremendous resources.[42]

The story of Marshall storming around the room has been interpreted as showing that he did not support the grassroots movement. But taking a conservative position and forcing people to argue with him was also his classic method of honing a legal argument. Lewis Sargentich, Marshall's Supreme Court law clerk during the 1970 term, said that when discussing cases, the "Marshall technique" was to "take [the] most conservative position & let clerks try to beat him down." This method required that the clerks "feel free enough to fight hard." It was a way of testing ideas and would challenge his clerks to come up with good counterarguments. With the LDF facing new legal hurdles, it would not be uncharacteristic for Marshall to adopt the least favorable argument as a way of challenging his colleagues to strengthen their own.[43]

Marshall may not have embraced the student movement with open arms, but he did put the resources and staff of the LDF behind the effort to defend the students in court. He quickly convened a three-day lawyers' conference to debate legal strategies for defending the demonstrators. The lawyers concluded that "the use of public force in arrest or conviction of students engaged in peaceful demonstration is in truth state enforcement of private discrimination." Government involvement in enforcing private discrimination, they argued, was a violation of the Constitution. This idea provided the basis for a legal defense. In the hands of the NAACP and LDF lawyers, charges of petty lawbreaking in the interests of justice took on constitutional significance.[44]

Nineteen-sixty was not the first time the LDF had backed students. On December 20, 1958, Bruce Boynton, an African American law student at Howard Law School, was on his way home to Alabama for Christmas. Instead, he ended up in a jail cell in Richmond, Virginia. Boynton's Trailways bus from Washington, DC, to Montgomery, Alabama, had stopped about 10:30 P.M. for a long break in Richmond. Boynton was hungry, and he stepped into a restaurant in the Trailways bus station. In Richmond, seating was segregated. The "colored" section was crowded, so Boynton sat down in the white section.[45]

He described what happened next: "One of the waitresses on duty came up to me and asked me to go over on the other side, that they had facilities over there." Boynton told her that the other side was crowded, and besides, since he was an interstate passenger, he could eat where he was sitting. The Supreme Court had held in *Henderson v. United States* that a federal statute governing interstate commerce made segregation unlawful in trains and buses that carried passengers across state lines. The waitress was not impressed. She told Boynton that she couldn't serve him. At some point the manager arrived. Boynton showed him his interstate bus ticket, but the manager also insisted that he move. Boynton refused and was arrested for trespassing.[46]

The sit-ins in Greensboro, North Carolina, in February 1960 sparked sit-ins across the South. This interracial group sitting in at a drugstore in Arlington, Virginia, is picketed by members of the American Nazi Party carrying racist placards, June 9, 1960. (© Wally McNamee/ CORBIS)

Boynton was not the first, and not the last, to sit down. Rosa Parks had more famously refused to move to the back of the bus in Montgomery, Alabama, in 1956, helping to set off the Montgomery bus boycott, a pivotal moment in the civil rights movement. There were others who never made national headlines, such as Edna Griffin of Des Moines, Iowa, who sat down at a segregated soda fountain in 1948, was kicked out, and inspired a local boycott that led to integration.[47]

Boynton himself was convicted of trespassing and fined $10. *Boynton v. Virginia* was Marshall's final case in the chambers of the U.S. Supreme Court as an LDF lawyer. Marshall argued the case, James M. Nabrit III remembered, in a way "designed to make the judges want to rule in his favor." Marshall previewed an argument that would become even more relevant to the 1960s sit-ins. While he argued the case on the grounds that the segregated restaurant violated the Interstate Commerce Act, he also argued that discrimination by a private company became public discrimination, in violation of the Fourteenth Amendment, when enforced by the police, and so Boynton's arrest for violating the restaurant's segregation rule was unconstitutional state action. Marshall's oral argument was heard in October 1960. Everyone knew that many sit-in cases were in the Court's pipeline. The Supreme Court did not take up the constitutional argument in its *Boynton* opinion, but instead held that under the Interstate Commerce Act, Boynton had a right to be served in the white section of the restaurant. But Marshall's use of the constitutional argument ensured that when the sit-in cases came before the Court in 1961—cases without the clearer statutory argument—the controversial constitutional argument had already had an airing.[48]

Boynton would not result in a landmark constitutional ruling. But the case connected one moment in the civil rights struggle and another. Boynton helped open a door to a new phase of the movement, which would focus on the streets. In February 1961, civil rights leader James Farmer found letters about the *Boynton* case waiting for him on his first day as CORE's new director. CORE staffers were already thinking about testing enforcement of the case. Soon they began organizing the historic Freedom Rides, integrated bus trips through the South that drew a stunningly violent reaction from segregationists. John Lewis recalled his first encounter with violence in Rock Hill, South Carolina. He walked into the white waiting room of a segregated Greyhound bus terminal. Young white teenagers playing pinball, in leather jackets and with ducktail haircuts, ordered him to the other side. "I did not feel nervous at all," Lewis wrote in his memoir. He told them he had a right to be there because of the *Boynton* case.

> I really did not feel afraid. "I have a right to go in there...on the grounds of the Supreme Court decision in the *Boynton* case."...
>
> "Shit on that," one of them said.
>
> The next thing I knew a fist smashed the right side of my head.
>
> Then another hit me square in the face.

Police eventually intervened and told the white boys to go home. Lewis had bruised ribs and lacerations and needed medical care, but first insisted on sitting in the white section and drinking a cup of coffee.[49]

WHEN MARSHALL SET TO WORK ON THE KENYAN BILL of Rights in January 1960, he was torn between two continents and two movements. These struggles for justice seemed so different. In one, a people tried to make a nation. In the other, supposedly free citizens fought for an equality long promised but never delivered. What drew these movements together was that in both places people sought social change in an environment laced with the possibility of violence.[50]

The difficulty for Marshall as an advisor was how to counsel a move forward in this threatening context. In Kenya, many feared that chaos would erupt and urged that change must be deliberate and slow. Others warned that without immediate progress, Kenya would face a violent upheaval. Kenya was framed always in terms of the latest African conflagration. First was the fear, in early 1960, that another Mau Mau rebellion might take place, throwing the colony back into the insurgency and counterinsurgency of the '50s. Then, violence in Congo became the new reference point for Kenya. A crisis erupted in that country after independence as Belgium, the departing colonial power, tried to retain a hold on a mineral-rich region and the new government attempted to establish control over divided factions. Ultimately, the independent nation's first prime minister, Patrice Lumumba, who had sought Soviet support, was murdered by a rival faction, with Belgian and U.S. involvement. The need for peaceful social change, the need for a just legal order, the means to transition to African majority rule—Kenyans viewed their future in the shadow of the Congo. Planning independence through the process of legal negotiations was seen as an effort to protect Kenya from the same fate. In this context, law and politics were not simply a path to governance; they were a means of avoiding bloodshed.[51]

The challenge for both the activists and their advisor was how to operate within a violent terrain. In the United States, this was an era when the story of Emmett Till was recent memory. When the mangled body of the Chicago teenager was retrieved from a river in Mississippi in 1955, his mother, Mamie Till, insisted on an open casket funeral, so that the world could see what they did to her son. Till had flirted with a white woman. In death, his battered face became a symbol of the way unwritten racial norms were enforced in corners of America. For those hoping to transform American race relations, Till's murder was an unsettling reminder of the danger of their work.[52]

Marshall was no stranger to violence. Racial violence had brought him to the town of Columbia, Tennessee, in 1946, where an altercation between a black Navy veteran and a white store clerk resulted first in the veteran's arrest for disturbing the peace. Later he was charged with attempted murder, a felony, and this inflamed tensions. A white mob gathered at the courthouse. Blacks gathered in the segregated black business district. White patrolmen entered the black district, and, after refusing a request to stop, were shot and injured. Although law enforcement prevented the worst white mob action, the black part of town was ransacked. One hundred African American men were arrested. Marshall assisted Tennessee lawyers Z. Alexander Looby and Maurice Weaver with their defense.[53]

One day after the trial, Marshall was driving to Nashville with his colleagues when his car was stopped by three carloads of Tennessee police. They searched the car for alcohol, found none, and let them go. At this point, Marshall asked Looby to take over the driving. The car was pulled over again. This time police asked for the driver's licenses of everyone in the vehicle. Although Marshall was sitting in the backseat, they ordered him out and arrested him for drunk driving. Marshall said he had not touched alcohol in two days, during the trial. The police told Looby to keep going. With Marshall in custody, the police drove down a back road. Marshall later recalled that much of the town had gathered by the river "for a party." But Looby trailed the police car, and the police finally changed course and drove instead into town, which was deserted. The officer told Marshall to go, alone, to the magistrate's office. Marshall said to him: "'If we go over, I'm going with you.' He said, 'Why?' I said, 'You're not going to shoot me in the back while I'm "escaping." I mean, let's make this legal.' So he said, 'Smart-ass nigger,' and things like that."[54]

The magistrate eventually concluded that Marshall was not drunk and let him go. On the way out of town, Marshall, Looby, and the others divided into three cars and went separate ways. Marshall left safely, but Looby's car was followed and the driver beaten. Marshall believed he had escaped a lynching party, and there were surely many in the towns where he appeared in Southern courtrooms who would have welcomed such an occasion.[55]

For Marshall, courts were a contained environment in which he could battle Jim Crow without physical violence. But his was not the only philosophy of social change. Gandhi first began to develop his idea of *satyagraha*, a philosophy of social change through nonviolence, in South Africa, battling discrimination against Indians. For Gandhi, truth was achieved "not by infliction of suffering on the opponent, but on one's self." Gandhi led thousands in nonviolent protests, helping to unhinge British rule. News of Gandhi's work in India was followed by many African Americans. Bayard Rustin was most prominent in bringing Gandhi's philosophy into the American civil rights movement, through his work with Martin Luther King Jr., beginning with the 1955 Montgomery bus boycott. King became the movement's most eloquent proponent of nonviolent direct action, arguing that "the Gandhian philosophy of nonviolence is the only logical and moral approach to the solution of the race problem in the United States."[56]

Gandhi showed the way a movement, by drawing violence, could ultimately bring about the undoing of a state. Americans tried their hand at nonviolent civil disobedience and debated whether civil disobedience or legal action was the best means of change. These were important questions in many nations, but not the only ones. In Kenya, some insurgents remained in the forests and would never see the land they fought for. For them, constitutional negotiations held no promise, and the effort to

construct Western-style legal institutions was simply a capitula-
tion. Gandhi was not their model. The question still remains for
some Africans whether creating a state that was truly African
required more of a revolution than the times would tolerate.[57]

The costs of social change were so apparent in 1960, on the
streets of American cities, or in African communities like Sharpe-
ville, South Africa, where a peaceful demonstration in March
ended in a hail of bullets. The risks and the consequences
weighed heavily on the minds of all who tried to overturn injustice. Perhaps the most important question was whether social
change and violence were interdependent, whether one could
not exist without the other.

For Marshall, any path to social change would be ineffective
if it did not reform the legal order. American history bore out
this idea, he believed. And so although Marshall would not try
to impose particular American laws on Kenya, his very notion of
the means of social change was forged in his American experience. At a time when the tools of the lawyers were under assault
in his own country, Marshall took to Lancaster House the project of law reform.

- 3 -

WRITING RIGHTS

[The Bill of Rights] should not entrench the position of those enjoying a privileged position, nor perpetuate a system that was basically unjust.
—Tom Mboya, 1960

I would suggest those who are not satisfied—like the seven at the lunch counter—return to their native Africa, and they'll find out they're doing a lot better here than they would in their native land.
—Louisiana Governor Earl Kemp Long, reacting to the sit-in movement, 1960

MIDAS MIGHT HAVE TOUCHED THE WALLS of Lancaster House and reached up to brush his fingertips across the ceiling, drenching it in gold. The brilliance of the fine, detailed gold engravings, enhanced in the principal meeting room by a massive crystal chandelier, nearly eclipsed the beauty of the fine paintings, mostly of elegant women and children and of angelic visions, gracing the walls. In its opulence, it was a setting designed, it would seem, for one ruler to impress another.[1]

Into these halls and up the gilded staircase came not only the British officials used to these accoutrements, but also the subjects of empire with very modest lives. The forces that had led to the gatherings at Lancaster House were in the streets of Britain's far-flung colonies, in the trading houses, in the camps of the insurgents. But it was in this gilded setting, around tables set with fine linens, that the British Empire negotiated the terms of its retreat. It was here that one form of global dominance pre-pared to be eclipsed by another.

Thurgood Marshall was more comfortable on the streets of Manhattan, amid the gray stone buildings at Columbus Circle, in the Legal Defense Fund offices. The grandeur there lay not in the appointments but in a view of Central Park. But he was used to navigating the chasm between a home in Harlem and the majesty of the American Supreme Court building. And he was not in London to be comfortable but to do his job.

As an American, Marshall might seem like an intruder in a conversation, in essence, between British ruler and subject. But his presence was a marker of an era. His nation had thrown off British rule, an example that inspired the new generation. Now African Americans challenged their country to live up to its democratic ideals. In the decades ahead, would the world's leading democracy bestow full democratic rights on all its citizens? As emerging nations attained sovereignty, would they follow America's early path of rights only for some, or make of all their people full citizens?

The task of those present in Lancaster House was to chart a rule of law to guide the future. But the setting said more about the role of power and privilege than equality under the law. Perhaps it was fitting, for this would not be a negotiation between free citizens about their future. Ultimately these proceedings would come to a close, and a constitution would be made, not with a vote of the people, but with the signature of a queen.

The beauty of the setting was at odds with the tenor of the proceedings. "Everybody was at everybody's throat," as Marshall put it. What mattered most to the Africans was democratic self-governance, and soon. Delay "would be disastrous," Ronald Ngala, leader of the African delegation, insisted. To reach that goal through constitutional negotiations, the Africans would have to address the problem of the rights of racial minorities. In the past, rights of the white minority had not needed legal protection because they held the reins of power. In the Kenyan government, their interests were formally recognized through reserved seats for racial groups in the legislature, giving the whites far more political power even though they were outnumbered. Now, the Africans wanted "one man, one vote." No special seats for particular groups. Legal rights, rather than reserved seats in the legislature, were the ideal way to protect minorities, the Africans repeatedly emphasized. They favored something that had a very American ring to it: "a Bill of Rights enforced by an independent judiciary." Protection for minority rights had been a long-standing position, argued Dr. Julius Kiano, and was not "developed merely to quiet the fears of those who were afraid of African domination." Oginga Odinga had included a call for complete equality in a 1957 election manifesto, and in 1958, the African Elected Members circulated a memorandum pledging support for a bill of rights. Kiano stressed that Africans intended that an independent Kenya should subscribe to the Convention on Human Rights. The African Elected Members stressed that they had just the person to help with this: Thurgood Marshall, minority rights expert.[2]

The position of the Africans was not quite good enough for Michael Blundell and other so-called moderates in the multiracial New Kenya Group. They could go along with majority African voting power as long as they had both a bill of rights and a guarantee of their seats in the legislature. Since whites would be disadvantaged by a simple majority voting system, they wanted some seats in the legislature reserved only for whites, and other seats reserved for other racial minorities. They wanted it all: guaranteed rights and guaranteed seats.[3]

Asians and Muslims, caught in the middle of the three-tiered racial politics of Kenya, with greater numbers than the whites but with less political power than either whites or Africans, lined

An entryway at Lancaster House, decorated with gold highlights
from floor to ceiling, lit with gold candelabra and a crystal chandelier.
(Photograph by the author, 2007)

up with the New Kenya Group. Special seats for minorities in
the legislature, they believed, was the only way they would have
a voice.[4]

The all-white United Party spoke for the hard-liners who
had not yet come to terms with the passing of an era. They
did not favor voting rights for Africans. Full enfranchisement,
they argued, would have to wait until more Africans had been
educated. If Africans had control, United Party leader L. R.

Briggs told the BBC, "they would make it 'virtually impossible' to farm, either by taxation or by political pressures." For white settlers like Briggs, "if a constitution were introduced which would have the effect of placing the Europeans under the dictatorship of the Africans, then we would naturally wish to enable our people to leave the country if they wished to do so."[5]

Colonial Secretary Ian Macleod thought that a bill of rights was only a second-best source of protection for minorities. He hoped to usher in an era of goodwill and fair dealing. A gradual transition in Kenya would give the races time to work together. "This should help to generate mutual goodwill, respect and understanding, which will afford more lasting assurance of European position than any constitutional safeguards."[6]

The parties soon got to work. Days of grand statements were accompanied by nights of behind-the-scenes negotiations. Through this process, Macleod developed a blueprint for majority rule in Kenya. A new legislative council would consist of thirty-three members elected for the first time to open (non–racially designated) seats. Twenty remaining seats in the legislature would be reserved for minority groups: ten for Europeans, eight for Asians, and two for Arabs. No seats were reserved for Africans because they would be the electoral majority. Based on their proportion of the population, whites would still be over-represented in the colonial legislature, but it was still a major victory for the Africans. For the first time the British government had embraced majority rule in Kenya.[7]

How had this dramatic change come about? In a press conference, Macleod gave his perspective: "In Kenya the groups mainly concerned had taken up positions which it seemed impossible to reconcile. Here in London, by talking out their differences together, they have come much closer to each other." He thought there was "a good chance that the wide measure of agreement" that he had long sought was now within reach.[8]

The Commonwealth Relations Office praised the New Kenya Group. By supporting majority rule if "reasonable agreement is reached on the safeguards," they had shown "great political courage in going beyond views of many supporters (of all races, but particularly of [the] European community)." Government officials hoped the party would "form an effective sandbag against African extremism" and also appeal to Europeans. But back in Kenya, it was unclear whether moderates could survive. Acting Governor Patrick Renison reported that European opinion was coalescing behind the United Party. The United Party opposed Macleod's proposals, but he was still hopeful, believing that "even they are anxious to join in the further discussions."[9]

Nationalist leader Oginga Odinga had a different view about the conference. He called Macleod "a skillful psychologist," able to manipulate all the parties to achieve his objectives. Macleod had held private meetings with each group, letting the Africans know that the British government was prepared to relax restrictions on colony-wide African political activity, but not to release Kenyatta. Macleod "appeared to be concerned with what was acceptable to Africans," and his approach "infuriated the settlers." The settlers' fury "impressed us that we were winning." But Odinga later realized that Macleod was playing the settler reaction against them. He was very patient. "We were at a constitutional disadvantage, he said. We should assist him in dealing with the settlers who were not prepared to give an inch of the way. He conscripted us into looking at the problem from his point of view."[10]

As rights became central to the conference, Thurgood Marshall, a supporting member of the Lancaster House cast of characters, found himself front and center. He was, after all, the "rights" man. A bill of rights was much more in this context, however, than a solemn commitment to future generations. The idea that rights could create a political climate in which all races in Kenya could coexist was what kept the conference going. It was the unseen adhesive holding adversaries together in one place. A contest over rights enabled conflict around a conference table. For these political figures, each of whom believed there was blood on the hands of the other, to do battle around a table, and with words and legal clauses, was no small accomplishment.[11]

It is not surprising that Marshall was enthusiastic about a bill of rights. The U.S. Constitution was amended to include a bill of rights protecting free speech, freedom of religion, and other important rights shortly after the nation was founded. It might seem curious, however, that the British government supported a bill of rights in the Kenyan constitution, since England did not have a written bill of rights. The path toward a bill of rights for Kenya was paved by the experience in Nigeria. Nigeria was the first British colony to adopt a bill of rights on the way to independence in 1960, but the proposal was not without controversy. At a 1953 conference on a constitution for that colony, Colonial Secretary Oliver Lyttleton "managed to laugh the Nigerians out of" a declaration of rights "by saying, 'Why not also put in God is love?'" Lyttleton thought that such a proposal was "not customary" and would be ineffective. Ultimately, however, concerns about minority rights in ethnically diverse Nigeria jeopardized the creation of a unified state. A bill of rights was the answer to the anxieties of minorities. In addition, as civil liberties came under attack in newly independent Ghana, human rights historian A.W. B. Simpson notes, "The failure of the Colonial Office to ensure that fundamental rights were to be protected now seemed to have been a mistake." The Colonial Office thought that a bill of rights for Nigeria would be particularly helpful in the predominantly Muslim north, but how could a document be drafted in a way that didn't cause one region to feel targeted? The answer was to turn to the European Convention of Human Rights, which already applied to Nigeria. A proposal based on the convention was then adopted with little controversy. According to Simpson,

"Though the purpose was to provide minority protection, the bill of rights was so drafted as to confer fundamental rights generally."[12]

Marshall's job of drafting a bill of rights at Lancaster House was not a neat and tidy task, confined to the pristine world of legal analysis. And the document would not inscribe rights that would last forever. Instead, it was bricks-and-mortar work, the laying of a political foundation. The Bill of Rights was most importantly a commitment on the part of the parties to each other, a commitment to politics. To craft rights was to help build a nation.[13]

On February 2, 1960, Marshall submitted his draft Bill of Rights to the Committee on Safeguards at Lancaster House. Although he was an advisor to the African Elected Members (AEM), Marshall submitted his memorandum on his own. "This proposal is solely mine," he wrote, "and has neither been discussed with nor approved or rejected by the African Elected Members or any other group. It is, therefore, submitted for use by all members of the Conference."[14]

Marshall's reasons for submitting it this way are not disclosed in the historical record. It may have reflected everyone's timing and priorities. The nationalists were tied up in negotiations leading to a compromise on representation and suffrage. They held press interviews and meetings, and did much work behind the scenes. Marshall also had to divide his time between his Kenyan work and ongoing responsibilities at the LDF. A bill of rights also raised many complicated issues that the nationalists did not have time to consider fully. And while Marshall and the African delegates supported each other's positions in discussions, Marshall was thought of as a Mboya man, so he was inevitably ensnared in group rivalries. At one point, Odinga was "reported denying rumours of clash between A.E.M. and Thurgood Marshall." But the British press often played up divisions in Kenyan politics, whether or not they existed. Ultimately, Marshall's sole authorship reflects more about his thinking than would a consensus document.[15]

In the end the nationalists were pleased enough with Marshall that when they prepared for a new Lancaster House conference in 1962, two competing nationalist groups named him as a possible advisor. One of the groups, the Kenya African National Union (KANU), the party of Mboya, Odinga, and Kenyatta, included Marshall's draft Bill of Rights among their constitutional demands. Marshall's appointment in October 1961 to the Second Circuit Court of Appeals, however, made him unavailable to serve.[16]

What did Marshall bring to the Bill of Rights? According to Juan Williams, Marshall said that to prepare for this work, he "looked over just about every constitution in the world just to see what was good." Pounding his fist on the desk, he exclaimed, "And there's nothing that comes close to comparing with this one in the U.S. This one is the best I've ever seen." Marshall's admiration for the American constitution was surely genuine. And Marshall assumed that some features of the U.S. constitutional system, such as judicial review, would be part of Kenyan law. But one of the more interesting turns of the story is that Marshall drew more heavily from other sources for his Kenya Bill of Rights. Many passages were identical to the Universal Declaration of Human Rights. Marshall was very familiar with international human rights due to NAACP involvement during the founding of the United Nations, as well as an NAACP petition to the United Nations written by W. E. B. Du Bois in 1948. And it surely helped that James M. Nabrit III, a young LDF lawyer, had thought to hand Marshall a copy before the trip. Marshall also learned about postcolonial constitutions during his work for the Kenyans. His Bill of Rights also borrowed from the independence constitutions of Nigeria and Malaya.[17]

Marshall explained to the Committee on Safeguards later that month that his proposals were intended "to protect the rights of every individual in Kenya, rather than the rights of any particular minority groups." Marshall put the most important principle in the Bill of Rights in the preamble: the principle of equality. "All persons are equal before the law and are entitled without any disorimination [*sic*] or distinction of any kind, such as race, colour, sex, language, religion, political or other opinion, national or social origin, property, birth or other status, to equal protection of the law." Marshall hoped that the preamble would "help the Courts when interpreting the particular provisions of the Bill by setting out general principles on which it would be based." It illustrates two of Marshall's fundamental priorities. The starting point, upon which other rights were built, was equality, not liberty. And independent courts would be part of the political structure that gave these rights meaning.[18]

Section I of the Bill of Rights protected freedom of religion, speech, press, and association. Section II, "Personal Security," protected rights to life and liberty, rights against slavery, and the right to equal protection of the law. Section III guaranteed rights to education, health, and welfare; Section IV protected the right to work; and Section V protected voting rights. Sections I, II, and V were similar in many ways to the U.S. Constitution, but Sections III and IV were different. The U.S. Constitution protects individuals against government misconduct. It protects against discrimination in provision of government services, but it does not require affirmative government assistance, such as health care or education. Marshall's Kenyan Bill of Rights, in contrast, included affirmative rights to protection of social welfare, including rights to education, health, and welfare. The right to work guaranteed a right to employment and to what would now be called a living wage, providing that "everyone who works has the right to just and favourable remuneration insuring for himself and his family an existence worthy of human dignity, and supplemented, if necessary, by other means of social protection." It also protected the right "to form and to join trade unions."

Marshall suggested that the conference should agree on general principles, with detailed drafting to be carried out later.[19]

The property rights clause was the most important provision at the Lancaster House conference. This provision had to balance two interests that seemed irreconcilable: private property rights and the need for land reform. Here Marshall recommended that provisions of the Nigerian Constitution be adapted to conditions in Kenya. His memo simply incorporated the Nigerian text because he thought its property rights clauses were "the best he had met." This section required that the government could only take private property for public purposes. Property could not be "taken possession of compulsorily" except by law, and a forced taking of property required "adequate compensation" and gave the property owner a right to contest the acquisition and amount of compensation in court. Ultimately the language would be modified to include a right to take a dispute over a taking of property directly to the highest court in Kenya. Allowing the government to take property left open the option of land reform, while the requirement of compensation protected minority settlers from government abuse. Because only a tiny number of indigenous Africans in Kenya were lawyers, placing property disputes in the hands of courts meant that property disputes would be resolved in most cases, for the time being, by Asian and European judges. Marshall realized this and thought it was crucial for Kenyan Africans to be trained as lawyers.[20]

The fairly straightforward language of this clause tapped a deep underlying division at the Kenya constitutional conference, a fissure that ran through independence politics in the colony. The most valuable land in Kenya had originally been in the hands of Africans and was now exclusively owned by white settlers. These farmers produced Kenya's agricultural exports, its principal tie with global markets. The settler community believed that the land belonged to them and that their property rights must be protected. Nationalists believed that a key objective of a postcolonial government must be land reform and resettlement, which would redress a historical injustice: the displacement of African peoples under colonialism. For the British, contemplating a continuing relationship with Kenya as part of the Commonwealth and hoping to protect British citizens who had settled in Kenya, any resettlement scheme could not interfere with settler property rights, and so must be based on just compensation.[21]

An argument broke out in committee: for what "public purposes" could the government take land? Some white settlers wanted this spelled out very clearly in order to limit the power of an independence government over land. But to do that seemed to require the Africans to develop a land reform policy on the spot—something they were not in a position to do. Humphrey Slade, a white settler with the New Kenya Group, thought that even if compensation was provided, the government's ability to take land should be restricted to public purposes, and "some definition of 'public purposes,' even if it were a negative one, should be included in the Bill of Rights."[22]

The nationalists balked at this. The new constitution should not tie the hands of a future government. The Bill of Rights "should not entrench the position of those enjoying a privileged position, nor perpetuate a system that was basically unjust," Tom Mboya argued. Instead the Kenyan government should have power to redress inequities. The meaning of "public purposes" should be defined by the courts. In any case, Mboya insisted, a broad understanding of "public purposes" was important. Ngala stressed that it should include "the acquisition of unused land for distribution to the landless of all races."[23]

As the delegates focused on property rights, the conference stalled. Colonial Secretary Macleod was worried that this issue threatened his ability to create a consensus. "We are bogged down over Safeguards," his office reported. "Conference pretty well agreed there should be a Bill of Rights...largely based on Nigerian model. But [the] hitch came, when we got on to property rights." Macleod explained in a memo to Prime Minister Harold Macmillan that the New Kenya Party had made their willingness to go along with the overall constitution conditional on acceptable safeguards. "By that they mean largely land." However, the Africans were "very resentful of the Europeans" for raising the land issue when they had already agreed to have a bill of rights. The Africans "had not come here to discuss land issues" and would not commit to any precise formula. A further wrinkle, Macleod said, was that "they are of course very much divided on the issue themselves."[24]

In spite of the impasse, nearly all the participants hoped to reach some sort of agreement, so that Kenyans of all races could return as soon as possible to Kenya where conditions were worsening. The Africans were unhappy, but willing to compromise, Macleod thought. They wanted to return to Kenya with an agreement, so were prepared to accept a portion of the proposal in spite of their dislike for it. The one thing they would not accept was language defining and limiting the public purposes for which land could be confiscated. Meanwhile, Acting Governor Renison warned of growing unrest among the Europeans in Kenya. "We are afraid that a band of hot heads may do something rash which will spark off a series of racial clashes which will do a good deal of harm particularly to [the] European community."[25]

In an effort at compromise, a new proposal for property rights was circulated to the committee. Under the draft, compulsory takings were limited to circumstances when "required for the fulfilment of contractual or other legal obligations" of the property owner or "circumstances in which such acquisition is justified in the general public interest." On the second page of the proposal, the limitations on the government's power to acquire property were spelled out. A taking would not be "justified in the general public interest" if the property was acquired to make it "available to another person or persons for his or their private advantage" unless the public benefit from the property outweighed the hardship to the property owner.[26]

The Africans said that they could agree to the first page of this language, but not to the second page, with its weighing of public benefits against private harms. The white settlers, especially Slade, held out for page two. Marshall insisted that he was prepared "to stake his reputation" that the language of page two would "add nothing" to the provisions the nationalists were comfortable with. For him, the proposed balancing of public interests against private ones was the obvious way to show that the "general public interest" was served when one person's property was taken for use by another. Still, the nationalists were reluctant. It is unclear whether balancing these interests was itself objectionable or whether, at this point, they simply felt they had been pushed too far.[27]

Macleod thought that the central obstacle to forging a compromise was less the New Kenya Party as a whole than Slade, whom Macleod described as "something of a fanatic" who viewed the issue as a matter of principle. Slade had earlier displayed his "willingness to be burnt to the stake for principle," as Blundell saw it, during the emergency. Slade represented a constituency on the border of the Aberdare Mountains, in the heart of the Mau Mau insurgency, and had demanded more extreme defensive measures than were forthcoming from the colonial government. During the state of emergency, Slade had battled with the British government over counterinsurgency methods. Now he turned to words in a constitutional compromise. As the political power of white settlers waned in Kenya, this was Slade's last place to stand his ground.[28]

Macleod thought that he might need to bring Slade to see Prime Minister Macmillan, and suggested that "an appeal to Slade on the wider grounds of the importance of the Kenya agreement to the whole of Africa, and indeed the whole Commonwealth," was the only way of getting through to him. "Reason alone will not do it." The Africans, he thought, could not go further "or they would be repudiated at home." In fact, "already they may have gone too far." It seemed as if this effort to negotiate had pushed the parties to the brink.[29]

For all the shouting, the nationalist leaders and their adversaries were locked in a debate that left out important interests. Women in Kenya petitioned to be included in the next round of constitutional talks, but they were ignored. And while there was consensus that some form of recognition of property rights of white settlers was essential, there was no discussion of the forest fighters, on the front lines of the independence struggle, and their demands to return to the land the settlers had long ago occupied. They were Mau Mau terrorists, in the eyes of the British, and any mention of their interests would have led to an impasse. And so those who had borne the harshest burdens in the struggle for an independent Kenya were left out of the project of building the nation.[30]

Perhaps this was a necessary compromise, but it was a pact between Kenya's new leaders and the British, at the expense of those on the front lines of the fight for independence. Although it enabled constitutional reform and a peaceful transition, it embedded an injustice in the political structure of the new nation, tainting the legitimacy of Kenya's founding movement. Such a compromise—a bargain between colonized peoples and colonizer—ensured the continuing impact of the British Empire on Kenya even as the country slipped from Britain's grasp. The limits of democracy in Kenya's founding resonate with the work of African politics scholar Claude Ake, who later asked whether in the deep shadow of Western influence, something that we might call democracy could ever come to the nations of Africa.[31]

As positions hardened at Lancaster House, Marshall was flying back and forth between London and New York. The civil rights struggle at home had taken a dramatic turn when students held a sit-in in Greensboro on February 1. A month later, seven students at Southern University in Baton Rouge, Louisiana, held the first Deep South sit-in. Before long, Thurgood Marshall would join with local counsel to represent them.[32]

Johnnie A. Jones vividly remembers the day. He had been practicing law in Baton Rouge for seven years and was at the district attorney's office to negotiate a plea bargain. Earlier that month, African American students from Southern University called and asked him to be their lawyer, though they wouldn't tell him why. It was on March 28, 1960, when he was in the DA's office, that Jones discovered that he was counsel to students in the first Deep South sit-in.

"They're sett'in!" a voice called through the hallways.

"Who's sett'in?"

"The Niggers! The Niggers are sett'in!"

The DA had no time for the plea bargain and quickly dropped all charges against Jones's client. Jones headed straight for the jail. The students, who had sat quietly at a whites-only restaurant counter, were arrested and detained for "disturbing the peace." Thousands of students would sit in that year, but it was these students who would find themselves the parties to sit-in cases in the U.S. Supreme Court.[33]

Nearly five decades later, it is hard for Jones to talk about those times. It had always been hard and dangerous to be an African American lawyer in Louisiana who took civil rights cases from the beginning of his practice. In 1960 it was worse. Even his wife was afraid to be with him—the threatening phone calls, the cars that blocked his on the railroad tracks when the train was coming, the attempts to force him off the road and make it look like an accident. The Deep South was the stronghold for hard-line white supremacy. Thurgood Marshall and the other Northern lawyers faced threats as well. But then they went home. For Jones, the Ku Klux Klan was not a distant threat but a part of his community. He lived it every day. "When you walk out your office, you meet them."[34]

The sit-ins involved civil rights lawyers in a new phase of the movement. It was not just that their old legal strategies did not fit. The lawyers felt a paternalistic desire to protect the students from the brutality of Southern jails. A legal brain trust worked to craft new legal arguments, and frontline lawyers worked with local communities to raise bail to get the students out of jail.

The students were well organized. "We'd read about North Carolina A&T in February," Janette Hoston Harris later recalled. Students met to discuss how they "could support North Carolina A&T College," but they kept their plans secret. On March 28, Hoston Harris was walking to her dorm when someone tapped her on the shoulder. "Come to a meeting," he said. "I knew then, that was it. . . . If anything happens," she told her roommate, "call my parents. Just take care of my things."[35]

Three coordinated sit-ins would happen over two days: at a Kress store, a Greyhound bus terminal, and Sitman's Drug Store. Hoston Harris went to Kress, along with six other students. She purchased cosmetics and went to the lunch counter. "I sat down and ordered a cup of tea," she recalled. "The woman was startled. She just looked at me. She didn't know what to do. I said, 'Maybe you didn't understand. I'd like to have a cup of tea.'" The waitress looked at her again. Then the manager said to the waitress, "Tell her we don't serve Colored at the lunch counter." He said they could order at the counter but must take their drinks to a table behind a curtain. Hoston Harris said, "No, I want to drink it here."[36]

This was enough for Kress to call in the Baton Rouge police. They may have already been on their way because one student had stayed back to call the police. They knew that their actions would inflame the white community. This was the Deep South, law student Kenneth Johnson emphasized. The Klan was active in nearby areas and "committed to segregation at any costs." The students knew that not only did they risk their individual lives, but that there were broader risks as well to their families and communities.[37]

It was only a matter of minutes before officers arrived, but for Johnson, also sitting at the lunch counter, "it felt like an eternity." He was happy to see the police, and "very happy to get arrested." It wasn't simply that this was a political statement and that the arrests were a part of this act of political theater. "Baton Rouge was a pretty rough place." In the mirror at the lunch counter, he could see whites picking up objects and see "the disapproval and hatred in their eyes." Johnson thought he would be killed. The press soon arrived as well. Reporters asked the students whether more demonstrations were coming. "We don't know," replied Donald Moss, one of the students. "This was an individual thing but we hope it will awaken seven million more colored students." Asked whether they were members of the NAACP, which at that time was banned in Louisiana, Moss answered that they were not. But they were "members of the human race."[38]

The students responded to the arrest order politely, the papers reported. They "stood up...and filed quietly out to the paddy wagon with police officers escorting them....The Negro men helped the two women up the steps into the paddy wagon." Janette Hoston Harris and JoAnn Morris found themselves sharing a jail cell with hard-core inmates, but the women reassured

Civil rights protesters who supported students in sit-ins, Baton Rouge, Louisiana, March 30, 1960. (© Bettmann/CORBIS)

them: "Don't worry. You won't be in here long." When the students were released on bond after about five and a half hours in jail, over thirty-five hundred celebrated with a rally on the Southern University campus. Students threatened to boycott if the demonstrators were expelled. But the students were expelled nonetheless and finished their degrees at other universities, traveling to and from Louisiana to attend their trial. Asked by the Southern University president to write letters to a member of the State Board of Education, apologizing and asking to be readmitted, they refused. "Who is to say," said JoAnn Morris, "that we were not born for this?"[39]

Later, Governor Earl Kemp Long of Louisiana issued a statement criticizing the students, calling them foolish. "I would suggest those who are not satisfied—like the seven at the lunch counter—return to their native Africa, and they'll find out they're doing a lot better here than they would in their native land." The students then issued a statement saying that since the governor's ancestors were from Europe, if he was not pleased with things in Louisiana, he could go back there.[40]

Upon hearing of the case, Thurgood Marshall contacted Louisiana lawyer A. P. Tureaud, who handled other cases for the NAACP Legal Defense Fund, and asked him to help. By this point, Marshall and his colleagues had organized a legal campaign to aid the students. After the sit-ins began in February, LDF lawyers consulted with leading constitutional law scholars at Columbia, Harvard, Howard, and Yale. Marshall organized an emergency legal conference at Howard University Law School in Washington, DC, from March 18 to 20. Sixty-two lawyers joined the seven members of the LDF staff to devise a new legal strategy to handle the sit-in cases. Among them were forty-two Southern lawyers who were committed to representing student demonstrators in their areas.[41]

The lawyers agreed that the convictions must be appealed. Student demonstrators were often charged with offenses like "trespass, parading without a license, violating fire regulations, blocking aisles." However, the attorneys concluded, the students' conduct demonstrated that "in almost all cases, the nuisance the laws were designed to punish did not take place." Law enforcement officials were therefore using existing statutes in a discriminatory manner. Discrimination by private individuals, such as store owners and restaurant operators, did not violate the constitution, and there was not yet a federal statute outlawing such conduct, but public officials were involved in these cases, which enabled the lawyers to develop the constitutional argument they needed. "The use of public force in arrest or conviction of students engaged in peaceful demonstration," the lawyers concluded, "is in truth state enforcement of private discrimination and is therefore in violation of the 14th Amendment." It was an argument, but by no means a certain one. No court had held that when police enforced a business owner's right to expel an unwanted customer, the police became complicit in the private business's discriminatory motive. What was difficult was finding a limit to such a principle. That this elite cadre of civil rights lawyers found themselves grappling with new and difficult legal arguments is apparent in the memo summarizing the outcome of their meeting. It is filled with as many questions as answers.[42]

Marshall's work was not confined to organizing the lawyers. On March 31, he sent a memo addressed to the "Friends of the Committee," asking for contributions. He would spend many hours in his final months at the LDF, before leaving in October 1961, trying to raise money to cover the costs of these cases. The student protests resulted in litigation costs "far in excess of our anticipated budget," Marshall wrote to prospective donors. The LDF was

> determined that every young person arrested as a result of a participation in a peaceful protest against racial segregation will have adequate legal defense. We can not protect these courageous youngsters from possible violent attack. They have knowingly accepted this risk. At the least, they should know that they will have adequate legal representation in the courts if they are arrested.[43]

In late March, the LDF and cooperating attorneys were representing over twelve hundred students from seven states. Their cases required a new legal strategy "to meet entirely new legal problems." Many of the students already represented by the lawyers had been convicted and sentenced. Their appeals required appeal bonds and expenses would increase as cases moved into higher courts. This new crisis had generated "thousands of small gifts" but the LDF needed more funds. Marshall appealed to the paternalism of his audience. "We are unwilling, if it can be avoided, to permit these students, particularly the young women, to be subjected to imprisonment under conditions prevailing in jails for Negroes in many southern communities."[44]

Marshall had reason to be concerned. Kenneth Johnson has never been able to forget a scene he witnessed in the five and a half hours it took Johnnie Jones to raise the extraordinary $1,500 bail each student needed for release. The inmates were nice to the students in the men's jail, but they believed that one inmate was a police informer. The inmates tried and convicted him in the jailhouse and carried out the sentence: gang rape. It was the first Johnson had ever known of sex between men, and the shocking memory of this rape scene has never left him.[45]

When the students returned to Louisiana for trial in July 1960, conditions were hostile and difficult. By then Marshall's work in London was completed, and he was focused full-time on American civil rights, with much of his attention devoted to the sit-ins. He advised the students to "stay strong and be careful in this environment." Three trials were held on July 5 in Baton Rouge. The courtroom was "packed with spectators, mostly Negroes," the local press reported. The difficulties that worried the lawyers when they plotted strategy at the Howard conference came out at trial in the Kress case. The students would have had a clear defense had they violated an unconstitutional law. But they were not charged with violating an illegal segregation ordinance. Instead, they were charged with disturbing the peace. Granted, they had "disturbed the peace" by desegregating the lunch counter. Segregation was Kress company policy, however, and discrimination by a privately owned store was not illegal in 1960. Jones tried hard to bring the state into the action against the students. Were Kress carrying out state policy, perhaps he could make a colorable claim that state action was involved, so that the students could invoke their rights under the Fourteenth Amendment, which protects against discriminatory action by state and local governments. "Did you consider these defendants violating the law while sitting at this café counter?" he asked the store owner at trial. An objection to the question was sustained: He had asked for the store owner's legal conclusions, and the owner was not a lawyer. "In asking or advising these defendants to go to the other café counter seat did you at any time think that you were acting according to law?" Objection sustained.[46]

Jones had more success in his cross-examination of the arresting officer:

Q. Did you know why they were placed under arrest?
A. Because they were disturbing the peace.
Q. How were they disturbing the peace?
A. By sitting there....
Q. And that is because they were members of the negro [*sic*] race?
A. That was because that place was reserved for white people.[47]

It was clear that the police had intervened because the students had crossed a race line. In *Shelley v. Kraemer* (1948), the Supreme Court ruled that it was unlawful for state courts to give force to private discrimination in housing, by enforcing racially restrictive covenants. The courts had not gone so far, however, as to rule that when the police carried out a shop owner's discriminatory wishes about whom to serve, this tarred the police with the shop owner's discrimination. Instead, shopkeepers had a historic right to serve or expel whomever they wished. Here was the legal dilemma facing Marshall and the other lawyers.[48]

The trial courts held that the Southern students' convictions were lawful. In the Greyhound bus terminal case, the court found that "the mere presence of Negroes in a white waiting room...was sufficient evidence of guilt."[49]

By the time the sit-in cases were argued in the U.S. Supreme Court in October 1961, Marshall had just left the LDF for a recess appointment on the Second Circuit Court of Appeals. His successor, Jack Greenberg, argued *Garner v. Louisiana,* the Baton Rouge case, pressing the points Marshall himself had made the year before in *Boynton.* The Supreme Court ruled in favor of all the Louisiana students. The Court, however, did not embrace the broad theory that all police action that enforced private discrimination made the state complicit in the act of discrimination. Instead, following a line of reasoning the Court had begun in seemingly unrelated cases, it ruled in *Garner* that there was simply no evidence that any breach of the peace had occurred. The standards of evidence in state trial courts are usually matters of state law, unreviewable by a federal court. But the Supreme Court found that federal constitutional rights were implicated. To convict the students without evidence was to deny them due process of law.[50]

When Michael Meltsner, a young lawyer and new member of the legal team, arrived in 1961, the LDF was deeply involved in sit-in cases. Still, tensions between the student movement and civil rights lawyers, surfaced in some cases. According to Jones, NAACP lawyer Tureaud, who had a demanding civil rights caseload, objected to the students' strategy and complained that he had "more important things to do" than represent them. But Kenneth Johnson thought the LDF lawyers were "just as committed as we were" to the cause of racial justice and that the students were "lucky, extremely lucky" to have the LDF involved in their case.[51]

Although the sit-ins brought different strains of the movement together, underlying differences over strategy and basic philosophy were soon to become larger than ever. Marshall spoke of Martin Luther King Jr. as a great leader who "came at the right time." But, as he told an interviewer, he didn't agree with King and the Southern Christian Leadership Conference, and he and King would argue over King's theory of civil disobedience. "I thought you did have a right to disobey a law," Marshall said, "and you also had a right to go to jail for it. He kept talking about Thoreau, and I told him, I said, 'If I understand it, Thoreau wrote his book in jail. If you want to write a book, you go to jail and write it.'" Perhaps Marshall underestimated King, who would be arrested many times for his civil rights work. And King would, of course, write one of the more memorable documents of the civil rights movement while incarcerated: "Letter from Birmingham Jail."[52]

Differences between the Southern Christian Leadership Conference and the LDF sometimes led to harsh words. For Marshall, civil rights reform was "men's work." He accused King and his followers of using "'the bodies of children' to achieve their civil rights objectives." Some activists dismissed Marshall. John Lewis of the Student Nonviolent Coordinating Committee, now a member of Congress, felt that the "old guard," including Marshall, didn't understand "the importance of creating mass movement."

> Thurgood had this abiding concern that we didn't need to continue to put ourselves in harm's way. I think that, more than anything else, was his idea. He wasn't saying be "patient" and "wait," he was just saying that this is the way that he would do it, through the courts, and that we didn't need to have people spitting on us, pulling us off lunch-counter stools, and putting lighted cigarettes out in our hair.

Lewis thought that Marshall came to appreciate the movement's power. And although the NAACP "was not there at the beginning,...when we would go to jail, even though Thurgood Marshall disagreed with our techniques, he would make available the legal expertise and the legal resources of the Inc. Fund."[53]

Ultimately, it was the actions of students and others in the grassroots movement that created the civil rights crises that demanded a response from a slow-moving federal government and captured the attention of the world. The activists created the conditions that would place within reach the legal change Marshall hoped for. They are sometimes cast as working in opposition to each other, and at times they saw it that way, but in 1960, the students and the civil rights lawyers continually reinforced each other's work.

IF SUCCESS WAS UNCERTAIN ON THE CIVIL RIGHTS FRONT at home, it was equally so back in London at the Kenya conference. After Marshall had departed, meetings continued on land and safeguards in mid-February, with the goal of crafting general principles that could be fleshed out later in Nairobi and London. But the highly emotional land issue blocked a resolution of the conference. As the *Times* of London reported, "the Africans agree on the principle of no expropriation without compensation: but other delegates ask how one judges the compensation, and whether it is right that it should be used for the settlement of Africans in the present agricultural system." According to the *Ghana Times*, the Africans wanted to make it "crystal clear" that they would protect property rights of all citizens regardless of race. Still, it quoted Ngala as saying, "We feel that the people of Kenya must preserve their right to carry out such land reforms as will accelerate economic betterment of the country." Many felt that there was now only one hope for a successful resolution. Macleod must take matters into his own hands and formulate a compromise.[54]

The conference ended in late February without resolving the major question of land and safeguards. It produced no final constitutional text, only Macleod's report summarizing the meeting's accomplishments and limitations. Though Marshall was no longer in London, his ideas continued to have an impact. Macleod's official report singled out two documents as particularly helpful: a discussion of the Nigerian constitution and "a very helpful paper by Dr. Thurgood Marshall outlining the kind of provisions which might help to meet the situation." The ideas contained within these documents would be put to use. It was "the firm view of Her Majesty's Government" that the Kenyan Constitution must protect human rights "on the lines of the provisions in the Nigeria (Constitution) Order in Council, taking into account the draft prepared by Dr. Thurgood Marshall and the special circumstances of Kenya."[55]

Although the negotiations over land rights were incomplete, the conference had achieved its most important purpose: an embrace of majority rule. Because of this, the *Ghana Times* called the conference "a victory for the African Nationalists, who were, after due thought and consideration, supported by the Colonial Secretary." For some settlers, Macleod's constitutional proposals represented "a Mau Mau victory." The all-white United Party "denounced [the] conference as [a] death-blow to [the] European community," and said that "the reported proposals would virtually mean that Europeans and Asians would no longer have genuine representation." Most of the major players, including the Africans, agreed to go forward with the agreements they had reached so far. Nevertheless the future remained uncertain. The U.S. Embassy in London was of the opinion that "Macleod has only just managed [to] avoid [a] conference breakdown and that local Kenya reaction to [the] positions of [the] three principal groups may jeopardize [the] results."[56]

Macleod's proposals were endorsed by the British government, and Kenya colony's constitution was now called the Macleod Constitution in the same way that earlier colonial

constitutions, the product of less negotiation, had been identified with previous British government officials. Although the
nationalists were on board at Lancaster House, they quickly distanced themselves from the document back in Kenya. The constitution represented a colonial position that would be the new
starting point for their arguments about further change. With
independence movements gaining power throughout Africa, the
U.S. consul in Kenya, Charles Withers, assessed the conference
this way: "It would appear that [Britain] has made up its mind
to divest itself of its colonial responsibilities in Africa as expedi-
tiously as feasible."[57]

What sort of decolonization did the British have in mind? Even
before the Lancaster House conference, the British government
was developing plans. British officials told Withers that they
were "trying now to establish such firm control of the Colony's
government departments that incoming African ministers would
be little more than figureheads." Nationalists, including Mboya,
were aware of the strategy. According to Withers, the British
planned to entrench British high-level civil service employees in
Kenya. When an African became a minister and wanted to do
something about financial or policy matters, the British officials
would say that this was "not the way things are done in a parlia-
mentary system of government," and that such matters were to
be handled by the permanent secretariat and civil service staff.
Kenya's future would depend on more than governing documents and political compromises; it would also depend on the
long-term impact of colonialism on the nation's infrastructure.[58]

With independence and an eventual African government on
the horizon, a new climate of negotiation emerged back in Nairobi. Colonial politics would be further complicated by a split
among nationalists and the formation of two principal nationalist parties, KANU and the Kenya African Democratic Union
(KADU). The New Kenya Group would ultimately propose a

formula for resolving the land issue. It involved Africans pur-
chasing land from white settlers with funds lent by the Kenyan
government. Money for this would be lent to Kenya by the
British government and the World Bank. This formula was
settled on by the multiracial New Kenya Group after the 1960
Lancaster House conference, once it became clear that African
majority rule was inevitable, and the nationalist leaders agreed
to it. There was, however, dissent. KANU's militant wing sought
land transfer with no compensation, so it might seem puzzling
that the African leaders agreed to the formula. According
to historian Colin Leys, there were several possible reasons,
including

> the fear of independence being delayed; the hope of chang-
> ing things after independence; a lack of interest in the detail of
> the negotiations; a fear that the rival party, the Kenya African
> Democratic Union (KADU), for whose supporters the land issue
> was less vital,... might agree to the proposed scheme first and
> perhaps manage to get KANU excluded from the transitional
> government; and finally, the risk of alienating the former forest
> fighters if they were not provided with land quickly.

Another factor was Kenyatta's moderating influence on nationalist politics after his release in 1961. Perhaps influenced by an
economic crisis in the colony, precipitated by progress toward
independence at the 1960 Lancaster House conference, Kenyatta emphasized that property rights would be protected by
the future Kenyan government, and that "we will encourage
investors in various projects to come to Kenya and carry on their
business peacefully, in order to bring prosperity to this country." Because of these developments, land and the compensation clauses, though dominant at the 1960 meeting, were not
major issues in later constitutional negotiations, which would

turn instead on regional versus national government, tribal politics, and federalism. The final 1963 independence constitution would contain very detailed clauses regarding confiscation of land for public purposes, along the lines that Marshall supported in 1960.[59]

But when constitutional negotiations came to a close in February 1960, all this was far from certain in Nairobi. Twenty Kenyan political leaders, including Michael Blundell and Ronald Ngala, were greeted by a crowd at the Nairobi airport when they returned from their work at Lancaster House. White settlers shouted at Blundell "Traitor" and "Thirty Pieces of Silver." A white man with a microphone yelled, "Congratulations, Mr. Ngala, you stood by your policies. Blundell, you have sold your own people." But Blundell also found support. An African shouted in response: "Blundell, you will get our votes if necessary. You have sold nobody. You are all right."[60]

In contrast, when Mboya, Odinga, and other nationalists arrived home a couple of days later, they had a different experience. They were met at the airport by thousands of Africans. The new constitution would not last, Mboya told the crowd. The "struggle [had] only begun," and a move toward independence would happen "immediately." There was a place in Kenya for all races, Mboya said, but "those who did not believe in democracy should sell out and leave." Kenya's destiny, Kiano emphasized, was "for [the] first time turned over to Africans."[61]

Twenty-five thousand people attended a gathering at the African Stadium held later that day. Mboya told the crowd that if they supported the stand on the constitution taken by the African delegation at Lancaster House, they should raise their hands. Around African Stadium, the American consul reported, "nearly every hand [was] raised." Not willing to let this moment slip away, as the leaders left the stadium, a jubilant crowd began to follow Mboya home. When they reached the city limits, police

A large crowd of cheering supporters greet Tom Mboya and his colleagues as they return from the Lancaster House conference, March 1, 1960. (Photo by Terrence Spencer/Time & Life Pictures/ Getty Images)

tried to turn them back. When they would not disperse, the "riot act [was] read." The American consul's telegram reporting next was very sparse: "tear gas used and baton charges made, crowd eventually disbursing [*sic*]." It is impossible to know how violent this confrontation was. In the end, only two people were reported to be injured. Perhaps the incident best illustrated the limits of colonial authority in Kenya in 1960. Colonial police might suppress a demonstration, but a spirit of independence was alive in Kenya, and no tear gas canisters or police batons could make it go away.[62]

MARCHERS, SEEKING FULL CITIZENSHIP, met with brutal force. It would be an all-too-familiar story in both Africa and America during the 1960s. This was not Thurgood Marshall's path to social change. Many observers looked upon these events with a combination of admiration for the courage of the demonstrators and dread at what destructive force might come their way. But in the 1960s, taking to the streets was a crucial element of democratization.

At this point, Marshall and Mboya turned to different tasks. For Marshall, the focus would be using law to expand rights to make his nation better. For Mboya and the other nationalists, their task was overturning an unjust order. It was not a matter of reform but of creating a new polity. Their different struggles would draw them apart, but they had forged a bond that would last their lifetimes. Marshall wrote to Mboya on March 15, 1960, with a simple request on behalf of a friend. Mboya answered him and said, "I do not know whether it will ever be enough to write letters to thank you for your good work at the London Conference. . . . I am sure I speak the mind of all of us, that you were the easiest man to work with, and that any of us who had apprehension before you came were easily disarmed as soon as we met you." Mboya thought that Marshall's work had "led to a greater understanding of the Negro/African problem."[63]

As for Marshall, when he first arrived in Kenya, he said that he had come home. Marshall's own biography had become central to the way his country thought of itself. Perhaps it was a sign that all was not well in America if a man thought to embody the American dream felt that he had found belonging on a distant continent.

-4-

DISCRIMINATING FRIENDS

Why do you call me a "guest,"
When here I have my home.
> —J. M. Nazareth, *Brown Man, Black Country* (1981),
> on the Asian experience in East Africa

Here is a Federal Judge, the very embodiment of our law, acting as
though he had turned in his judicial robes for a pair of sneakers and
a CORE sweatshirt.
> —*St. Louis Globe-Democrat*, on Thurgood Marshall, 1964

IT MUST HAVE SEEMED BRIGHT, the morning sun on the Nairobi
airstrip, as the small plane carrying the judge and the young lawyer touched down. They had flown through the night, but the
occupants of the plane were very much awake.

July 1963. The runway cut the same path across the flat plain
south of the city as it had before. But much had changed in the
three years since Thurgood Marshall had last been to Kenya.
In early 1960, independence had been a demand. Now it was
an inevitability, with ceremonies scheduled for December. Jomo
Kenyatta, still in detention in 1960, his influence feared by the
British and Americans, had instead emerged as a moderating
voice after his release in 1961. He had carried the Kenya African
National Union (KANU) to power, and was now prime minister
during the colony's short period of self-rule. As for Marshall,
bruising Court of Appeals confirmation hearings were now

behind him. The civil rights lawyer had settled into life on the court. But most surprising on that July morning was that the cabin of the airplane could contain him.[1]

Berl Bernhard, staff director of the U.S. Commission for Civil Rights, had been listening to Marshall's stories on the long flight from Rome. He knew that Marshall had worked with Kenyan nationalists in 1960 and had written a bill of rights that had played an important role at the 1960 constitutional conference. Some parts of Marshall's handiwork had been retained in the Kenya Independence Constitution, soon to be finalized. But Bernhard wasn't sure how many of this great storyteller's yarns to believe, and he was skeptical of Marshall's insistence that in Nairobi, a red carpet would be laid for their arrival. But there it was.[2]

So excited to be back, Marshall nearly burst out of the plane. He stood at the top of the stairs, arms extended, savoring the moment. "This is my country," he said to Bernhard, before descending. It was certainly his red carpet. No colonial officers would bar him from meetings on this trip. Thurgood Marshall was returning, triumphant.[3]

THE PAST THREE YEARS HAD NOT ALWAYS seemed so full of promise, either for Marshall or for the civil rights struggle in America. A charismatic young president, John F. Kennedy, had been elected in 1960 after courting the black vote with promises. He said that an executive order banning discrimination in federal housing programs could be accomplished "with the stroke of a pen." After the election, when no order was forthcoming, civil rights activists sent thousands of pens to the White House.[4]

The civil rights movement had escalated from 1960 to 1963. After the lunch counter sit-ins of 1960 came the Freedom Rides of 1961. Desegregation cases continued to provoke reaction and make headlines, including James Meredith's successful effort to integrate the University of Mississippi. The movement itself was motivated as much from within individual communities as it was engaged with national organizations. Even when focused on local struggles, the movement had ramifications for the nation and the world. This was illustrated most powerfully in Birmingham, Alabama, in May 1963.[5]

Civil rights activists targeted Birmingham and by early May the jails were full of protesters. Police Commissioner Bull Connor felt that he was running out of options. He thought that eventually Martin Luther King Jr. would, as he put it, "run out of niggers." But on May 3, fifteen hundred schoolchildren skipped school to march into the city, singing movement songs like "We Shall Overcome." They disobeyed police and marched in peaceful, orderly lines into white Birmingham. Connor could not throw them in jail, so he had the fire department turn high-powered hoses on the children. Demonstrators were tossed to the ground and pinned in doorways by the force of the blasts. One girl was rolled down the street by the spray. Then Connor said, "Bring the dogs." Images of police dogs lunging at demonstrators appeared on television and on front pages of newspapers across the country. "I've never seen anything like this in my life," said R. W. "Johnny" Apple, an NBC television reporter.[6]

Before long, the brutality in Birmingham was worldwide news. Disturbing images appeared on television in Kenya, and newspapers there carried headlines like "Riots Flare in U.S. South—Infants Sent to Jail." The U.S. Embassy in Accra reported that the United States had lost credibility in Ghana due to the events in Birmingham. The Soviet Union made the incident a focus of its anti-U.S. propaganda, devoting one-fifth of its radio programming to the story.[7]

A civil rights demonstrator is pursued by a police officer as firefighters spray others with high-powered hoses in Birmingham, Alabama, May 1963. (Photo by Charles Moore/© Black Star/Alamy)

Birmingham coincided with the first meeting of the Organization of African Unity. African leaders gathered in Addis Ababa diverted their attention from the crucial task of African solidarity to debate their reaction to the events in the United States. "Nothing is more paradoxical," Milton Obote of Uganda wrote in an open letter to President Kennedy, "than that these events should take place in the United States and at a time when that country is anxious to project its image before the world screen as the archetype of democracy and the champion of freedom." The conference passed a resolution expressing concern about race discrimination and calling upon the United States to put an end to "these intolerable mal-practices which are likely seriously to deteriorate relations" between Africans and Americans. Birmingham, like Little Rock before it, was both a domestic and a foreign affairs crisis. The Kennedy Administration had to address its impact on the community, the nation, and the world.

Birmingham and other 1963 civil rights crises propelled the president to adopt a more aggressive civil rights agenda in the final months of his presidency.[8]

Amid this turmoil, Thurgood Marshall backed out of the front lines of the civil rights movement. He was in his early fifties and had been litigating civil rights cases for more than two decades. It was not that he had tired from this work, although many were awed by how endlessly he labored. Instead, he thought it was time to move on. As the movement shifted focus, Marshall had come to question his own role. He had practical concerns as well. He had a family to support, and civil rights practice was not a path to financial security. And there were new horizons: The federal judiciary was yet to be meaningfully integrated. Marshall hoped to bring his civil rights experience into the closed quarters of the federal courthouse.[9]

On September 23, 1961, President Kennedy nominated Marshall to a new seat on the Second Circuit Court of Appeals in New York. Kennedy initially had intended to nominate him to a district court, but Marshall did not want to be a trial court judge and held out for an appellate position. Early the next month, during a congressional recess, the president gave Marshall and seven other judicial nominees recess appointments, meaning Marshall would serve as a judge through 1962. Kennedy officials thought that placing Marshall on the court and enabling him to serve as a judge would ease the confirmation process. Senators could see the civil rights advocate in the staid and impartial judicial role.[10]

Marshall was thrilled with the appointment, but it turned out to be an ignoble introduction to the federal judiciary. The confirmation hearings dragged on. Southern Democrats, Marshall's principal opponents, used the hearings as political theater to show that they were holding the line against civil rights incursions. The Kennedy administration seemed to benefit from the delay as well. So long as the Marshall hearings were in the press, they were a reminder that the administration was doing its best to integrate the judiciary by putting Mr. Civil Rights himself on the bench. In the meantime, life at Foley Square, the federal courthouse, was not what Marshall would have liked. As a recess appointee, he did not have a permanent office. He and his law clerk, Ralph Winter, shuttled from one spare office to another. Some colleagues only welcomed him after the eight-month confirmation process was over.[11]

It was a difficult year. Finally, after an exhaustive FBI investigation turned up no evidence of a connection to communism or other evils, and after many infuriating days spent before a subcommittee of the Senate Judiciary Committee, which passed on the nomination with no vote, Marshall was approved by the Judiciary Committee, and then by the full Senate, 54–14, on September 11, 1962.[12]

Marshall had aspired to be a judge, but his new role meant making sacrifices. There would be no more poker games with his LDF buddies. Even charitable boards were off-limits. He did not want to have to recuse himself from civil rights cases, and so avoided anything that might lead to the appearance of a conflict of interest. The court opened new doors but closed the social circle of a gregarious man.[13]

Although Marshall backed out of direct involvement in the movement, there was simply no escaping engagement with civil rights in America in the early 1960s. And Marshall didn't try. Perhaps it says something about the state of civil rights, and what the nation had been through, that he did something uncharacteristic: When the Episcopal Church gathered for a national convention in 1964, among the Episcopalians, he protested on behalf of civil rights protesters.[14]

He was elected as a delegate from his diocese to the triennial national convention, the first African American to represent the

Episcopal Diocese of New York. The meeting convened amid concern over civil rights and divisions within the church over its responsibility. A year before, the worldwide Anglican Congress adopted a manifesto that warned "that the old paternalism of home churches to the mission fields" and the "assumption of white superiority" had to stop. In his opening address, presiding bishop Arthur Lichtenberger spoke of the hundreds of letters he had received from church members, in a "mood of dark despair," complaining that he wanted them to "get mixed up with minority groups [and] with issues that have nothing to do with religion." Lichtenberger admonished them, as historian Gardiner Shattuck has written, that "instead of retreating into houses of worship...church people needed to step out into the world and involve themselves in politics and the fight against injustice."[15]

In keeping with Lichtenberger's sentiment, the convention officially honored Martin Luther King Jr., who was about to leave for Norway to receive the Nobel Peace Prize. King addressed the convention's House of Deputies, calling upon Episcopalians to help with the civil rights struggle in the South. He was "generally well received," says Shattuck, but some white deputies refused either to stand for King or to applaud.[16]

The trouble occurred afterward at the House of Deputies meeting, when a resolution was introduced that spoke to the principles of King's philosophy of nonviolent civil disobedience. The resolution "recognized the right of persons to disobey segregation laws that are in 'basic conflict with the concept of human dignity under God.'" Civil disobedience had to be nonviolent, done only after "earnestly seeking the will of God in prayer." Many in the clergy supported the proposal, but a number of lay deputies opposed it. "This is the first time in all of the history of this church that we have been asked to take a position that recognizes the right of people to disobey the law," a Minneapolis deputy complained. "This is the way to chaos." Reverend Gordon E. Gilett of Illinois responded: "One of my ancestors picked up a musket at Lexington and fought the British and I am certain we agree that was one of the greatest acts of civil disobedience." When the measure came to a vote, it had the support of a majority of the clergy but did not receive enough support from lay deputies. The resolution was rejected. In protest, Marshall walked out.[17]

Marshall's walkout made headlines in New York and St. Louis. The Right Reverend Horace W. B. Donegan, bishop of the Diocese of New York, was "distressed" over the "unfortunate" incident and urged Marshall to stay. But Marshall was upset and angry. He was "just disturbed," said another participant in the meeting, "and I don't blame him." He was also surprised; he had expected clergy to be more conservative than lay members. The *St. Louis Globe-Democrat* blasted Marshall for his walkout:

> Here is a Federal Judge, the very embodiment of our law, acting as though he had turned in his judicial robes for a pair of sneakers and a CORE sweatshirt. The spectacle is ludicrous and not a little hypocritical.
>
> This is a man who sits upon the United States Circuit Court of Appeals asking his church to encourage followers who violate selected laws "for reasons of conscience."
>
> The terrible danger of such an official endorsement of civil disobedience is that it leaves to the individual to judge what laws to violate, and individuals have different ideas of "human dignity under God."
>
> This endorsement would have been an invitation to anarchy!

Meanwhile, the paper said, the South contained "a good half-million people...who think that God is the Original Segregationist." The editorial concluded:

God help this country, Judge Marshall, if some Sunday morning
the white preachers take to their pulpits and tell those wool hats
from the Alabama backwoods to go follow their Segregationist
God and not that "integrationist Congress"—because that Monday
morning it'll take all Lyndon's paratroopers, and then some, to
enforce that Civil Rights Act.[18]

George L. Cadigan, bishop of Missouri, defended Marshall and
publicly apologized on behalf of his city and his diocese, the host
of the conference. He announced that the House of Bishops, in
a rejoinder to the vote of the House of Deputies, had adopted a
strong pro–civil rights statement after Marshall left the convention, on the "classical doctrine of obedience to God's law, and
its corollary, the right of conscience under extreme laws which
deny human dignity." Cadigan thought the attack on Marshall
in the *Globe-Democrat* was unfair and ignored Christian teach-
ings. The departure of Marshall, "our distinguished brother in
Christ" was "a judgment on us all."[19]

Marshall was very angry when he got home to New York. But
after sparking this controversy, he refused to comment on it.
Reached at home in Manhattan, he told a reporter, "I just came
out of there, that's all. There are no conclusions to be drawn
from that."[20]

Marshall knew that whenever he said something about
civil disobedience within earshot of a reporter, it would make
news. The next spring, Marshall's civil rights views figured in
a *Time* magazine story about a dramatic voting rights march in
Selma, Alabama, even though Marshall himself was not present and did not speak to reporters. Demonstrators gathered in
Brown's Chapel to debate whether or not to march in violation
of a federal court order. Princeton University Religion Professor
Malcolm Diamond was among them. As *Time* reported it, Diamond "announced that he would march" and "quoted Federal

Judge Thurgood Marshall, a Negro, as once having said, 'I am not defying the sovereignty of my country. I am making witness within the framework of the law of my country.'" The next day, peaceful demonstrators were savagely beaten by police when they tried to cross the Edmund Pettus Bridge, an event that helped prompt Congress to enact a voting rights bill. Seeing Marshall's name in *Time*'s coverage, Diamond was concerned that the magazine had quoted him out of context, making the judge look bad, and later wrote to the editor:

> In fairness to Judge Thurgood Marshall I should note that when I quoted him at Brown's Methodist Chapel in Selma, Alabama, I was not quoting from a text but from something he said on a television program. When asked whether the non-violent Civil Rights demonstrators were not, on occasion, guilty of defying the law even as members of the White Citizens Council defy it, Judge Marshall replied (roughly) as follows: "When Civil Rights demonstrators break the law to protest against an unjust social order they are willing to pay the price—to go to jail if necessary—in order to witness to what they believe in. I wonder if the members of the White Citizens Councils are willing to do the same?"[21]

Much had happened in the movement and in the nation from the time when Marshall had stormed through the LDF office criticizing sit-in demonstrators to the time when he walked out on the Episcopalians in support of them. High school students had been hosed down and chased by dogs in Birmingham, when that city seared the conscience of the nation in 1963. And breaking the law in the face of segregation could not look evil to many Americans who read of the girls incinerated in the Birmingham church bombing later that year or saw the young faces of three civil rights workers missing for weeks and found murdered and buried in Neshoba County, Mississippi, in July 1964. The nation, and with it the views of many, was changing.[22]

Marshall faced different risks than the demonstrators did when he supported civil disobedience, of course, but his position on this issue was not without its costs. He had looked violence in the face before, when he represented black defendants in Southern courtrooms in the 1940s in spite of threats, and when he went to the front lines in Korea to fight discriminatory treatment of African American soldiers. By the mid-1960s, everyone knew he was under consideration to be the first African American Supreme Court justice. This was so widely expected that when President Lyndon Baines Johnson held an impromptu press conference to announce Marshall as his nominee for Solicitor General in 1965, reporters, thinking instead of the Court, asked each other who on the Court had resigned. Marshall was careful about the way he was perceived, knowing that any folly would be negatively used against him by critics. Civil disobedience would be at the center of later efforts to discredit him. Still, in St. Louis, in defense of civil disobedience, he walked out.[23]

LEAVING CAN BE A WAY OF SPEAKING. For some African Americans, as legal historian John Fabian Witt has argued, Africa was part of an American exit. Joining the colonization movement, leaving America for Africa, was a way of expressing a deep dissatisfaction with the place the nation had made for its black citizens.[24]

Africa had held various meanings at various moments in American history. In the 1960s, to those in the civil rights movement, it became a Mecca, a respite, a place for renewal. Countless activists found their way to Africa, seeking a break from the intensity of the movement at home and the glare of the media spotlight. In August 1964, after the Mississippi Freedom Democratic Party had challenged the legitimacy of the Mississippi delegation at the Democratic Convention, Fannie Lou Hamer and other members of the party traveled to Africa, where Hamer said she was "treated much better" than she was in the United States. Civil rights leaders also turned to independent African countries for support of the movement. Malcolm X attended the 1964 meeting of the Organization of African Unity, hoping to convince the organization to bring the issue of American race discrimination before the United Nations. African independence continued to inspire American civil rights activists, even as some Americans working there found themselves at odds with newly independent African governments more interested in consolidating power than in protecting rights.[25]

For Marshall, returning to Kenya was deeply meaningful. He called it his "homeland." But perhaps more than anything, it was a place where he could be something that escaped African Americans in his own nation. Derrick Bell later reimagined the framing of the U.S. Constitution, placing an African American woman in the room with the nation's founders. In Kenya, no imagining was required. Marshall had been there, along with Mboya, Odinga, and the others. Africans and an African American had debated the framing of a nation. And now he was returning to see what they had made.[26]

Marshall's arrival was front-page news in Nairobi. "Welcome for Famed U.S. Judge," was the *Daily Nation* headline, followed by a photograph of Marshall at the airport with nationalist leader Tom Mboya and others. Kenya looked good to Marshall, and Marshall looked good to his hosts. "For 25 long, weary years," John Dumonga wrote in the Nairobi paper, "a tall well-dressed American Negro with a greying crop of thick hair, and bushy eyebrows battled through the courts of the United States so that Negroes should have a place in the sun." Marshall, he wrote, "touched greatness" in the legal battle resulting in *Brown v. Board of Education*.[27]

On his first trip to Kenya, Marshall had simply been a private citizen, invited by nationalists to serve as an advisor during constitutional negotiations. In 1963, he was a federal judge traveling

Judge Thurgood Marshall and Berl Bernhard, staff director of the U.S. Civil Rights Commission (left), are greeted at the Nairobi airport by Tom Mboya, Kenyan Minister of Commerce and Industry Julius Kiano, and U.S. Consul General Laurence Vass, July 10, 1963. (Associated Press)

at the request of the U.S. State Department. It had been a difficult year in the United States, and the world was still reeling from the terrible photographs of police violence against civil rights demonstrators in Birmingham, Alabama, that May. The State Department sent speakers around the world to place Birmingham in context, and to emphasize the U.S. government's support of civil rights reform. Marshall and Supreme Court Chief Justice Earl Warren were just two of those enlisted. As Berl Bernhard explained to reporters, their purpose was "to explore and discuss with people here the role of law in our own country in trying to solve some of our problems of race relations, trying to gain new ideas and have an open and free exchange of viewpoints."[28]

Thurgood Marshall was the perfect sort of American ambassador to repair U.S. prestige in Africa. His mere presence illustrated an argument long made in U.S. government pamphlets on race prepared for foreign audiences: He demonstrated that African Americans could attain prestigious posts, that, in spite of past discrimination, the nation had achieved racial progress, and that the legacy of racism did not confine African Americans to the bottom rungs of society. It is a great irony that a man who would spend most of his life challenging American inequality would be asked to serve as an illustration of the nation's racial progress, but there was propaganda value in Thurgood Marshall the moment he simply stepped off the plane.[29]

When he was a civil rights litigator, Marshall was once asked whether he thought perhaps the civil rights movement

Prime Minister Jomo Kenyatta welcomes Thurgood Marshall to Kenya, July 11, 1963. (Associated Press)

was moving too far, too fast in the 1950s. "The Emancipation Proclamation was issued in 1863," he said wryly, "ninety-odd years ago. I believe in gradualism. I also believe that ninety-odd years is pretty gradual." When he addressed the Nairobi Rotary Club in 1963, he seemed more accepting of the slow pace of social change in the United States. He had come, the press reported, "to give the story of how the United States Government operates in the field of civil liberties." He invoked British Prime Minister Harold Macmillan's speech from three years before, about the "wind of change," meaning nationalism and independence "blowing across Africa." "The winds of change are sweeping all over the world in the area of personal and individual rights," Marshall said. The form democracy took in the United States was different than in many other countries, however, because of the American separation of powers and federalism. It would take time for "great change" to be achieved. "I believe the operation of government is based on time."[30]

Marshall seemed to justify gradualism, and he emphasized that some forms of change took longer than others. This was very much in keeping with an argument the U.S. government had stressed in overseas information programs, especially in the context of civil rights crises. The U.S. federal government was behind civil rights, countless speakers and pamphlets had argued. The nature of American federalism, however, meant that progress in some states (i.e., the South) lagged behind in an inevitable march of progress. Under this line of reasoning, civil rights violations in Southern states simply meant that they were progressing more slowly and should not be seen as indications that American democracy itself was flawed.[31]

Marshall was briefed by the State Department before and after the trip, and he was well aware of the damaging impact of American racial problems on U.S. standing in Africa. The briefing would have made clear the department's concern about the importance of Kenya as a cold war ally in Africa and their concern about the impact of communism in the colony. Marshall had not developed a fondness for gradualism on the American scene, but he was a believer in American democracy, and a critic of communism. In a 1961 Voice of America Radio Program, Marshall acknowledged civil rights problems, but he said that it was clear that "in America, in the eyes of the law, the Negro is the equal of any other citizen." Problems in Little Rock and elsewhere might cause observers to think it wasn't so, but "the law says it is, and it is just a matter of time before practice is brought into complete conformity with the law, and that should occur now within the next few years." In Kenya, he was happy to do his part to present a positive image of the U.S. system of government to his friends.[32]

The State Department got Marshall to Kenya, and his schedule included the sort of speaking engagements common to such trips, but Marshall's own objectives were different. He wanted to see how "his" Bill of Rights was working. Not everything he found met with his approval. As Marshall and Bernhard drove through Nairobi, Bernhard remembered, they saw signs that made it look as if "the Indians and Pakistanis were being thrown out of the country." Marshall was "very upset about it." Indians and Pakistanis were a sizeable minority in Kenya. Many were middle-class business owners. The new Kenyan constitution was supposed to protect minorities from discrimination, but Asians seemed to be running into trouble.[33]

"Forced to Leave" was the sign in a shop window Marshall and Bernhard saw on the way to make a speech. Marshall wanted to know what was going on, and they went into the shop to investigate. The shop owner, who was Indian, said that he was being boycotted. "No one was going to buy their stuff," Bernhard recalled. Marshall was irate. Asian shopkeepers throughout Nairobi felt vulnerable. This was not what Marshall expected.

And it was not what he had worked so hard to achieve for Kenya at Lancaster House. He said, "Well, I don't know what's going on. They're supposed to protect their property. I'll talk tonight when we see the [Prime Minister]."[34]

The year had begun with optimistic pronouncements. Kenya's new colonial governor announced that the British government would "lose no time in making all the practical arrangements which are necessary" for Kenya's independence. Jomo Kenyatta gave a press interview aimed at reassuring whites. "Any white settler who is willing to join with us and identify himself with us will be welcome in the Kenya of tomorrow," he said. "What we want is to take over the Government. But people of all races, provided they co-operate, will be welcome in Kenya." Just what it meant to "join" with Kenyatta and "co-operate" remained unclear.[35]

When the colony became a nation, colonial subjects would become citizens. One contentious issue in Kenya was just who those citizens would be. Would everyone living in Kenya automatically become citizens? Or would everyone have the choice to decide whether or not to become Kenyan citizens? Europeans, as the whites in Kenya were called, tended to support the idea that citizenship should be awarded by positive action, so that no "non-African" would become a citizen automatically. Prominent Asians wanted to make as many non-Africans citizens as possible, although, Chanan Singh observed, the Asian rank and file was largely indifferent. Dual citizenship appealed to many but was rejected by African nationalists as suggesting divided loyalties. The 1963 Independence Constitution incorporated many different ideas, making automatic citizens of the second generation born in Kenya before independence and allowing other Kenyan residents to register as citizens within two years. But the constitution also drew a line between those with citizenship and those without: It expressly exempted noncitizens from protection against discrimination.[36]

For Marshall, equality was central. His draft Kenya Bill of Rights had made equality its guiding principle. The preamble read: "All persons are equal before the law and are entitled without any discrimination or distinction of any kind, such as race, colour, sex, language, religion, political or other opinion, national or social origin, property, birth or other status, to equal protection of the law." Marshall thought that this wording would "help the Courts when interpreting the particular provisions of the Bill by setting out general principles on which it would be based." He had intended that other aspects of the text would be read in light of the preamble, so that the overriding norm of equality would carry through. As he told the Committee on Safeguards, "the intention of his paper...was to protect the rights of every individual in Kenya, rather than the rights of any particular minority groups." As it turned out, the most important equality protection hammered out at Lancaster House was not the preamble or even the explicit equality rights in the text. Instead, it was the constitution's "takings clause." That provision had survived the rounds of redrafting since Marshall first submitted it at Lancaster House in 1960. The preamble, on the other hand, had been lost on the cutting room floor along the way, as had the broad social welfare rights Marshall's idealistic Bill of Rights had sought to entrench.[37]

The focus of attention at Lancaster House had been the rights of whites, who were about to lose political power and were concerned about the way that loss would affect their property rights. They remained wary as the handover neared. Their interests had been addressed, however, through a land buyout scheme and the right to emigrate to England. Kenyatta promised to protect the property of those who stayed, since he viewed them as key to Kenya's economic growth.[38]

The minority group whose rights seemed more unsettled was Asians (Indians and Pakistanis), the in-between race in a rigid class and race hierarchy. Like Africans, they had been barred from owning land in the White Highlands and were paid less when they held the same jobs as whites. Yet as much as they had challenged white supremacy, white rule gave them their political and economic power in Kenya's tiered racial structure. Independence meant that the old racial hierarchy would be replaced. But "Africanization" would be the focus as the new government quickly tried to train Africans for the sort of civil service positions Asians had traditionally held.[39]

Immigrants from India and what is now Pakistan had established trade with the east coast of Africa long before European colonization, and Asian communities settled first in coastal cities, including Mombasa. Later the British brought Indian indentured workers to East Africa to work on the Uganda railroad, laid across Kenya in the 1890s. According to constitutional scholar Yash Ghai and sociologist Dharam Ghai, Asian settlement in Kenya did not consist principally of these workers, most of whom returned home. Instead, most settlers came of their own initiative "to set up trade, mostly in the form of the small general store known to this day as the *duka*, from the Indian word, *dukan*, meaning a shop." These shopkeepers brought a market economy to new areas. They were "instrumental in opening shops even in remote parts of the country, buying local African produce, creating a demand for imported goods and helping to spread the use of money."[40]

India traditionally took an interest in the welfare of diaspora Indians. The government took up the cause of Kenyan Indians at imperial conferences, leading to a 1921 resolution that India's status as an equal member of the British Empire was incompatible with unequal treatment of Indians in parts of the empire. This would change with India's independence. India continued to play a strong role in criticizing racial policies in South Africa, but the independent Indian government, "anxious to lead the

Third World, encouraged nationalist activity in Africa," Ghai and Ghai write, "and once the African countries became independent, showed itself even less anxious to get involved in the question of the Asians."[41]

As Kenyan independence neared, Asian immigrant communities were apprehensive. They had fewer options than other immigrants. Europeans might leave Africa without great difficulties, but for Asians, resettlement in Britain was uncertain as concerns about increased immigration of nonwhites led to new immigration restrictions. Many Asians had never lived outside of Kenya, and feared that a move to India or Pakistan would mean poverty.[42]

The uncertainty *Uhuru* would bring had not kept many Asians from working for it. Since Gandhi's struggle against South African apartheid, Indians had long opposed racial hierarchy and colonial rule in Africa, and Indians had worked alongside Africans in the nationalist movement in Kenya. But tensions between Asians and Africans in East Africa had deep roots. When the "Scramble for Africa" took place, Britain's main colony was India. In East Africa, the indigenous peoples worked the land and there was no market for labor, so labor was brought in from the outside, and England turned to India to supply it. Indians came as imperial soldiers and then as laborers on the railway from Uganda, a source of natural resources, to the Kenya coast. Others arrived to work as clerks and petty traders. "Together they [the Asians] extended the horizons of the empire and built its fences," writes anthropologist Mahmood Mamdani. "The strategy of colonial rule was that an ethnically different people were used as a means of coercion in a colony." This meant that contact between the races in Kenya happened "in the market place: between seller and buyer, trader and customer, master and servant, subject and ruler. Significantly, these were all relations of power." In East Africa, writes Mamdani, "the equation in those times was simple. He is an Asian; he is rich. I am an African; I am poor."[43]

The compartmentalization of society into racial groups was "one of the most striking features of colonial rule in East Africa," write Ghai and Ghai. Africans, Europeans, and Asians were separated, living in different residential areas, going to separate schools and hospitals, and they were separated politically, as seats in the colonial legislature were designated according to racial group. Racial ordering permeated economic life, with a racial salary structure in public employment and racial restrictions on land ownership. These policies strengthened European dominance in East Africa, keeping the Asians in a middle tier and the Africans at the bottom.[44]

As independence neared, some Kenyan Asians wondered whether, in working for *Uhuru*, they were ultimately working against their own interests. Jagdish Sondhi, a Kenyan Asian, described it this way in 1962:

> Fear grips the heart of the Asian community in this country....It is a common feeling among the community that we are prostituting ourselves for the fruits of friendship with African leaders. I am all for statesmanship and am fully conscious of the necessity of exercising it in the interests of our community but we must not lose sight of our own rights....While being fully desirous of wanting development in the country there is no need to offer ourselves as a sacrifice to the future happiness of the indigenous people.[45]

Whatever they might do, the fate of the Asians would soon depend on the new Kenyan government.

The Asians' in-betweenness meant that their interests were squeezed from both sides as groups in Kenya jockeyed for position. Not long after the 1960 Lancaster House conference,

Chairman A. T. Culwick of the United Party, representing hard-
line whites, publicly admonished the Asians. "The way you are
going I fear there is no hope for you in this country," he said.
"It is no good for any community in this country to go on sitting
on the fence placating and appeasing in the hope that it may be
allowed to survive." Culwick warned that serious consequences
would result if the Asians did not support European interests.
"Unless you pull your weight, things may go very wrong. If the
European farmer goes from this country the source of your
wealth will have been removed. You will then have little alternative but to eke out an impoverished existence as a downtrodden,
intimidated, persecuted community."[46]

Then, troublesome news percolated through Kenya as the
colony approached its first multiparty, reasonably free election.
For years, colony-wide political organizing had been banned.
With the future leadership of Kenya up for grabs, groups with
no experience with electoral politics sought allegiances. Their
methods were not always appealing.

KANU would soon emerge as the leading party. While dominated by the Kikuyu, the tribe in Kenya at the center of the Mau
Mau resistance movement, KANU also had leaders from other
tribes, including Mboya and Odinga, who were Luo. The Kenya
African Democratic Union (KADU) emerged as an alternative
to KANU and attracted some of the smaller tribes concerned
about Kikuyu dominance, as well as some whites. KADU would
play an important role in 1962 negotiations, resulting in a draft
constitution that recognized regional authorities. Regionalism
was discarded in early postindependence amendments to the
constitution, out of a concern that the new country needed a
stronger national government.[47]

Before the elections sealed KANU's role, support for the
KADU party by some Asians led to tensions. In February,
KANU organizing secretary John Keen called for a boycott of

Asian shopkeepers who had supported KADU. When Keen's remarks were criticized, he responded: "The fact that cannot be ignored and cannot be challenged by any African leader is that the Asian dukawallahs [traders] have exploited Africans for the last 60 years. The ordinary African businessman must be given the opportunity to run his business without competition from these Asians with their large capital." The KANU leadership favored a moderate tone in the final months before independence, but Keen said it was instead time for a new movement: "Us for us," meaning that "Africans should buy only from Africans." This would continue, he insisted, until Asian "fence-sitters" supported "the nationalist cause." For Keen, this meant support for the KANU party. Keen later became more conciliatory, agreeing that "some Asians had helped the Africans and had fostered the nationalist cause of political and economic independence." What Keen objected to was "'fence-sitters' who drained the economy of Kenya, exploited the Africans and sent their money to Bombay." The Asians "live at the top," he said. "They make a big margin of profit on the goods they import to sell here while the African goes barefooted." Keen did not want to deport Asians but to reduce their economic power.[48]

The options for Asians in an independent Kenya were unclear. Some bought farmland, as the removal of racial restrictions opened land ownership in white areas to Asians as well as Africans. The departure of whites meant that valuable land was available at bargain prices. But Asian leader N. S. Toofan warned that by becoming landowners, Asians were "playing with fire." For the most part, the Asians were not farmers but land speculators. "Land-hunger has become a serious malady in many parts of Kenya," he wrote. "Instead of helping to cure it, the Asians seem bent on making it worse."[49]

Tensions about the Asians spilled over into electoral politics. The *Daily Nation* reported in February 1963, "Allegations that a large number of letters written by a local Kanu official have been sent to Asians in Mrogi—warning them to join Kanu or quit the country—are being investigated by South Nyanza police." There was more: The letters warned Asians to give up their licenses to sell one of their staples, an unrefined sugar traditional in India, because it was allegedly used for making gin. The same day, a separate story in the *Daily Nation* reported that Asians were joining the KANU party. Keen, the party organizing secretary, claimed that one thousand Asians had joined KANU in the previous two weeks, but "he declined to say whether this was a result of his recent threat to boycott Asian shops." Instead, he called the move "very encouraging." Asians who had joined the KANU party, he said, were "the true sons of Africa."[50]

More troubling news came in March, when there was picketing outside the Nairobi shop of Nizarali Sayani. "We demand your deportation, Sayani," read one placard. The picketers had been arrested and released on bail, enabling them to return to picket again. Among them was John Wasswa, who had been charged with assaulting Sayani. The *Daily Nation* reported that the dispute was over which ethnic group would operate the shop. It had been purchased by the government "to establish African traders in the area." Sayani had refused to give up his lease while exploring his legal options. So the picketers intended to "try to dissuade" people from entering the shop. If they persisted, a spokesman said, "We will dissuade them further." If that failed, "We shall call the boys."[51]

Tensions reached such a pitch that KANU leader Tom Mboya stepped in. Mboya had learned that some Asian business owners had purchased membership cards for the three most prominent political parties. Shopkeepers would pull out a KANU card for a KANU patron, a KADU card for a KADU patron, and so on. Mboya insisted that party membership to avoid harassment was "absolutely unnecessary." He tried to reassure Asians, telling them that "there would be no wholesale nationalisation of business in an independent Kenya." But as much as Mboya might believe his own assurances and wish for clean elections, the difficulty, of course, was that others were prepared to use any means necessary to ensure that voters of all ethnicities came to the conclusion that their party, whether KANU or KADU, was right.[52]

A resounding electoral victory for KANU elevated Jomo Kenyatta to the post of prime minister in May 1963. Kenyatta welcomed Asians to join KANU in a speech shortly after the elections. He "recalled how for nearly 40 years he and the late M.A. Desai had fought together as brothers for the rights of Africans and Asians in Kenya." Kenyatta invoked memories of meetings with Mahatma Gandhi, Jawaharlal Nehru, and other Indian nationalists "when we sat together and planned the future of our countries." He stressed that it was KANU's hope that Asians would join in building a Kenya in which "African and Asian [could] live together, work together and plan together." Kenyatta sounded a similar theme at a meeting with Asians and whites in Nakura three days later. He stressed that a KANU government would protect their businesses and that Asians had "nothing to fear." Kenyatta hoped to dispel rumors that Asians who did not support KANU would be evicted. Anyone who did this would be "punished worse than under the British," Kenyatta insisted. "We will try to follow the Constitution to the best of our ability."[53]

When constitutional clauses were negotiated at Lancaster House, it must have seemed to Thurgood Marshall that he and the nationalists shared the same vision. This belief in their apparent common values was reinforced when Kenyatta, on his release from years of detention in August 1961, called for unity and insisted that an independent Kenya "would respect foreigners [*sic*] property and give them the same equal rights as Africans." For Marshall, independence was the most crucial issue,

Kenyan Premier Jomo Kenyatta (right, foreground) waves his ceremonial fly whisk as he and cabinet members Tom Mboya (minister of justice and constitutional affairs), A. Oginga Odinga (minister for home affairs), and James S. Gichuru (minister for finance) (left to right) greet a crowd of supporters celebrating the beginning of internal self-government in Kenya, in Nairobi, June 1, 1963. (© Bettmann/CORBIS)

and equality was the central value going forward. He must have seen his vision reflected in Kenyatta, who insisted, "We shall not steal anything from them except our freedom." When Kenyatta attended constitutional negotiations in 1962, he pledged that KANU would "treat as sacred provisions of the Constitution [and] Bill of Rights which will guarantee to all persons the fundamental freedoms, and equality before the law," and would "recognize and respect rights in private property." This rhetoric sounded good to an American interested in equality rights, but Marshall and Kenyatta had different objectives in 1963. As Africans took power in Kenya, Kenyatta's central concerns were about sovereignty and national unity, about pulling new Kenyan citizens together around the common goal of nationhood, rather than entrenching group-based identities or empowering individuals to use law to question government action. In this territory marked out years before by colonialists, which had never been a country, a real danger was that the divisions of race and tribe would undermine the creation of an independent Kenya. The need to create a national identity was in tension with an American conception of individual rights.[54]

THIS WAS THE CONTEXT THAT THURGOOD MARSHALL walked into in July 1963, a context that affected the ability of Marshall and his Kenyan colleagues to see constitutional rights in the same way. At the end of their first day in Kenya, Marshall and Berl Bernhard attended a reception and dinner in their honor at the home of Tom Mboya, who now held a cabinet post in the new government. Marshall fulfilled his promise to the Indian shop owner. Bernhard recalled,

> About halfway through the cocktail hour, Thurgood got ahold of Kenyatta and said: "Jomo, what the hell you doing?" and I thought, my God, . . . and he said: "I spent all my time busting tail in that wet place in London writing a constitution for you with a bill of rights. And you don't go around taking people's property without *due process of law*. And I've only been here one afternoon, and what is the first thing I see. You're beginning to make it impossible for Indians and Pakistanis to stay in Kenya and operate their business. What are you going to do about it?"[55]

Bernhard described Kenyatta as a very impressive man, "very cool, very elderly." Kenyatta told Marshall that they were looking into it. Marshall wasn't mollified. "No, it's not 'looking into,'" he replied. "It's *doing* something about it." He called Mboya over and said to him, "Your responsibility is to see that despite what the Prime Minister wants to happen, that we're going to protect property rights in the country."

"Tom Mboya said, 'Well we are going to do that, Judge, and...'"

Marshall cut in: "'You're *not* doing it.'"[56]

Bernhard was taken aback. "Never in diplomatic history has an American treated another nation's head of state this way!" he thought to himself. But Marshall had a touch that worked with these men, whom he thought of as colleagues. He as quickly berated Kenyatta as he teased him. "They *loved* Thurgood," Bernhard recalled.[57]

Kenya was not the only country to be criticized for inaction on rights that evening at Mboya's home. Marshall and Bernhard were concerned that there was so much anger in Kenya over treatment of African Americans in the United States that it "would spill over and ruin the trip." When these issues came up in discussions with Kenyatta and others, Bernhard remembered, Marshall explained "how bad the situation was, not just for the people in the U.S., but the impact overseas, that this was really hurting the United States." He was concerned about whether the United States could "ever have decent relations with the African nations, the African continent, when we had these problems at home." Marshall's approach was to face the problem, rather than deny its existence. "The problems are there for all to see," he said. But he stressed to the Kenyans, "It's what we're *doing* about it, and what you may *not be doing* about your own constitution."[58]

Marshall defended his country and quarreled with Kenyatta and Mboya over the rights of Asians. But this was his return to his "homeland." Although Marshall was deeply disappointed in what he had found, it did not displace his joy at being a part of Kenya's founding moment, at being with the ones who had helped carry the colony over a crucial political threshold.

African Americans in other African nations sometimes found themselves at odds with their hosts. Civil rights lawyer Pauli Murray worked in Ghana after that country's independence. Kevin Gaines describes growing tension between Murray and President Kwame Nkrumah's government. Trouble came about in part because Murray took on the role of responding to negative press treatment of the United States. She also clashed with Nkrumah over the 1958 Preventive Detention Act, which enabled the government to detain without trial persons deemed to be security risks, and other government restrictions on civil liberties. The law classes she taught in Ghana were attended both by members of the opposition interested in her critique and by government intelligence agents monitoring her activities. She became more strongly associated with Nkrumah's opponents just as the Congo crisis increased the president's concerns about security. Ultimately Murray left Ghana, Gaines writes, "just ahead of what would certainly have been her expulsion."[59]

Murray's effort to defend the American image in Ghana at a time when American civil rights problems were eroding U.S. international prestige led to difficulties for her. Murray was in Ghana as a private citizen. Marshall, in contrast, was sent to Kenya by the State Department for the purpose of burnishing the American image. His activities seemed to solidify his place in Kenya rather than undermine it. The difference in their experiences turned in part on the politics of the African nations they worked with. Most important was that many Kenya nationalists hoped to benefit from a relationship with the United States, whereas Ghana was critical of the U.S. role in Africa. It was also more difficult for women to play a role in global politics in both Africa and America in the early '60s. Compared to Murray, Marshall had more freedom in Kenya in 1963, in stark contrast to his own experience there three years earlier. The greater acceptance of Marshall is illustrated by the way he could turn diplomatic occasions to his own purposes. At an appearance at a Kenyan television station, for example, Marshall goaded Bernhard, his young white companion, to say the word *Uhuru* on the air. A slogan of the anticolonial movement, the word was an affront to the white settler community. When uttered on television by a U.S. government official, if only the staff director of the Civil Rights Commission, it created a stir in diplomatic circles. Marshall couldn't have been more pleased, but Bernhard got muzzled.[60]

Marshall had great fun in Kenya, sometimes at Bernhard's expense. He refused to attend a meeting in the White Highlands with white settlers and sent Bernhard alone. When Bernhard returned and joined Marshall at an event, Marshall announced loudly to all present: "The white settler has returned!" And then there was the matter of the leopard. Marshall insisted that a leopard skin must be found for his wife, Cissy. "Which leopard?" asked Kenyatta, and a leopard was shot just for this purpose. The trip gave a legendary storyteller a treasure trove of material he would draw upon thereafter.[61]

Beyond the stories, Marshall's Kenya trip engaged his life passion: equality under law. What he saw enraged him. The greatest puzzle is that this episode did not diminish Marshall's excitement at Kenya's independence and his great pride in having played a hand in crafting rights for this new country. He was thrilled to be at Kenya's independence ceremonies later that year with Cissy. They were among the very few special guests whose expenses were paid by the new Kenyan government. Marshall's affection for Kenyatta was genuine, and yet Kenyatta was focused less on rights than on consolidating national power and unity, to make a nation. When the Constitution stood in the way of his political objectives, he would be quick to cast it aside. In the years following independence, a large number of whites and Asians would leave Kenya. Those who remained faced discrimination, especially if they did not become Kenyan citizens, and some Asian citizens of Kenya even faced deportation, although nothing near the scale of deportation of Asians in neighboring Uganda. Marshall later had harsh words for the Asians in Kenya. He thought they were foolish when they delayed becoming Kenyan citizens due to concerns about discrimination. He clearly felt that they should have cast their lot with the independent government. But as Donald Rothchild and others have shown, independence led to a crisis over citizenship for Asians and whites, and Asians had legitimate fears that citizenship in Kenya would not protect them from discrimination and deportation. In later years, controversy over the role of minorities in the government and economy continued.[62]

Marshall's hope to see rights working in Kenya came up against the exigencies of a new government attempting to gain sovereignty for the first time, and after decades of brutal colonial rule. Constitutionalism had achieved a great deal by the time of Marshall's trip in 1963. In hammering out the details of the Kenya Bill of Rights, adversaries had negotiated with each other over core values and problems. As violence erupted in other parts of Africa, in Kenya these negotiations created a context for peaceful regime change, as different groups battled over land and political power, not with weapons of violence but with constitutional clauses. But the result was a flawed legal order, entrenching a system of property inherited from the colonial years. And once the Constitution was in place, rights under the new government depended on much more than a text; they depended on a culture of rights, on an engaged citizenry that would demand that the government adhere to limits on its own power. Kenyans would later take to the streets in the early twenty-first century, demanding that their government respect constitutional limits. But during the early years of nation building, constitutional rights gave way to political expediency as a new and fragile government worked to consolidate its power. In later years, when Daniel arap Moi became president, the text was no barrier to Kenya's slide into authoritarian government and political corruption. This is not to say that constitutionalism did not work in Kenya in the independence era, but it could not accomplish what Marshall had hoped for: the entrenchment in Kenya of the rights he still hoped for in America.[63]

Berl Bernhard later said that Marshall attributed "more goodness across the board to Kenyatta than I had ever read or heard was appropriate." The reason seemed to be Kenyatta's focus on the task at hand: bringing a subject people to independence. Marshall later explained that he had "the greatest respect for him." If not for Kenyatta, he thought, Kenya would have experienced "one of the damnedest bloodbaths you ever saw in your life. He was the one thing that stood in the way of that."[64]

Bernhard told Marshall, "This guy's not all clean," and Marshall said, "What do you expect?" Bernhard stressed that Marshall "wanted to protect that freedom, period, and he wasn't going to listen to a lot of carping about the method."[65]

IN DECEMBER 1963, BOTH MARSHALL and G. Mennen Williams, undersecretary of state for African affairs, traveled to Kenya for the independence ceremonies. That December was a difficult time for American diplomats. It was a month after the Kennedy assassination, and their job was to reassure the world that America was not falling apart.[66]

Kennedy had taken a stronger civil rights stance in the summer of 1963, calling for landmark civil rights legislation. The domestic and international reaction to Birmingham had been so intense that he had to act. His efforts helped shore up the U.S. image internationally. Race in America had become such an important world story in 1963 that many in Africa and elsewhere worried that the president's assassination stemmed from his support for civil rights. There was deep concern about what his loss would mean for the future of racial equality in America. In his address to a joint session of Congress, on November 27, 1963, an address to the nation and the world as well, the new president, Lyndon Baines Johnson, was careful to reassure his audience that there would be consistency not only in U.S. foreign policy but also in U.S. civil rights policy. Johnson promised the world that he would follow through on Kennedy's civil rights bill.[67]

This was the message that Williams took to Nairobi in December 1963. And he wrapped together the challenge of race in America and race in Kenya. Both nations faced challenges, he emphasized; both nations strove to move forward. It went without saying that discrimination continued in both countries. Williams was not there to point fingers. And he was certainly in no mood to have fingers pointed his way.[68]

By weaving together the racial fates of both nations, Williams simultaneously extended the hand of friendship to a new ally and created a buffer against criticism of American civil rights problems, at least from the new Kenyan government. Human rights problems would continue to plague both nations; Kenyatta and American leaders would continue to talk about it. When it came to the politics of the cold war, nations with common interests closed ranks. A new alliance would not be derailed by the problem of the Asians.

– 5 –

ANARCHY IS ANARCHY

What is striking to me is the importance of law in determining the condition of the Negro. He was effectively enslaved, not by brute force, but by a law which declared him a chattel of his master.... He was emancipated by law, and then disfranchised and segregated by law. And, finally, he is winning equality by law.
—Thurgood Marshall, June 1, 1966

Power is the only thing respected in this world, and we must get it at any cost.
—Stokely Carmichael, 1966

NINETEEN SIXTY-SIX WAS HOT. St. Louis, Missouri, faced record temperatures and heat-related deaths that summer, setting tempers on edge. Racial tensions had boiled over already in Cleveland that June. Amid days of rioting, fires consumed blocks of homes and businesses until more than two thousand Ohio National Guardsmen were called in to restore order. Chicago and other cities also faced riots that summer. What was it about the heat of the summer that set cities on edge, when the underlying catalysts of poverty and injustice spanned the year?[1]

Once merely a Los Angeles neighborhood, Watts became a national symbol of urban unrest in 1965. Hundreds of homes and storefronts burned to ashes; dozens were killed and more than a thousand injured. According to the California Governor's Commission on Watts, as many as ten thousand were involved in what has variously been called a riot and a rebellion. The violence, though centered in South Central LA, spread out to cover over forty-six square miles of the Los Angeles area.[2]

There was an urgent need for government response but little agreement about the direction action should take. Commissions urged that dollars be poured into the inner city. But many Americans felt the priority should instead be law and order. To some, police were the problem; to others, the solution.[3]

Thurgood Marshall found himself in the middle. Throughout his career, Marshall had been a consistent critic of police misconduct and racism. Then, in 1965 he was named solicitor general, one of the nation's top legal officials. President Lyndon Baines Johnson, who seemed genuinely committed to civil rights, called on him for advice, both about civil rights proposals and about how to stem the violence. But there was another dimension to Marshall's role. He had come to believe that law

Smoke rises in the evening sky as rioting breaks out in Detroit, July 24, 1967. (© Bettmann/CORBIS)

structured the lives and opportunities of African Americans and that it was through legal reform that real change would come. The crowds in the streets rejected this vision. And the political climate had changed, in part a negative reaction to urban violence, undermining the political context for new civil rights legislation. Within the Johnson administration, Black Power and urban violence were seen as detrimental to civil rights reform.[4]

Marshall was back in the spotlight. Since 1961 he had been relatively sequestered on the bench. Now, as one of the two top-ranking African Americans in the federal government, he was again a public figure, but this time from within the establishment. As Wallace Terry of *Time* magazine put it, "Marshall has become a part-time spokesman-strategist for the Administration on civil rights and Negro progress." And as the movement became more militant, Marshall became "Washington's leading critic of 'black power.'"[5]

Although differences in philosophy had always characterized the civil rights movement, Black Power was a departure from the nonviolent and inclusive rhetoric of Martin Luther King Jr. It burst on the national scene during a civil rights march in Mississippi in 1966. The march had not been planned; initially James Meredith intended to walk alone across Mississippi. He was shot and seriously injured on the second day, prompting civil rights leaders to come to Mississippi to continue his demonstration.[6]

There were tensions between King and the younger, less polished leader of the Student Nonviolent Coordinating Committee (SNCC), Stokely Carmichael, but they were largely contained until one night in Greenwood, Mississippi, when local police arrested Carmichael after a dispute involving the demonstrators' campsite. He was angry when he arrived at an evening rally, straight from the jailhouse. "This is the twenty-seventh time that I've been arrested," he told the crowd. "But I ain't going to jail no more. The only way we gonna stop them white men from whuppin' us is to take over. What we gonna start sayin' now is Black Power!" Soon "Black Power" became the slogan of a more militant wing of the civil rights movement.[7]

Not long after, Carmichael appeared on the CBS news program *Face the Nation*. He was peppered with questions about whether Black Power was a recipe for violence. "You seem to be arguing that wherever the Negroes cannot get what they wish they are entitled to use violent methods to achieve it," interviewer Martin Agronsky insisted. "I have never said that," responded Carmichael. "When I talk about black power I talk about black people in the counties where they outnumber them to get together, to organize themselves politically and to take over those counties from white racists who now run them."[8]

But before long, as historian Peniel Joseph put it, "Black Power would scandalize American politics." *Time* called it a "'racist philosophy' that preached segregation in reverse. *Newsweek* called it a 'distorted cry' that frightened whites." Social critic Harold Cruse wrote in 1967, "A new threat fell across the land like an ominous shadow even though the exact concept of Black Power has not yet been clearly defined." For civil rights leader Julian Bond, it was a "natural extension of the work of the civil rights movement for the past few years; from the courtroom to the streets in favor of integrated public facilities; from the streets to the backroads in the quest of the right to vote; from the ballot box to the meat of politics, the organization of voters into self-interest units." But to Cruse it was a strategic retreat, as deep economic change seemed elusive and white backlash hampered civil rights reform.[9]

The impact of Black Power could be seen in the way groups across the political spectrum positioned themselves in relation to it. According to Joseph, Martin Luther King Jr. "distanced himself from the slogan, but refused to censure the meaning behind the message or the messenger," while John Lewis, drawn to King's philosophy of nonviolent civil disobedience, resigned from the SNCC shortly after the march. The Congress of Racial Equality endorsed Black Power at its annual convention in the summer of 1966 and defined it this way:

> Black Power is effective control and self-determination by men of color in their own areas.
>
> Power is total control of the economic, political, educational, and social life of our community from the top to the bottom.
>
> The exercise of power at the local level is simply what all other groups in American society have done to acquire their share of total American life.[10]

Groups further afield from the Southern civil rights movement also reacted. Alpha Phi Alpha, an established African American fraternity that was the face of the black male middle-class elite, released a statement on Black Power at its August 1966 annual conference in St. Louis, Missouri. On one hand, the fraternity embraced the idea of Black Power. "Alpha Phi Alpha has been a black power for many years since its organization in that our ritual emphasized black Africa and our membership was composed of descendants of Africa." Also, the organization believed in "the words of Lord Byron that 'they who would free themselves must strike the blow.'" This was not a radical stance but deeply American, "the way upward in American life." However, the fraternity rejected the separatism of the Black Power movement. African Americans must not, they said, "make our power so exclusive that it is discriminative against whites. Nor must we have divisions of mulattoes, darker people or, for that matter, any class group." Instead, Alpha Phi Alpha urged that its members "close ranks along all lines, and move forward together with all distinctions as to colors and classes abolished. The power of positive and enlightened community effort should take the place of either white power or black power." In essence, the fraternity tried to reclaim the rhetoric of "black power" from the left. That they made this attempt illuminates the attraction of the idea of black power, and the recognition by this elite group that the Black Power movement was having an impact.[11]

Marshall traveled to St. Louis to address Alpha Phi Alpha's 1966 conference. His role in the meeting began with a pilgrimage to the Old Courthouse in St. Louis, in memory of the *Dred Scott* decision. Scott, a slave, had first sued for his freedom there in 1846, only eventually to lose his case in the U.S. Supreme Court. The Old Courthouse was a monument to the nation's legacy of slavery and the long battle for freedom. It was also an imposing architectural reminder of the imprimatur of law on the lives of African Americans.[12]

Marshall spoke, as he often had before, about responsibility, the theme of the fraternity's meeting. "Go down into the ghetto," he told his audience. "We know where it is, a whole lot of us started there—sit down with these people and say, 'We are not only with you, we are here.'" The black middle class needed to "determine what needs to be done for the poor," and pressure the government to get it. Support for poor communities must also come from black communities themselves. "It is time the Negro himself has to take over some of this responsibility," he insisted.[13]

The *St. Louis Globe-Democrat*'s front-page coverage did not emphasize the part of Marshall's speech about going into the ghetto. Instead it focused on his criticism of rabble-rousers. "Standing in the rotunda of the Old Courthouse at Fourth and Market streets," the paper reported, "the famed civil rights leader denounced the 'rock throwers' and 'Molotov cocktail throwers!'" The words that would be widely quoted were: "Lawlessness is lawlessness. Anarchy is anarchy is anarchy. Neither race nor color nor frustration is an excuse for either lawlessness or anarchy." If he meant it for the African American community, the speech nevertheless resonated with others who had tired of black anger on the heels of a decade of civil rights reform. "We won't settle for less than equality," Marshall warned, but "to replace 'white power' with 'black power' is an aim based itself on inequality." He insisted: "Negroes and other friends of democracy must not panic in the face of this new minority (black power advocates) who have nothing to offer but violence."[14]

Black Power was often equated with violence, but the role of armed struggle was highly controversial within the Black Power movement itself. In 1962, civil rights activist Robert Williams published his controversial volume *Negroes with Guns*, spelling out his philosophy that violence must be met with violence. By 1964, the Deacons for Defense began armed vigils, providing protection for civil rights marchers. For others, Black Power was less about fighting back and more about voting strength in majority black districts, and about pride in black culture. If the strands of Black Power came together around one thing, however, it was opposition to the form of social change Marshall had championed, in which the goal was integration with whites rather than strengthening black identity and achieving political power. But in the popular imagination in the late 1960s, any nuance was lost when youths throwing rocks or Black Panthers with rifles shouted "Black Power."[15]

Marshall was now an insider, but the problem of racial violence was not new to him. He had seen a city burn before. He had been a young lawyer working for the NAACP under Charles Hamilton Houston when Detroit erupted in violence in 1943. African American workers had migrated there in search of jobs in wartime defense production. Racial tensions spun out of control that August. Whites targeted blacks and blacks targeted whites, but the real cause of the violence lay elsewhere,

Central State University students raise their fists in the Black Power salute during a protest at the Ohio State House, Columbus, Ohio, May 22, 1969. (© Bettmann/CORBIS)

Marshall wrote in an editorial in *The Crisis*. "Riots are initially the result of many underlying causes yet no single factor is more important than the attitude and efficiency of the police." In that conflagration, "much of the blood spilled in the Detroit riot is on the hands of the Detroit police department," because the police "enforced the law with an unequal hand." In the end, seventeen African Americans were killed by police, but not a single white. The entire record of mistreatment of African Americans by police in Detroit, Marshall believed, "reads like the story of the Nazi Gestapo."[16]

The dilemma for a civil rights lawyer of Marshall's generation was that the law enforcement officers who were so often a source of injustice were also the ones charged with protecting rights. Through the 1940s, Marshall repeatedly challenged the Justice Department and the FBI for failure to prosecute those involved in lynchings. It was his determined efforts to get federal officials to pursue cases of race-based violence that first made Marshall a target of the FBI, leading to a voluminous record of FBI surveillance of him. For Marshall, there was nothing inherently just or unjust in law enforcement. What mattered was who held the reigns of power, and to what purpose they used them. As solicitor general, Marshall had become one of the nation's top law enforcement officers. If ever law enforcement could be a force for good, it had to be in his administration. And so the blistering critic of law enforcement became its defender.[17]

As the nation became increasingly divided over the war in Vietnam and over the nature of dissent at home, a national commitment to solve the trouble in the cities seemed elusive. The McCone Report called for improvements in employment, education, and public services in African American neighborhoods in Los Angeles, as would reports in other cities. But this kind of ambitious reform was beyond the political will of local and national leaders.[18]

The riots weighed heavily on Marshall. The blocks that burned were similar, often, to the segregated Baltimore neighborhood of his childhood. And it was African Americans, the people whose rights he championed, who struck the match. He had argued before that violence would come if peaceful means did not create a fairer society. But now that American cities were burning, Marshall, one of the nation's highest officers of the law, could not stand aside or tell American leaders that a cause of the ash in the cities was their own inaction. He was now, himself, an American leader. It had never been his way to lead by the barricades. But Thurgood Marshall took to this battle with a microphone.

"Anarchy is anarchy is anarchy," Marshall had insisted in the Old Courthouse in St. Louis on that hot August night in 1966. He would use almost the same language three years later, this time as Supreme Court justice, when addressing the centennial celebration at predominantly African American Dillard University in New Orleans. Marshall said many other things during these years, of course, but again it was this message that the American press latched onto. "Marshall Warns Negro Militants: Says 'Anarchy Is Anarchy' and 'Should Be Punished'" was the *New York Times* headline. "Negro militants who defied the law should be made to face the consequences," Marshall continued. "You can't use color for an excuse for not doing what you should be doing." It is a sign of how much mainstream America longed for this message that Marshall's anarchy speech at Dillard made it on two of the three national television networks. ABC and NBC carried his voice into countless American homes. "Nothing will be said over the gun," Marshall insisted. "Nothing will be said over the firebomb. And nothing will be said over the rock because the country will not be able to survive if it permits it to go unpunished."[19]

Marshall saw the legal process as an alternative to violence, but he had often warned that for people to seek out law instead of violence, they needed to see law working for them. For Marshall, the promise of progress through legal channels was still palpable. "So far as race problems go and minority rights go, the problems are not yet solved, and I have no idea when they will be," he told his audience. "But there has been some progress. The seeds are here."[20]

In the minds of Americans, these were the two poles of race in America. There was Thurgood Marshall, the face of moderation, who, in his earlier years, had threatened to change America but now occupied a terrain that seemed more palatable in comparison. Then there were Stokely Carmichael and Black Panther Huey Newton, the raised black fist seeking a world not of belonging with whites, but of power to challenge them. Whites could see themselves in Marshall's vision, the vision of an earlier generation of civil rights leaders. It wasn't that Marshall embraced a centrist position. Rather, the philosophy that had guided him for decades had shifted to the center.[21]

Marshall's faith in the law as a vehicle for social change was not based on a belief in the inevitability of legal progress. Neither was it a naive belief that cases would turn out right, that good would prevail. Instead, as he explained at a White House conference on civil rights in 1966, one of history's lessons was that the law had marked the place of African Americans in the world:

> What is striking is the importance of law in determining the condition of the Negro. He was effectively enslaved, not by brute force, but by a law which declared him a chattel of his master, who was given a legal right to recapture him, even in a free territory. He was emancipated by law, and then disfranchised and segregated by law. And, finally, he is winning equality by law.

If law had determined the place of African Americans in the world, then legal reform was essential to changing it. Marshall added that "there is very little truth in the old refrain that one cannot legislate equality. Laws not only provide concrete benefits; they can even change the hearts of men—some men anyway—for good or for evil." The lesson of history, he emphasized, was that "the hearts of men do not change of themselves."[22]

Marshall's opposition to Black Power, then, was not simply based on the tendency to conflate Black Power and violent resistance. Instead, Black Power seemed to reduce history to a raw dynamic of power. The idea that only a power shift could markedly alter material conditions for African Americans was at odds with his core beliefs. It denied the rule of law itself.

THE UNITED STATES WAS, OF COURSE, not the only place where the rule of law was under siege in the late 1960s. As new African nations turned from nationalist politics to the business of governance, their new constitutions and laws were put to the test. The superpowers were helpful when it came to certain forms of development assistance, but creating a political culture supportive of democratic governance was an entirely different matter. It was not in the interests of the United States to criticize a nation it needed as a cold war ally. Kenya quickly found that when it came to abuses of government power, its new friends would look the other way.

One of the more curious turns in Kenya's political evolution was that the man once feared as the "leader to darkness and death," in Patrick Renison's words, came to be embraced so warmly by Western leaders. When it first became clear that Jomo Kenyatta had a popular mandate and would surely become the nation's first president, the British and Americans assumed he would be a transitional figure. He was an old man of seventy-four when Kenya achieved independence in 1963, far exceeding Kenya's average life expectancy, which was at that time under fifty. But he endured.[23]

In the eyes of American officials, Kenyatta's principal value lay in his willingness to stave off communist influence in Kenya. His biographer, Jeremy Murray-Brown, writes: "He preached unity to his people and pointed out how the British had won their empire through a policy of divide and rule; but he showed that he had learnt enough from them to apply the same technique to his own government." Kenyatta sought aid from both East and West but would crack down on any perceived signs of communist infiltration. Not long after Kenya's independence, Americans were wishing him well. Benjamin Read wrote to National Security Advisor McGeorge Bundy that Kenyatta "exercised a moderate role in Kenya and has maintained a balance between conflicting elements in the Government. Should his leadership fail control would almost certainly go to the pro-communist

Minister of Home Affairs Oginga Odinga, and Kenya would probably come quickly under communist control." Read urged that the United States "must continue to assure Kenyatta of our friendship and support." In July 1964, the Central Intelligence Agency prepared a report on "Leftist Activity in Kenya," detailing great concern about Odinga's ties with communist countries and the fact that Odinga was now the only one who seemed to have the political power to succeed Kenyatta. The only course was to back Kenyatta. American support for the new president paid off. Before long, foreign largesse was evident in Nairobi's rising skyline, "where a new Hilton Hotel symbolized American faith in Kenyatta's regime." With World Bank support, Kenya was soon the most prosperous nation in East Africa.[24]

President Johnson and Kenyatta maintained a warm correspondence, often commenting on their common efforts to combat racial oppression, and the way the action of one nation could affect the other. Kenyatta wrote to Johnson in May 1965, expressing support for LBJ's civil rights efforts. This was not long after violence in Selma, Alabama, had captured the world's attention yet again, as peaceful demonstrators were beaten by police when trying to march across the Edmund Pettus Bridge. President Johnson called for landmark voting rights legislation, declaring that "we shall overcome." "It is always easy for those in power to oppress minorities," Kenyatta wrote Johnson, "and it takes special courage to denounce entrenched interests and selfish groups." His own country had "experienced similar circumstances and it is the policy of my Government, backed by the Bill of Rights enshrined in the constitution, to defeat racialism whenever it raises its ugly head." But Kenyatta wrote that his own efforts "will be made easier if your government will overcome this racial problem, especially in the Southern States."[25]

Johnson wrote to Kenyatta in 1966 that Americans "especially admire your efforts to build a multi-racial society where prejudice and bitterness will be swept away by free men working together as equals. Kenya serves as a good example for all those countries of the world where racial or ethnic minorities are to be found." The Johnson administration surely knew at this point that Asians in Kenya were in trouble. Kenyatta shared the resentment many Africans harbored for Asians, seen as the merchants of colonial capitalism. Asians who had not become citizens suddenly could not obtain work permits. The need to "Africanize" jobs that Asians traditionally had held denied Asians their livelihood. Some left for England, but then Britain refused them unrestricted entry, even though they held British Commonwealth passports.[26]

It was not only Asians who felt the full weight of Kenyatta's governing hand. Kenyatta had the difficult task of uniting divided tribes into a common sense of nationhood. For years, Kenyatta himself, and demands for his release, had been a uniting force of the nationalist cause. Kenyatta became the symbol of his nation. This might have aided national unity, but of course there was a dark side. It was a short step from the confluence of Kenya and Kenyatta to a sense, as Murray-Brown writes, "that one's patriotism was implicated in the way the president was treated." A major street in Nairobi was named for Kenyatta. His statue was erected, replacing one of a settler. These changes might have been expected. But soon his photograph was to be seen everywhere, including on the new currency, and "the legislature made it a crime to show disrespect for Kenya's leader."[27]

Kenyatta's desire to maintain unity by suppressing opposition would ultimately ensnare even Oginga Odinga, who had so loyally championed Kenyatta when he was detained. Odinga broke with the president in 1965, forming his own political party, the Kenya Political Union. His goal was to create a left-wing alternative to the Western-oriented, increasingly conservative, Kenya African National Union–dominated government. KANU responded by amending the Kenya constitution in one day to require members of the legislature who changed parties to resign and face an election. The result was devastating to Odinga's party, which lost all but nine of its twenty-nine seats. The constitutional amendment remained on the books, an effective tool to control opposition in future years.[28]

The commitment of Americans to close ranks with Kenyatta, and in fact to do their best to protect his presidency, was apparent following a strange incident in January 1968 in Nairobi. Vice President Hubert Humphrey and his entourage stopped in Kenya on a trip through Africa that year. Kenyatta hosted a luncheon for Humphrey on January 8. The luncheon featured all the ceremony of an important state visit, and many guests were present. As fate would have it, soup was on the menu. A waiter accidentally spilled it on Kenyatta's coat. Kenyatta stood up and hit the waiter with a karate chop. The waiter fell to the floor and had to be carried from the room. The luncheon then simply continued. Shortly afterward, word went out from the State Department that American personnel at the luncheon were not to speak to the press about it. If the karate chop story got out, the source would not be a U.S. government one.[29]

DURING THE LATE 1960s, AFRICA KEPT ITS HOLD on the black imagination. African American leaders continued to travel to Africa, and Stokely Carmichael pledged to lead a pan-Africanist revolution from his new home in Guinea. More than a geographic location, Africa informed black culture. In Los Angeles, black nationalist Ron Karenga urged African Americans to reclaim a lost African past through wearing African dress, learning the Swahili language, and engaging in African cultural practices, including an African American holiday, Kwanzaa. By 1974, Peniel Joseph suggests, pan-Africanism "became the dominant mode of radical black activism around the country."[30]

As Africa changed in the years after independence, engaging specific African nations became more complicated. In Ghana, for example, Kevin Gaines writes that a coup overthrowing the Nkrumah government and its aftermath "drastically altered the outlook" of African American expatriates in the nation "toward an African people they had once regarded as progressives." Throughout the continent, political differences divided newly independent nations. And some of the heroes of the independence era had blood on their hands. Perhaps this is one reason why American attention came to focus especially on South Africa, where apartheid made the lines easy to see. It was clear on which side good and evil lay. African leaders from independent countries, not necessarily needing Western saviors but seeking dialogue, fit more awkwardly into American conversations. It proved hard for a real African to negotiate what Africa had come to signify.[31]

Tom Mboya found this out in the spring of 1969, when he came to New York. Mboya confided how difficult things were in Kenya to three American friends, including Frank Montero and William Scheinman, whom he had known before Lancaster House. His enemies wanted to block his influence, he said. He thought the risk of assassination was growing. They told him he should hire a better bodyguard; they wanted to pay. The promise of *Uhuru* had devolved into a politics of survival. Mboya had come across the Atlantic to do business but also to seek support. "Tom was usually a stoic guy," Montero recalled. "He was embarrassed to be showing his feelings." His enemies were getting "nervous and desperate," Mboya later wrote Scheinman from a secure location. "Security will become more urgent now."[32]

But Mboya was still free to walk the streets of Manhattan. It must have been a joy to be back in this place where he had triumphed. And then it was a great disappointment to find himself under attack in a different way, in the United States, and in, of all places, Harlem.

Americans still thought of Mboya as "heir apparent to President Jomo Kenyatta," as the *Pittsburgh Courier* called him, even though within Kenya his political fortunes were now more muddled. He spoke at the Countee Cullen Library in April 1969, discussing developments in independent Kenya. The nation was "a modern model of equality for all races and religions," he said. Because of "modern communications, commerce and transportation, 'the whole world has become as small as a little village with no room for those who would isolate themselves.'"[33]

Mboya took questions after his prepared remarks. That is when the trouble started. "I was once asked whether I support the movements of Afro-Americans from the United States to Africa," he said.

> My answer was, no. I do not believe that there should be a movement. I do not believe that we should run away from the struggle. I believe that Africans should have the right to move to other lands. I also believe that the cosmopolitan atmosphere which has been established in Africa and elsewhere must be established all over. Africa has shown the white nations that there is no place for racialism.

Mboya's remarks "stirred up a hornet's nest among his audience," which included many black separatists. Reaction was so strong that New York City police were called in, though no arrests were made. Mboya later said that some people had approached him before the meeting, and his remarks were a response to them. He "decided to comment on the proposal for a mass movement of black Americans to Africa. I began by rejecting the proposal, but before I had a [chance] to elaborate, I was noisily interrupted by two or three people, one [of whom] projected four or five eggs in my direction." Fortunately, Mboya added, "His aim was as bad as his manners."[34]

"You're not the same Mboya that we knew! You're not the same Mboya that we fought for! We fought for Kenya," shouted one woman. "Throw him out!" shouted others. Odeyo Ayaga, head of the African Students Union, thought Mboya was wrong. He told the press: "If we are to be self-sufficient, we must rely on black scientific brains and must create an atmosphere in Africa to welcome blacks from America. They did not choose to be where they are and have every right to return to Africa." An editorial in the *Chicago Defender* argued that Mboya was

> caught in a cross-fire between two schools of thought—those who advocate black power as a separate entity and those who insist that the black man has a constitutional right to be part and parcel of the American society. The former look upon Africa's resurgence as the ideal pattern of independence for the separatist movement of the U.S. blacks. Thus, they look upon modern, independent Africa not only as a classic example but as a corner of the world where they would be welcome should they decide to return to the ancestral homeland.

In other words, Mboya satisfied neither integrationists nor separatists. The *Defender* expected an imminent showdown between these schools of thought, with one "bound to prevail at the expense of the other." As for Mboya, the *Defender* thought the misunderstanding might have been avoided if he had "spoken of black power as a political reality in the context of world affairs." Perhaps a focus on power itself could "bridge the moat between black power militants and civil rights crusaders."[35]

Mboya's comment had a context that might not have been clear to some observers. The previous year, a motion had been offered in the Kenyan legislature awarding automatic Kenyan citizenship to any African American who wanted to settle there. The motion was tabled and rejected. Mboya later explained, "even Africans coming from neighbouring states cannot acquire automatic citizenship in Kenya." Kenyan citizenship requirements were set forth in the Kenyan Constitution. A bill discriminating in favor of one group would have violated the citizenship clause. The rejected proposal was raised at the Harlem meeting, and some participants were angry at the Kenyan government for the outcome.[36]

Africa as home figured powerfully in the imagination of a new generation of African Americans, but it would be difficult to see that continent as a homeland if African nations refused to welcome them. And how could a transnational African identity persist when African nations drew lines of citizenship that bolstered nation building but made African Americans into aliens?

Mboya was upset by this incident and addressed it in a long essay. It was also the reference point of lengthy remarks he sent to the annual meeting of the NAACP. Many miles had been traveled since he first came to America, but, reflecting on the state of Africa and of America, Mboya saw them facing the same struggle:

> Our slogan during the independence struggle was "Uhuru Sasa," and I do not think it is a coincidence that its English translation, "Freedom Now," was the slogan for the Civil Rights Movement in America. For the black American struggle in the 1950s and 1960s was very similar to our own. The objective of both was political liberty for black people. In America the black people demanded the abolition of Jim Crow segregation and the right to vote, and they won their fight through courageous and inspiring political protest. But like their African cousins who must meet the challenge of development they now confront the more difficult task of achieving economic equality.

"I have seen the black ghettos in America," Mboya wrote. Black poverty was "more outrageous in America...because it is surrounded by unparalleled wealth." Because of this, "the problem of equality looms larger than the problem of development" for African Americans, but these problems were "similar in that the achievement of both requires massive institutional changes."[37]

Nonetheless, there were differences between the African and African American struggles. "African nationalism is by its very nature integrationist. Its primary objective is to mold numerous tribes into a single political entity." Tribal differences, Mboya argued, had been an obstacle to independence and had facilitated the colonial strategy of divide and rule. "Just as the African must reconcile the differences between his tribal and his national identity," Mboya believed, "so too must the black American realise to the fullest extent his potential as a blackman and as an American." Although the task was "extraordinarily difficult, African Americans must "assert the right for equal rights and opportunities and to be treated as equal citizens," rather than to seek a separate state. Ultimately, "freedom for both Africans and Americans is not an act of withdrawal but a major step in asserting the rights of black people and their place as equals among nations and peoples of the world."[38]

Mboya turned to the words of Bayard Rustin, who argued that the reason for the back-to-Africa movement had "less to do with the Negro's relation to Africa than to America." Separatism was "always strongest at the very time when the Negro is most intensely dissatisfied with his lot in America. It is when the Negro has lost hope in America—and lost his identity *as* an American—that he seeks to re-establish his identity and his roots as an African." Rustin wrote that these cycles of despair followed periods of hope. The new separatist mood "has come after a decade in which the Negro achieved enormous and unprecedented gains through the civil rights struggle, and it has coincided with a right-wing reaction that has obstructed further measures toward equality." The pattern of "progress, aroused hopes, frustration and despair" had led many to "withdraw into separatism and to yearn for Africa."[39]

Mboya called for communication between Africans and African Americans, though he himself would have little time to participate. His last letter to the NAACP, marking the Association's sixtieth annual convention, was not a typical letter of congratulations. In it Mboya referred again to the confrontation in Harlem and stressed the need for a dialogue. Then he drew his message for the convention from a long passage from the late Martin Luther King Jr.'s *Where Do We Go from Here?* King described speaking in Chicago and being booed by members of the Black Power movement. "Why would they boo one so close to them?" King asked. But then he came to an understanding of the source of the anger. For years, civil rights leaders had held out promises of progress. "I had preached to them about my dream," he said, and "their hopes had soared." Now they were booing because these promises had not been realized. For King, the answer to Black Power was to renew hope for the future. "We need the vision to see in this generation's ordeals the opportunity to transfigure both ourselves and American society."[40]

Using King's reflections, Mboya drew a lesson from his own travels to America. "In 1956, I flew from New York to London in the propeller-type aircraft that required nine and a half hours for a flight now made in six hours by jet," he wrote. "Returning from London to the United States, the stewardess announced that the flying time would be twelve and a half hours. The distance was the same." The reason for the difference was the wind: They would have a strong tailwind going to London, but on the way to New York a strong headwind against them. Mboya wrote, "We must not permit adverse winds to overwhelm us as we journey across life's mighty Atlantic; we must be sustained by our engines of courage in spite of the winds." The hallmark of a great movement for Mboya was "this refusal to be stopped, this 'courage to be.'"[41]

For King, it was a matter of vision; for Mboya, endurance. Each man's message reveals how he viewed his own challenges as that promising decade lengthened and times became harder. Mboya revealed as well the way his work had changed him. Independence leaders empowered their people, even as their own personal power weakened the ties between a leader and his community. He had come a long way from the sisal plantation of his youth. Mboya drew in his audience with a story, but it was a story only the elite could identify with in 1969—a transatlantic flight, not even to Africa, but between New York and London, Western centers of power.

In spite of his experience in Harlem, Mboya came away from his last American visit "very impressed by the strength of the black people's movements in the United States as well as the movements of the young people at universities." He wrote to his colleagues in Kenya that "these are the new forces that cannot be ignored and it is in the interest of every country abroad to get to understand more closely what is going on in the United States." Although they had differences, the student movement and Mboya appeared to share the view that the time had come for one generation's vision to be eclipsed by another. His hopes for the future did not rest with his old friend Thurgood Marshall. Mboya thought that African leaders should be associated with America's new black leadership rather than "the old leadership whose survival in my view is very doubtful." He was optimistic, expecting "tremendous change in the institution and structure of society in America in the next ten years as a result of this movement."[42]

The last public photograph of Tom Mboya was taken at an airport outside of Nairobi, on Friday, July 4, 1969. It did not capture the dread he had shared with his American friends. Perhaps there were surveillance photos, but at this point they were unnecessary. Plans had clearly been laid. When Mboya stepped out onto a Nairobi street at midday on Saturday, there were two shots. One hit him in the shoulder. The other tore through his aorta. "He never uttered a word. He fell into my arms and began to fall to the ground," said his friend Mohini Sehmi Chhani, whose shop Mboya had just visited. "He must have been hit before he knew there was a gunman. . . . I held his head and asked him 'Are you all right?' but there was no sound from him. . . . He never spoke." Mboya was dead on arrival at the Nairobi hospital.[43]

As news quickly spread, an emotional crowd surrounded the hospital. People "threw themselves about with grief," a local paper reported. Nairobi was tense, and the entire police force was mobilized. They used tear gas and clubs to disperse the crowds. The next day, as Mboya's body was driven to his home, thousands lined the route. A requiem mass was held at Holy Family Cathedral, attracting a crowd of twenty thousand, mostly from Mboya's Luo tribe. When Kenyatta arrived, police could not contain the crowd. Mourners beat the car with stones, sticks, and shoes. "For the first time in his long life Jomo Kenyatta was jeered by his country men," Goldsworthy writes. The hope of a Kenya in which all would unite across ethnic lines to make a nation seemed to collapse amid the chaos. "Mboya's murder was bringing to a head all the tensions he had spent his life fighting." Rioting spread from the cathedral through the streets of Nairobi.[44]

A Kikuyu man, Nahashon Isaac Njenga Njoroge, was arrested and convicted of the crime, satisfying public speculation of a tribal motive. But when police came for him, he asked, "Why do you pick up me? Why not the big man?" Njenga went to the gallows without disclosing who the "big man" was. Speculation over Mboya's murder continues in Kenya to this day.[45]

"The bullet is stronger than the ballot" (cartoon by Mahood), July 8, 1969. (Solo Syndication/Associated Newspapers)

"Son of a bitch," Thurgood Marshall said bitterly to Berl Bernhard, upon hearing the news of Mboya's assassination. "It was Moi." He was wrong about the big man behind Mboya's killing, but his reaction surely reflected tensions he had noticed between these political rivals. Daniel arap Moi, then Kenya's first vice president, would succeed Kenyatta and lead the country into a period of political repression and authoritarian rule from which it is still recovering.[46]

IT WAS MARSHALL'S FATE TO BE NOMINATED for the Supreme Court in 1967, a year writer Robert L. Allen would call "an important turning point in the history of black America. It was a year of unprecedentedly massive and widespread urban revolts. It was the year that so-called riots became an institutionalized form of black protest."[47]

The Court was not immune to the actions in the streets. In June 1967 the justices issued an important ruling about the rule of law and civil rights protest. *Walker v. City of Birmingham* involved a peaceful civil rights march in Birmingham, which had been led by Martin Luther King Jr., Ralph Abernathy, and Fred Shuttlesworth. The city had obtained a preliminary injunction against the marchers, but the protesters, believing that the injunction and underlying city ordinance were unconstitutional, violated the injunction and marched. The Alabama trial court found them in contempt for ignoring the injunction and sentenced them to jail. The protesters challenged the ruling, but the Supreme Court held that they were bound to follow the lower court order and challenge it through the judicial process, rather than violate it and question its constitutionality afterward.[48]

Writing for the majority in *Walker*, Justice Potter Stewart saw the case as involving the fundamental idea of a rule of law. "This Court cannot hold," he argued, that the demonstrators "were constitutionally free to ignore all the procedures of the law and carry their battle to the streets." Their "impatient commitment to their cause" might be understandable, "but respect for judicial process is a small price to pay for the civilizing hand of law, which alone can give abiding meaning to constitutional freedom."[49]

Justice Brennan saw it differently. "We cannot permit fears of 'riots' and 'civil disobedience' generated by slogans like 'Black Power' to divert our attention from what is here at stake," he wrote in a dissenting opinion. The case was not about "violence or the right of the State to control its streets and sidewalks," but whether Alabama could insulate from judicial review unconstitutional restrictions on civil rights protest. The Court was "arming the state courts with the power to punish as a 'contempt' what they otherwise could not punish at all."[50]

Although the march's leaders had rejected a Black Power philosophy, Brennan's opinion shows that the fear of African

American militancy affected the Court. Justices differed in *Walker* on which path would lead to law, which to anarchy. The majority felt that allowing demonstrators to disobey a court order, even if patently unconstitutional, was a recipe for chaos. For the dissenters, a true rule of law was one that constrained rulers as well as ruled. To expect compliance, enforced by federal courts, the government must issue orders that were lawful.

Handed down June 12, 1967, *Walker* was a 5–4 decision. Retiring Justice Tom Clark was in the majority. President Johnson nominated Marshall the next day.[51]

When Marshall's Supreme Court confirmation was debated in the Senate, *Walker v. City of Birmingham* was argued again. Senator Strom Thurmond of South Carolina first drew the attention of his colleagues to the case. On June 15, 1967, he introduced into the Senate record an editorial from the *Washington Evening Star* titled "Dr. King's Conviction." The editorial argued that the *Walker* ruling was sound and hoped it would last as controlling precedent. But, it added, "This would be a very dubious assumption in view of the President's nomination of Thurgood Marshall to replace Justice Clark." With Marshall on the Court, there was "a high probability that the holding in the case of Dr. King will be overruled by a new 5 to 4 decision." Senator Sam Ervin of North Carolina put the *Evening Star* editorial first on the list of six sources cited in his opposition to Marshall when the nomination was debated in the full Senate. Two of Ervin's other sources also raised *Walker*. "Certainly the Rev. Martin Luther King and eight other clergymen might not be going to jail if Marshall had been on the court last week when it upheld contempt convictions of the ministers," Clayton Fritley wrote in the *Washington Evening Star*. James J. Kilpatrick's op-ed simply asked, "Would Marshall have voted to send Martin Luther King to jail?"[52]

The man who had called for an end to "anarchy" was now attacked for being a source of it. Marshall's nomination was directly linked by members of Congress to the turbulence of the times. Congressman John Rarick of Louisiana argued that the nomination was "more salt" in the "despairing wounds" of a country "already subjected to racial riots, civil disorders, and an ever-increasing national crime wave." For Rarick, Marshall was "one of the originators and activists of the problem that now plagues America."[53]

Others used Marshall's nomination as a vehicle to critique the Warren Court. Senator Spessard Holland of Florida thought Marshall "would further destroy the balance of the U.S. Supreme Court and would further entrench the ultraliberal activists among its members." Senator Robert Byrd justified voting against Marshall by saying that "if we want to really come to grips with the spiraling crime rate, the place to start is in the appointments to the Supreme Court."[54]

Most senators saw it differently, however. Wayne Morse of Oregon thought Marshall's nomination "a shining moment for American democracy," evidence of the nation's progress and reflecting "our growing maturity as a people and a nation." Thomas Kuchel, Republican from California, argued that Marshall's nomination "reflects the American tradition in its finest sense." While many stressed that Marshall's appointment was due to his experience, not his race, Kuchel thought that "the world and the American people will not ignore completely the fact that as a member of an ethnic minority, he will now sit on our supreme tribunal." Marshall's nomination exemplified the American dream of "equal justice and opportunity under law." By confirming Marshall, argued Kuchel, the Senate would "express confidence in the American dream, a dream which says that every man, regardless of race, color, or creed, may achieve the goals he seeks in a free society."[55]

Thurgood Marshall's nomination to the U.S. Supreme Court was confirmed by the Senate by a vote of sixty-nine to eleven, on August 30, 1967. Compared with his difficult and drawn-out confirmation to the Second Circuit in 1961–62, it had been easy sailing. Still, Marshall said of LBJ: "I don't see how he got it through, but he did."[56]

"This is a shining hour," Senator Michael Mansfield said in announcing the news to Johnson. "We have come a long, long way toward equal access to the Constitution's promise," but the nation would go "further along that way" with Marshall on the Court. For Marshall himself, a wide chasm remained between the ideal of constitutional equality and the actual conditions under which African Americans lived. He hoped that the Court would provide new opportunities to move the nation forward. For many Americans, his appointment was instead a sign that the American dream had already come true.[57]

MARSHALL, AS SUPREME COURT JUSTICE, would withdraw further from civil rights politics. He felt that he needed to, so that he would not be required to recuse himself from civil rights cases. But Marshall had one more day to work with civil rights leaders. It was April 5, 1968, the day after Martin Luther King Jr. was assassinated. There had been too many deaths already in the 1960s. In his last speech, King had urged justice for Memphis, Tennessee, sanitation workers, placing their struggle in the context of liberation struggles elsewhere. In American cities, and in Nairobi, Johannesburg, and Accra, Ghana, he said, "The cry is always the same—'We want to be free.'" The world he had embraced reacted in horror at King's murder, while in the United States many took to the streets as the cities again exploded.[58]

News of the assassination swept through Nairobi. The National Assembly stopped its business for two minutes of silence in King's honor. Editorials in Kenyan papers pondered whether violence would now be seen as the only effective means of social change. The United States itself was the target of a *Daily Nation* editorial. "If America wants to export democracy, why can she not have it at home for over 20 million Negroes?" the paper asked. In Nigeria, a paper carried the headline: "Black America Fights Back."[59]

President Johnson called civil rights leaders together for an emergency meeting at the White House on April 5. With Marshall at his side, he declared a national day of mourning. At the same time, drawing upon his powers as commander in chief, he called upon the military to help restore order in the cities. The president and civil rights leaders held a press conference after their meeting. "The dream of Dr. Martin Luther King Jr. has not died with him," Johnson insisted. Everyone must work together, "to let all the forces of divisiveness know that America shall not be ruled by the bullet, but only by the ballot of free and of just men." Justice Marshall said it was "important to get the country out of this mood of depression," and it was "the duty of all responsible people to help on this." The president would hold a bill-signing ceremony later that month to note the passage of the Civil Rights Act of 1968, a fair housing bill, which he stressed was a sign of progress.[60]

It would be Marshall's task to try to move his Supreme Court colleagues to redress American injustice. The communities that had ignited could only believe in change through law if they could see it working for them, he believed. But as the troops withdrew from American neighborhoods, there seemed no way to fill the void left by King's passing. The Kenyan *Daily Nation* captured the sentiment of many in America as well as Kenya in saying, "It may well be that the era (of non-violence) has died with its prophet."[61]

EPILOGUE

Our nation is moving toward two societies, one black, one white—
separate and unequal.

—Kerner Commission Report, 1968

You have engaged yourself in activities and utterances which are
dangerous to the good Government of Kenya and its institutions.

—Detention order for novelist Ngũgĩ wa Thiong'o, 1978

IF THURGOOD MARSHALL'S GREATEST TRIUMPH was reaching
the Supreme Court, it was also at the Court that he would experience his greatest frustration. The tools of constitutional change
could bring about a just America, he thought. He was now in a
position to see it happen. And then, before his eyes, something
went terribly wrong.

If one case stood out as the harbinger, it was a school desegregation case from Detroit. Three decades earlier, Marshall
had flown to Detroit to assess the circumstances of the city's
race riots in 1943. The intervening years had not been kind to
the city. As Detroit's bedrock industries declined and moved to
the South and the suburbs, the city's tax base eroded. The concentration of poverty increased as the middle class, of all races,
moved out. By the mid-1970s, Detroit's population was 70 percent African American. The great racial disparity in the schools

Supreme Court Justice Thurgood Marshall meets with President
Lyndon Baines Johnson and civil rights leaders at the White House
on the day after Martin Luther King Jr.'s assassination, April 5, 1968.
(Lyndon Baines Johnson Library)

was not within in the city, but between schools in the city and
suburbs.[1]

The Detroit city schools were intentionally racially segregated,
a federal district court found in 1971. The issue was what could
be done about it. In *Swann v. Charlotte-Mecklenburg Board of
Education* in 1971, the Supreme Court upheld crosstown busing
as a remedy to desegregate schools in a large metropolitan district. The NAACP sought something similar for the plaintiffs in
the Detroit case. If schools within the city limits could be paired
with suburban schools, meaningful racial integration could be
achieved. But Detroit was different from Charlotte, North Carolina. In Charlotte, the city and suburban schools were part of
one large school district. In Detroit, the inner city and suburban
districts were separate.[2]

The district court had ordered a metropolitan school integration plan that called for busing between the city and suburbs, but the Supreme Court struck it down in 1974 in a 5–4 decision, *Milliken v. Bradley*. Justice Warren Burger, writing for the majority, noted that the case was not like *Swann*, because it raised the question of when courts could require a desegregation plan that went beyond a single school district. This implicated the important issue of local control: "No single tradition in public education is more deeply rooted than local control over the operation of schools."[3]

The outcome of the case turned on the traditional idea that the "scope of the remedy is determined by the nature and extent of the constitutional violation." The constitutional violation (segregation) occurred in the city school district. The remedy therefore must be restricted to that school district, absent evidence that district lines were drawn or used for the purpose of maintaining segregation. The Court rejected arguments made by dissenters and the NAACP that the State of Michigan was ultimately responsible for and had participated in creating the conditions in the schools in Detroit, and therefore the state could be held responsible for a broader remedy. For the Court majority, segregation had happened only within the city of Detroit, so any remedy must happen there, even though Detroit was rapidly becoming so segregated that racial balance in Detroit alone was likely to achieve little.[4]

It was the first time since *Brown v. Board of Education* that the Court had "handed down a ruling that will mean less, rather than more integration," Warren Weaver Jr. wrote in the *New York Times*. Suburban parents rejoiced at the ruling, as did President Richard Nixon who, beleaguered in the Watergate scandal, took it as a needed victory. But others were troubled about the future. NAACP counsel Nathaniel Jones called it "a giant step backward toward the separate but equal doctrine." The Supreme Court "has said to black people: 'You have rights, but you don't have a remedy.'" For many, it seemed the end of an era. Legal historian Lawrence Friedman would later write, "The world was made safe for white flight.... Official, legal segregation indeed was dead; but what replaced it was a deeper, more profound segregation."[5]

The case prompted Marshall to deliver an oral dissent from the bench, which the *New York Times* called "unusually bitter." It had been just over twenty years since he had stood in the same chambers, arguing *Brown*. Twenty years earlier he was victorious. This time he seemed defeated.[6]

The Court had recognized in *Brown*, Marshall said, that "remedying decades of segregation would not be an easy task." Since then, the nation had seen that prediction bear bitter fruit. Still, the Court had hewed to its task of making a "'living truth' of our constitutional ideal of equal justice under law." But now, in *Milliken*, after two decades of "small, often difficult steps toward that great end," he said, the Court had taken "a giant step backwards." This was a blow not only for the plaintiffs but also for the entire nation. "The rights at issue in this case are too fundamental to be abridged on grounds as superficial as those relied on by the majority today," Marshall insisted. At stake in *Milliken* was "the right of all our children, whatever their race, to an equal start in life and to an equal opportunity to reach their full potential as citizens." The Court's ruling was not in the nation's interest, for "unless our children begin to learn together, there is little hope that our people will ever learn to live together and understand each other."[7]

Friends of Marshall have said that *Milliken* was the second of two cases that broke his spirit. The first one was *San Antonio Independent School District v. Rodriguez*, decided the year before—another school case in which the majority rejected the idea that poor children, as a class, warranted special scrutiny from the Court. Marshall dissented. If Marshall was disheartened by these developments, it was hard to know how the future would unfold. Nixon was one president, one political cycle since the Warren Court era, and the Republicans would be weakened by Nixon's resignation in August 1974. The long road ahead with Republican dominance of the White House, increasingly using the Court to cater to a hard right constituency and having the political power to do so, ultimately filling seven of the Court's nine seats—all this was yet to unfold.[8]

Marshall also was finding that his vision held less appeal for some in the younger generation. Derrick Bell, once a young Legal Defense Fund lawyer who called Marshall "Boss" in his affectionate letters, and now a law professor at Harvard, told the press after *Milliken* that the strategy of "integrating every public school that is black perpetuates the racially demeaning and unproven assumption that blacks must have a majority white presence in order to either teach or learn effectively." Bell thought that the civil rights bar had taken a wrong turn in *Milliken*. Lawyers were serving their own vision, he soon argued in an influential article, rather than the interests of their clients, who wanted instead community control in good schools. His footnotes reflected new Black Power ideas and priorities, but African American communities had long been divided about broad-based integration remedies.[9]

The Court's failure to ratify Marshall's vision of equal justice did not result from the inherent nature or capacity of the Court. It was not an inevitable development but was historically contingent. It had much to do with particular turns of history, with the events of 1968, when President Johnson, weakened by Vietnam, announced that he would not run for reelection in March and then Chief Justice Warren announced his resignation in June. In the words of advisor Clark Clifford, Johnson "really was not conscious of how much his power had diminished." Rather than nominate someone safe to replace Warren, Johnson

miscalculated. He sought to elevate Associate Justice Abe Fortas and maintain a strong liberal in the chief justice position.
This would require two Senate confirmations, since Fortas's
seat was now open. Johnson nominated his Texas friend Homer
Thornberry, a Fifth Circuit Court of Appeals judge and a former member of Congress. Thornberry would appeal to Southern Democrats, Johnson hoped, and having reached a deal on an
unrelated matter with Republican Senate leader Everett Dirk-
sen, Johnson expected to have Republican support as well. But
some Republicans, knowing that the president was weakened
and hoping for a victory in the November presidential elections,
balked. A combination of Republican desire to have the newly
elected president fill the vacancy, opposition to liberal Court rulings on criminal procedure and pornography, and political mis-
steps led to the downfall of Johnson's strategy. A toxic election
year was no time to solidify the Court's liberal vision.[10]

That 1968 was a difficult year in American history is, of
course, an understatement. It is impossible to know how events
might have unfolded if a bullet had not ended the life of Robert
Kennedy on the night he won the California Democratic primary, if the Democratic Convention in Chicago had not been
the occasion for chaos. One thing is clear: the war in Vietnam
pervaded American politics, domestic and international. An
impact of the war was that a weakened president handed two
open Court seats to his successor. Rather than Fortas, the new
chief justice would be Warren Burger. Instead of Thornberry,
there would be Harry A. Blackmun. In 1972, Richard Nixon
named Lewis Powell to replace Justice Hugo Black, and William
Rehnquist to replace Justice John Marshall Harlan. With the
new appointees in the majority, in 1974, *Milliken v. Bradley* was
decided 5–4.[11]

Battles over rights would continue in the years until Marshall's
retirement from the Court in 1991, but they would not always

reflect the needs of the most vulnerable. The most enduring difficulties were in Detroit and other cities. The problem was diagnosed most bluntly by the National Advisory Commission on Civil Disorders (the Kerner Commission), appointed by President Johnson in 1967 in the wake of that summer's riots. "Discrimination and segregation have long permeated much of American life; they now threaten the future of every American," the commission warned. If underlying problems were not addressed, the nation's major cities faced a "system of 'apartheid.'" Even before *Milliken* brought the era of *Brown* to a close, the Kerner Commission drew back the curtain on poverty and injustice in America's cities, exposing an anarchy the courts would not touch. Equality under law was a powerful thing, but it would not keep the cities from eroding.[12]

And so, while Thurgood Marshall had worked on one problem of race in America, others were festering. This is not an indictment of Marshall, of course, whose life's focus was undoing the constitutional embodiment of Jim Crow, surely one of the impediments to equality. To move the nation toward a fuller vision of racial justice in the 1960s required other tools than those Marshall possessed, and this required a deeper commitment from a broader political coalition. What had once seemed possible was out of reach by 1968, just as the Kerner Commission issued its report. A nation torn apart over war and divided over domestic politics was not to be united around the vision of its 1960s leaders. It was a cruel irony that in shining a light on the cities, the Kerner Commission Report seemed a reverse echo of *Brown*: "Our nation is moving toward two societies, one black, one white—separate and unequal."[13]

THURGOOD MARSHALL WOULD HAVE MANY MORE YEARS on the Court until, at the age of eighty-three, he retired in 1991. Historian John Hope Franklin, who had worked with Marshall on *Brown v. Board of Education* and other cases, heard from Marshall from time to time when he had questions about history. Franklin got a call in 1978, and Marshall seemed especially glum. Franklin asked him what was the matter. "If you knew what I know, you would be glum, too," Marshall replied. Later that year, the Supreme Court handed down a ruling in *Regents of the University of California v. Bakke*, striking down the U.C. Davis medical school's affirmative action plan. Justice Lewis Powell provided the fifth vote, enabling a majority and allowing some forms of affirmative action to stand. But even Justice Powell believed that the Court must apply its highest bar to any government-sponsored programs that took race into account, even programs meant to overcome racial discrimination.[14]

Justice Marshall wrote an angry response. "Three hundred and fifty years ago, the Negro was dragged to this country in chains to be sold into slavery," he wrote. Slavery was "etched into" colonial self-government and into the founding document of the United States. Marshall described the long history of discrimination and disenfranchisement that followed. The position of African Americans in contemporary society, he argued, "is the tragic but inevitable consequence of centuries of unequal treatment," making the achievement of equality "a distant dream." Because of this history, bringing African Americans to full citizenship should be "a state interest of the highest order." The Court must allow government to act to redress this history of injustice, he argued; otherwise the nation would remain forever divided.[15]

Nine years later, Marshall would again call on Franklin. He needed sources on the history of slavery. This time the research was not for a case before the Court, but because 1987 was the bicentennial of the U.S. Constitution. Chief Justice Warren Burger headed the national commission for a three-year celebration of the document. Marshall, again, found himself a dissenter. The framing of the constitution in 1787 was not to be celebrated, Marshall thought, for the framers had created a government "defective from the start" that embraced slavery and also disenfranchised women. "These omissions were intentional," he argued, and led to a government that could only be repaired after a civil war and fundamental changes to the constitutional order.[16]

Marshall's criticism was aimed at the American framers, not at what the Constitution had become in later years. The framers had forged a political compromise, a trade-off between northerners seeking broad national power over commerce and southerners seeking to preserve slavery. Marshall thought that the nation should celebrate not the birth of the Constitution but "its life . . . nurtured through two turbulent centuries of our own making."[17]

If the American framers were wrong to compromise, what of Kenya, where Marshall himself had helped forge a compromise? During the 1960 negotiations, he wrote a clause that entrenched property rights acquired through discriminatory colonial land policies. The lesson of his work in Kenya might be that nation building required trade-offs, that righting all wrongs is inconsistent with creating a shared sense of national unity, that even historic injustices must sometimes be accommodated to achieve a more fundamental purpose, even though such a process taints a nation's founding moment. In one case it was the entrenchment of white property rights to land in Kenya; in the other it was the entrenchment of rights to own American slaves. When Marshall embraced Jomo Kenyatta, he seemed to accept the notion that sometimes political realities must triumph over principle.

But perhaps the lesson Marshall took away from Kenya was different. "When you can give to the white man in Africa what you couldn't give the black man in Mississippi," he said in 1977, "that, to my mind is really working toward democracy. . . . That's good." Marshall was talking about himself, of course, since he was the one who had worked in both Africa and Mississippi. What he tried to take to Kenya that was missing in his own country was protection of the rights of a group destined to lose out in majoritarian politics. He tried to embed this principle in the Kenyan Constitution, placing in the preamble of the Bill of Rights the idea that equality was paramount, an idea that would inform so much of his work on the U.S. Supreme Court.[18]

Compromise was central to his experience with constitution writing, but there were limits to compromise. He drew the line at the issue of equality. In Kenya itself, the project of nation building would be more successful than protection of the principles so important to Marshall. When individual rights were compromised not long after independence, Marshall either could not or would not see it.

IN HIS LATER YEARS, THURGOOD MARSHALL still talked about Kenya. He would take out a cloak from Kenya made of monkey skin and tell stories of how he was made an "honorary chief" on one of his visits. Embedded in this cloak were so many memories, of a place, of a time when all things seemed possible.[19]

Marshall would travel once more to Kenya. He was part of the U.S. delegation to the funeral of Jomo Kenyatta in 1978. He said that he was "happy to find that the Schedule of Rights that I drew for the Kenyan Government was working very well."[20]

The Kenyan Constitution actually was not working so well in 1978. While Marshall was in Kenya, the country's leading novelist and chair of the Department of Literature at the University of Nairobi, Ngũgĩ wa Thiong'o, was in prison. His crime was to put on a play. *Ngahaahika Ndeeda* (I Will Marry When I Want), coauthored with Ngugi wa Mirii and written in the Kikuyu language, opened at a community-based theater in Limuru. The play attacked the government's policy toward the poor and was an effort to preserve the Kikuyu language. According to Kenyan scholar B. A. Ogot, Ngũgĩ was "the first Kenyan intellectual to be detained because of his works." He was never charged with an offense or put on trial. His detention order, signed by Vice President Moi, said that the grounds for detention were engaging "in activities and utterances which are dangerous to the good Government of Kenya and its institutions." He was held behind the stone walls of the Kamiti Maximum Security Prison for a year. Ngũgĩ wrote, "12 December 1978: I am in cell 16 in a detention block enclosing eighteen other political prisoners.... Here I have no name. I am just a number in a file: K6,77." There were many such numbers, and not all would endure the months or years intact. "Detention and conditions in detention, including the constant reminder of one's isolation, can drive, in fact are meant to drive, a former patriot into a position where he feels that he has been completely forgotten, that all his former words and actions linked to people's struggles, were futile gestures and senseless acts of a meaningless individual martyrdom; yes, reduce him to a position where he can finally say: *The masses have betrayed me, why should I sacrifice myself for them?*"[21]

"Kenyatta sheds *Petals of Blood*," read a sign held by a protester outside the Kenya High Commission in London, quoting one of Ngũgĩ's titles. But Marshall did not see these signs, did not follow this news, did not know of Ngũgĩ's next novel, written on hoarded pieces of toilet paper—as much a means of survival as a creative expression during that year behind steel bars and stone walls.[22]

The Kenya he remembered was the Kenya of 1963, the moment the flag was raised and power transferred. "He wanted to protect that independence, period," Berl Bernhard emphasized, reflecting on the early 1960s. This became what he knew about Kenya. As with so many memories, as the years went by, he looked upon it through an imperfect lens. He saw a Kenya frozen in time; he saw himself at the height of his powers. His challenges became harder, as the Court shifted further away from his vision and the infirmities of age took their toll. Through it all, Marshall held on firmly to a memory of a time when he had helped frame a constitution that made a colony a nation. This vision was with him to the end, wrapped up in his Kenyan cape, found in his office after his death in 1993, draped over an armchair at the window in the morning sun.[23]

APPENDIX

Thurgood Marshall's Draft Bill of Rights for Kenya, 1960

THURGOOD MARSHALL'S DRAFT BILL OF RIGHTS FOR KENYA, which he wrote in January and early February 1960, was based on three documents: the Universal Declaration of Human Rights (1948), the Malayan Independence Constitution (1957), and the Nigerian Independence Constitution (1960). The Nigerian Constitution in turn drew on the European Convention of Human Rights (1950). Some sections of the Draft Bill of Rights have no parallels in these documents. As discussed in *Exporting American Dreams*, much of Marshall's draft was not retained in the final Kenya Independence Constitution (1963).[1]

This copy of the Draft Bill of Rights is annotated to provide citations to the sources Marshall borrowed from.

---

1. Universal Declaration of Human Rights, G.A. Res. 217A, at 75, U.N. GAOR, 3d Sess., 1st plen. mtg., U.N. Doc. A/810 (Dec. 12, 1948); Nigerian (Constitution) Order in Council (1960) (Nigerian Independence Constitution); Proposed Constitution of Federation of Malaya (Malayan Independence Constitution) (Kuala Lumpur, 1957). See also *Malaya and Singapore, The Borneo Territories: The Development of their Laws and Constitutions,* ed. L. A. Sheridan (London: Stevens & Sons, 1961).

CONFIDENTIAL

<u>K. C. (S) (60) 2</u>   COPY NO. 98
<u>2nd February, 1960</u>

KENYA CONSTITUTIONAL CONFERENCE, 1960
COMMITTEE ON SAFEGUARDS
<u>Note by the Secretaries</u>

The attached paper by Dr. Thurgood Marshall is circulated
for the consideration of the Committee.

                                        (Signed)   J. A. SANKEY
                                                        T. M. HEISER

PROPOSED DRAFT OF BILL OF RIGHTS
PRELIMINARY STATEMENT
BY DR. THURGOOD MARSHALL

Here is a rough draft of a Proposed Bill of Rights for Kenya. This proposal is solely mine and has neither been discussed with nor approved or rejected by the African Elected Members or any other group. It is, therefore, submitted for use by all members of the Conference.

All persons are equal before the law and are entitled without any discrimination or distinction of any kind, such as race, colour, sex, language, religion, political or other opinion, national or social origin, property, birth or other status, to equal protection of the law.

I
FREEDOM OF RELIGION, SPEECH, PRESS AND ASSOCIATION

1. Everyone has the right to freedom of thought, conscience and religion; this right includes freedom to change his religion or belief, and freedom, either alone or in community with others and in public or private, to manifest his religion or belief in teaching, practice, worship and observance.[2]

2. Everyone has the right to freedom of opinion and expression; this right includes freedom to hold opinions without interference and to seek, receive and impart information and ideas through any media and regardless of frontiers;[3] and the right to freedom of peaceful assembly and association. No one may be compelled to belong to an association.[4]

---

2. Universal Declaration of Human Rights (UDHR), Article 18, is identical to this section. The Nigerian Independence Constitution, Chapter III, Section 23 (1), is similar.

3. UDHR Article 19 is identical to this passage. There are some similarities with the Nigerian Independence Constitution, Chapter III, Section 24 (1).

4. UDHR Article 20 is identical to this passage.

3. No one shall be subjected to arbitrary interference with his privacy, family, home or correspondence, nor to attacks upon his honour and reputation. Everyone has the right to the protection of the law against such interference or attacks.[5]

4. Neither the legislature, the executive nor the judicial branch of government may interfere with any of the aforementioned rights and shall take all necessary steps to protect said rights from interference by individuals.

II
PERSONAL SECURITY

Everyone has the right to life, liberty and the security of person:

1. (1) No person shall be deprived of his life or personal liberty save in accordance with law.

   (2) Where complaint is made to the Supreme Court or any judge thereof that a person is being unlawfully detained the court shall inquire into the complaint and, unless satisfied that the detention is lawful, shall order him to be produced before the court and release him.

   (3) Where a person is arrested he shall be informed as soon as may be of the grounds of his arrest and shall be allowed to consult and be defended by a legal practitioner of his choice.

   (4) Where a person is arrested and not released he shall without unreasonable delay, and in any case within twenty-four hours (excluding the time of any necessary journey) be produced before a magistrate and shall not be further detained in custody without the magistrate's authority.

   (5) Clauses (3) and (4) do not apply to an enemy alien.[6]

---

5. UDHR Article 12 is identical to this section.
6. Sections 1–5 of Part II are identical to the Malayan Independence Constitution (1957), Part II, Sections 5 (1) to (5).

2. (1) No persons shall be held in slavery.

   (2) All forms of forced labour are prohibited, but Parliament may by law provide for compulsory service for national purposes.

   (3) Work incidental to the serving of a sentence of imprisonment imposed by a court of law shall not be taken to be forced labour within the meaning of this Article.[7]

3. (1) No person shall be punished for an act or omission which was not punishable by law when it was done or made, and no person shall suffer greater punishment for an offence than was prescribed by law at the time it was committed.

   (2) A person who has been acquitted or convicted of an offence shall not be tried again for the same offence except where the conviction or acquittal has been quashed and a retrial ordered by a court superior to that by which he was acquitted or convicted.[8]

4. (1) All persons are equal before the law and entitled to the equal protection of the law.

   (2) Except as expressly authorised by this Constitution, there shall be no discrimination against citizens on the ground only of religion, race, descent or place of birth in any law or in the appointment to any office of employment under a public authority or in the administration of any law relating to the acquisition, holding or disposition of property or the establishing or carrying on of any trade, business, profession, vocation or employment.[9]

---

7. The Malayan Independence Constitution, Part II, Sections 6 (1) to (3), is virtually identical to this section. UDHR Article 2 and the Nigerian Independence Constitution, Chapter III, Section 19, also prohibit slavery and involuntary servitude, but their provisions are different.
8. The Malayan Independence Constitution, Part II, Sections 7 (1) and (2), is identical to this section. UDHR Article 2 and Article 11, Section 2, and the Nigerian Independence Constitution, Chapter III, Sections 21 (7) and (8), cover similar issues but use different language.
9. The Malayan Independence Constitution, Part II, Sections 8 (1) and (2), is identical. The first sentence of UDHR Article 7 is similar to this subsection.

5. The right of the people to be secure in their persons, houses, papers, and effects, against unreasonable searches and seizures, shall not be violated, and no warrants shall issue, but upon probable cause, supported by Oath or affirmation, and particularly describing the place to be searched, and the person or things to be seized.

6. Excessive bail shall not be required, nor excessive fines imposed, nor cruel and unusual punishments inflicted.[10]

III
<u>EDUCATION, HEALTH AND WELFARE</u>

1. Everyone has the right to education. Education shall be free, at least in the elementary and fundamental stages. Elementary education shall be compulsory. Technical and professional education shall be made generally available and higher education shall be equally accessible to all on the basis of merit.[11]

2. Education shall be directed to the full development of the human personality and to the strengthening of respect for human rights and fundamental freedoms. It shall promote understanding, tolerance and friendship among all nations, racial or religious groups.[12]

3. Parents have a prior right to choose the kind of education that shall be given to their children.[13]

4. Everyone has the right freely to participate in the cultural life of the community; to enjoy the arts and to share in scientific advancement and its benefits.[14]

---

10. Sections 5 and 6 of Part II do not appear to be borrowed directly from Marshall's non-U.S. sources and instead are similar to American law. See Lawrence Friedman, *Crime and Punishment in American History* (New York: Basic Books, 1993).

11. UDHR Article 26, Section 1, is identical.

12. UDHR Article 26, Section 2, is identical, except that there is additional language in the UDHR indicating that education "shall further the activities of the United Nations for the maintenance of peace."

13. UDHR Article 26, Section 3, is identical.

14. UDHR Article 27, Section 1, is identical.

5. Everyone has the right to the protection of the moral and material interests resulting from any scientific, literary or artistic production of which he is the author.[15]
6. Everyone has the right to adequate health and welfare facilities.[16]
7. All educational facilities, hospitals and other health facilities and all provisions for the general welfare shall be open to all without regard to race, colour, sex, language, religion, political or other opinion, national, or social origin, property, birth or other status.[17]

IV
RIGHT TO WORK

1. Everyone has the right to work, to free choice of employment, to just and favourable conditions of work and to protection against unemployment.[18]
2. Everyone, without any discrimination, has the right to equal pay for equal work.[19]
3. Everyone who works has the right to just and favourable remuneration insuring for himself and his family an existence worthy of human dignity, and supplemented, if necessary, by other means of social protection.[20]
4. Everyone has the right to form and to join trade unions for the protection of his interests.[21]

---

15. UDHR Article 27, Section 2, is identical.
16. UDHR Article 25 has much broader protection for health and welfare. While Marshall's text focuses on facilities, the Declaration relates to a "standard of living adequate for health and well being." Marshall's Bill of Rights includes a right to what we might now call a "living wage" and to public assistance if needed in Part IV, Section 3, on the "Right to Work."
17. A narrower right to nondiscrimination in education is protected in the Malayan Independence Constitution, Part II, Section 12 (1).
18. UDHR Article 23, Section 1, is identical.
19. UDHR Article 23, Section 2, is identical.
20. UDHR Article 23, Section 3, is identical.
21. UDHR Article 23, Section 4, is identical.

V
<u>RIGHT TO VOTE</u>

1. Everyone has the right to take part in the Government of his country, directly or through freely chosen representatives.[22]

2. Everyone has the right of equal access to public service in his country.[23]

3. The will of the people shall be the basis of the authority of government; this will shall be expressed in periodic and genuine elections which shall be by universal, and equal suffrage and shall be held by secret vote or by equivalent free voting procedures.[24]

VI
<u>PROPERTY RIGHTS</u>[25]

Here I suggest we use the following language from the Nigerian Constitution. If it is agreeable the language may be changed to conform to Kenya. The Nigerian Constitution provides:

(1) No property, movable or immovable, shall be taken possession of compulsorily and no right over or interest in any such property shall be acquired compulsorily except by or under the provisions of a law which, of itself or when read with any other law in force—

    (a) requires the payment at adequate compensation therefor;

---

22. UDHR Article 21, Section 1, is identical.
23. UDHR Article 21, Section 2, is identical.
24. UDHR Article 21, Section 3, is identical.
25. The Property Rights section is taken from the Nigerian Independence Constitution, Chapter III, Section 30. The UDHR has a property rights clause, but it is much less detailed. Article 17 of the Declaration states: "(1) Everyone has the right to own property alone as well as in association with others. (2) No one shall be arbitrarily deprived of property."

(b) gives to any person claiming such compensation a right of access, for the determination of his interest in the property and the amount of compensation, to the Courts;

(c) gives to any party to proceedings in the Court relating to such a claim the same rights of appeal as are accorded generally to parties to civil proceedings in that Court sitting as a court of original jurisdiction.

(2) (a) Nothing in this section shall affect the operation of any existing law.

(b) In this subsection the expression "existing law" means a law in force on the thirty-first day of March, 1958, and includes a law made after that date which amends or replaces any such law as aforesaid (or such a law as from time to time amended or replaced in the manner described in this paragraph) and which does not,

    (i) add to the kinds of property that may be taken possession of or the rights over and interests in property that may be acquired; or

    (ii) add to the purposes for which or circumstances in which such property may be taken possession of or acquired; or

    (iii) make the conditions governing entitlement to any compensation or the amount thereof less favourable to any person owning or interested in the property; or

    (iv) deprive any person of any right such as is mentioned in paragraph (b) or paragraph (c) of sub-section (1) of this section.

(3) Nothing in this section shall be construed as affecting any general law—

(a) for the imposition or enforcement of any tax, rate or due; or

(b) for the imposition of penalties or forfeitures for breach of the law whether under civil process or after conviction of an offence; or

(c) relating to leases, tenancies, mortgages, charges, bills of sale or any other rights or obligations arising out of contracts; or

(d) relating to the vesting and administration of the property of persons adjudged bankrupt or otherwise declared insolvent, of persons of unsound mind, of deceased persons, and of companies, other corporate bodies and unincorporate societies in the course of being wound up; or

(e) relating to the execution of judgments or orders of courts; or

(f) providing for the taking of possession of property which is in a dangerous state or is injurious to the health of human beings, plants or animals; or

(g) relating to enemy property; or

(h) relating to trusts and trustees; or

(i) relating to the limitation of actions; or

(j) relating to property vested in statutory corporations; or

(k) relating to the temporary taking of possession of property for the purposes of any examination, investigation or inquiry; or

(l) providing for the carrying out of work on land for the purpose of soil conservation.

(4) The provisions of this section shall apply to the compulsory taking of possession of property, movable or immovable, and the compulsory acquisition of rights over and interests in such property by or on behalf of the Crown.

(5) The provisions of this section shall apply in relation to the Southern Cameroons and Lagos as they apply in relation to

a Region and for that purpose references in subsection (1) to a Region shall be construed as if they were references to the Southern Cameroons or to Lagos, as the case may be.

Lancaster House, London, S.W.1

2nd February, 1960.

Source: Proposed Draft Bill of Rights, attachment to J. A. Sankey and T. M. Heiser, Note by the Secretaries, February 2, 1960, Folder: Kenya Constitutional Conference, 1960 Committee on Safeguards, Memoranda, CO 822/2362, Public Records Office, National Archives of the United Kingdom, Kew, England.

Reprinted with permission from Mrs. Cecilia Marshall.

NOTES

Manuscript and Archive Collections:
Abbreviations and Locations

ACOA Papers	Papers of the American Committee on Africa, Amistad Research Center, New Orleans, Louisiana
Amistad Research Center	Amistad Research Center, New Orleans, Louisiana
Bentley Historical Library	Bentley Historical Library, Ann Arbor, Michigan
Hoover Institute	Hoover Institute Library and Archives, Stanford, California
JFK Library	John F. Kennedy Library, Boston, Massachusetts
Kenya National Archives	The National Archives of Kenya, Nairobi, Kenya
LBJ Library	Lyndon Baines Johnson Library, Austin, Texas
LOC	Library of Congress, Washington, DC
NAACP Papers	Papers of the National Association for the Advancement of Colored People, Library of Congress, Washington, DC
National Archives	National Archives and Records Service, College Park, Maryland

NYU Archives   New York University Archives,
                          Tainament Library, New York, New York

TNA, PRO   The National Archives of the United
                          Kingdom, Public Records Office, Kew,
                          England

Reuther Library   Walter P. Reuther Library, Wayne State
                          University

Introduction

1. Tom Mboya to Thurgood Marshall, March 25, 1960, Folder 25.6,
General Correspondence with Foreign Countries, Correspondence with
USA, vol. 1 (For/1/v. 1) 1960 March–April, Box 25, Tom Mboya Papers,
Hoover Institute; Mark V. Tushnet, *Making Civil Rights Law: Thurgood
Marshall and the Supreme Court, 1936–1961* (New York: Oxford
University Press, 1994), 8; Juan Williams, *Thurgood Marshall: American
Revolutionary* (New York: Times Books, 1998), 18; Michael D. Davis
and Hunter R. Clark, *Thurgood Marshall: Warrior at the Bar, Rebel at
the Bench* (New York: Birch Lane Press, 1992), 30–31.

2. Thurgood Marshall, "The Reminiscences of Thurgood Marshall,"
Columbia Oral History Research Office, 1977, reprinted in *Thurgood
Marshall: His Speeches, Writings, Arguments, Opinions, and
Remembrances*, ed. Mark V. Tushnet (Chicago: Lawrence Hill, 2001),
443; James T. Campbell, *Middle Passages: African American Journeys to
Africa, 1787–2005* (New York: Penguin, 2006), xxi–xxiv; Claude A. Clegg
III, *The Price of Liberty: African Americans and the Making of Liberia*
(Chapel Hill: University of North Carolina Press, 2004).

3. Tom Mboya, Press Release, "Kenya Leader Wants Whites in Africa,
but as Equals," April 8, 1959, Folder: 36, Correspondence [U.S.A.] April
6–7, 1959, Box 13, ACOA Papers, Amistad Center.

4. Campbell, *Middle Passages*, xxiv. Daniel Rodgers uses "Atlantic
Crossings" to frame the relationship between Americans and Europeans
in his magisterial book on the influence of European ideas on Americans
during the Progressive and New Deal eras. Daniel T. Rodgers, *Atlantic
Crossings: Social Politics in a Progressive Age* (Cambridge, MA:
Harvard University Press, 1998). Much transnational work in U.S.
history is conceptualized within the frame of the "Atlantic world." See,
for example, Bernard Bailyn, *Atlantic History: Concept and Contours*

(Cambridge, MA: Harvard University Press, 2005). The Atlantic is a useful heuristic for some transnational work, just as the idea of borderlands informs scholarship on the United States and Mexico. Gloria Anzaldúa, *Borderlands/La Frontera: The New Mestiza,* 2nd ed. (San Francisco: Aunt Lute Books, 1999). All of these framing devices have their limits, however, since global impacts on U.S. history are not confined to these geographic regions. See, for example, Mae M. Ngai, *Impossible Subjects: Illegal Aliens and the Making of Modern America* (Princeton, NJ: Princeton University Press, 2003); Thomas Bender, *A Nation among Nations: America's Place in World History* (New York: Hill and Wang, 2006). It would be awkward to call the comings and goings in this book "Atlantic crossings." The principal characters in the narrative did fly across the Atlantic, but their journeys were to and from Kenya, which is on the Indian Ocean. They were bound together not by the Atlantic, but by relationships across continents based on politics, ideology, and international relations. There is no perfect term in historical studies to capture these relationships, but "transnational" seems a better term than one focusing on trans-Atlantic dimensions.

5. Mary L. Dudziak, *Cold War Civil Rights: Race and the Image of American Democracy* (Princeton, NJ: Princeton University Press, 2000), 77–114. On *Brown v. Board of Education,* see James Patterson, *Brown v. Board of Education: A Civil Rights Milestone and Its Troubled Legacy* (New York: Oxford University Press, 2001); Robert J. Cottrol, Raymond T. Diamond, and Leland B. Ware, *Brown v. Board of Education: Caste, Culture, and the Constitution* (Lawrence: University Press of Kansas, 2003).

6. "Chief Justice Warren in India," *Baltimore Sun,* October 1, 1956, India 1956 Correspondence, Clippings, Photographs Folder No. 1, Foreign File, Personal Papers, Papers of Earl Warren, LOC; Dudziak, *Cold War Civil Rights,* 109.

7. Genna Rae McNeil, *Groundwork: Charles Hamilton Houston and the Struggle for Civil Rights* (Philadelphia: University of Pennsylvania Press, 1983); Constance Baker Motley, *Equal Justice under Law: An Autobiography* (New York: Farrar, Straus, and Giroux, 1998); Jack Greenberg, *Crusaders in the Courts: How a Dedicated Band of Lawyers Fought for the Civil Rights Revolution* (New York: Basic Books, 1994); Kenneth Mack, "Rethinking Civil Rights Lawyering and Politics in the Era before *Brown,*" *Yale Law Journal* 93 (2006): 256–354.

8. Harry S Truman, "Special Message to Congress on Greece and Turkey: The Truman Doctrine," March 12, 1947, in *Public Papers of the*

Presidents of the United States, Harry S. Truman, 1947 (Washington, DC: Government Printing Office, 1963), 176–179; Dudziak, *Cold War Civil Rights,* 18–46, 79–114; Thomas Borstelmann, *The Cold War and the Color Line: American Race Relations in the Global Arena* (Cambridge, MA: Harvard University Press, 2001), 53–61, 74–84, 93–94.

9.   Keith Kyle, *The Politics of the Independence of Kenya* (Hampshire: Palgrave Macmillan, 1999), 8–9, 23; *Decolonization and Independence in Kenya, 1940–93,* ed. B. A. Ogot and W. R. Ochieng' (Athens: Ohio University Press, 1995). Very little is written on Marshall's work on African constitutions. Juan Williams briefly covers Marshall's trips to Africa in *Thurgood Marshall: American Revolutionary,* 284–286, 307–309. See also Roger Goldman with David Gallen, *Thurgood Marshall: Justice for All* (New York: Carroll & Graf, 1992), 139, 153, 178–179; Tushnet, *Making Civil Rights Law,* 313.

10.   *The Anatomy of Bomas: Selected Analyses of the 2004 Draft Constitution of Kenya,* ed. Kithure Kindiki and Osogo Ambani (Nairobi: Clairipress Limited, 2005); P. L. Agweli Onalo, *Constitution-Making in Kenya: An African Appraisal* (Nairobi: Transafrica Press, 2004); Joel D. Barkan and Njuguna Ng'ethe, "Kenya Tries Again," *Journal of Democracy* 9 (1998) 32–48; Joel D. Barkan, "Kenya after Moi," *Foreign Affairs* 83 (January/February 2004) 87–100; Joel D. Barkan, "Kenya's Great Rift," January 9, 2008, http://www.foreignaffairs .org/20080109faupdate87176/joel-d-barkan/kenya-s-great-rift.html; "Current Events in Kenya," interview with Makau Mutua, University of Illinois Public Radio, January 16, 2008, http://will.uiuc.edu/am/ focus/archives/08/080114.htm. On democratization in Africa in the late twentieth century, see *Democratization in Africa,* ed. Larry Diamond and Marc F. Plattner (Baltimore: Johns Hopkins University Press, 1999).

11.   Makau Mutua, *Kenya's Quest for Democracy: Taming Leviathan* (Boulder: Lynne Rienner, 2008); Walter O. Oyugi, Peter Wanyande, and C. Odhiambo Mbai, eds., *The Politics of Transition in Kenya: From KANU to NARC* (Nairobi: Heinrich Boll Foundation, 2003). For a critical examination of the concept of tribalism in Africa, see *The Creation of Tribalism in Southern Africa,* ed. Leroy Vail (Berkeley: University of California Press, 1989). On African culture and identity, see Kwame Anthony Appiah, *In My Father's House: Africa in the Philosophy of Culture* (New York: Oxford University Press, 1992). While many writers avoid using the term "tribe" and instead use "ethnicity," it would be difficult to do so in this history. Different layers of ethnic

politics (race and tribe) figure in the story. Because of that, it might confuse the reader if the term "tribe" was not used.

12. Saidiya Hartman, *Lose Your Mother: A Journey along the Atlantic Slave Route* (New York: Farrar, Straus, and Giroux, 2007), 34; Kevin K. Gaines, *American Africans in Ghana: Black Expatriates and the Civil Rights Era* (Chapel Hill: University of North Carolina Press, 2006), 1–26; Campbell, *Middle Passages*, 211–212.

13. Paul D. Carrington, *Spreading America's Word: Stories of its Lawyer-Missionaries* (New York: Twelve Tables Press, 2005).

Chapter 1

1. Bernard Taper, "A Reporter at Large: A Meeting in Atlanta," *The New Yorker*, March 17, 1956, pp. 78–82.

2. Ibid. The effectiveness of the work by Marshall and other civil rights lawyers has been questioned in recent years by scholarship seeing courts as inherently unable to change society, and questioning the emphasis placed on litigation by Marshall and others. See, for example, Michael Klarman, *From Jim Crow to Civil Rights: The Supreme Court and the Struggle for Racial Equality* (New York: Oxford University Press, 2004). The LDF lawyers did have faith in the power of courts to change society but also understood that litigation was only one part of a broader social change agenda. Court rulings can establish legal principles, but they are not self-enforcing. And careful studies have shown that courts can shape the social environment in positive ways, for example by raising consciousness about rights, which aids political mobilization. Michael W. McCann, *Rights at Work: Pay Equity Reform and the Politics of Legal Mobilization* (Chicago: University of Chicago Press, 1994). How history might have evolved if historical actors had made different choices is always difficult to say. All those who worked to change the nation faced serious obstacles, including the limited commitment to civil rights for most of the twentieth century on the part of all branches of government, and the continuing pervasiveness of racism in American society. In this environment, the lawyers used the tools in their hands to try to change it. On the LDF legal campaign, see Mark V. Tushnet, *The NAACP's Legal Strategy against Segregated Education, 1925–1950* (Chapel Hill: University of North Carolina Press, 1987). For a particularly thoughtful critique of the LDF by a former member of the legal team, see Derrick A. Bell Jr., "Serving Two Masters: Integration Ideals and Client Interests

in School Desegregation Litigation," *Yale Law Journal* 85 (1976): 470–516.

3. *Brown v. Board of Education*, 347 U.S. 483 (1954); Constance Baker Motley, *Equal Justice under Law: An Autobiography* (New York: Farrar, Straus, and Giroux, 1998), 110; *Time*, September 19, 1955, front cover; Constance Baker Motley, interview by author, New York, New York, November 8, 2004.

4. *Brown v. Board of Education*, 349 U.S. 294, 301 (1955) [*Brown II*]; *Griffin v. County School Board*, 377 U.S. 218, 234 (1964); Juan Williams, *Thurgood Marshall: American Revolutionary* (New York: Times Books), 284; Charles T. Clotfelter, *After Brown: The Rise and Retreat of School Desegregation* (Princeton, NJ: Princeton University Press, 2004), 56; Bureau of the Census, U.S. Department of Commerce, *Statistical Abstract of the United States: 1965* (1965), 122 table 162; Mark V. Tushnet, *Making Civil Rights Law: Thurgood Marshall and the Supreme Court, 1936–1961* (New York: Oxford University Press, 1994), 295; Manning Marable, *Race, Reform, and Rebellion: The Second Reconstruction in Black America*, 3rd ed. (Jackson: University Press of Mississippi, 2007), 12–37.

5. Taper, "Reporter at Large," 82.

6. Ibid., 83–84.

7. Ibid., 106.

8. Ibid., 115.

9. Tushnet, *Making Civil Rights Law*, 8; Williams, *Thurgood Marshall*, 15; Carl T. Rowan, *Dream Makers, Dream Breakers: The World of Justice Thurgood Marshall* (New York: Little, Brown, 1993), 31.

10. Tushnet, *Making Civil Rights Law*, 11; *Murray v. Pearson*, 169 Md. 478 (1936).

11. Genna Rae McNeil, *Groundwork: Charles Hamilton Houston and the Struggle for Civil Rights* (Philadelphia: University of Pennsylvania Press, 1983); Jack Greenberg, *Crusaders in the Courts: How a Dedicated Band of Lawyers Fought for the Civil Rights Revolution* (New York: Basic Books, 1994); Kenneth Mack, "Rethinking Civil Rights Lawyering and Politics in the Era before *Brown*," *Yale Law Journal* 93 (2006): 256–354.

12. Taper, "Reporter at Large," 119.

13. Ibid.

14. Ibid., 98, 106–107, 119.

15. George Houser, telephone interview by author, May 22, 2007; George Houser to Mary Dudziak, e-mail, July 5, 2007.

16. Leo Silberman, "Mboya in America: Not-So-Innocent Abroad," *Central African Examiner*, August 1, 1959, Folder: 10, Kenya—Writings—1951–1960, Box 90, ACOA Papers, Amistad Research Center.

17. Tom Mboya, "America in the Eyes of an African," n.d. (circa 1956), Folder: 9, Kenya—Writings—Tom Mboya—ca. 1956–1961, Box 90, ACOA Papers, Amistad Research Center; Tom Mboya, "Our Revolutionary Tradition: An African View," *Current History* 31 (December 1956): 343–347, Folder: 10, Kenya—Writings—1951–1960, Box 90, ACOA Papers, Amistad Research Center. The impact of the American Revolution around the world is explored in David Armitage, *The Declaration of Independence: A Global History* (Cambridge, MA: Harvard University Press, 2007).

18. Mboya, "America in the Eyes of an African"; Mboya, "Our Revolutionary Tradition."

19. "Political Awakening in Africa," Flyer, World Affairs Council of Philadelphia, 1956, Folder: 20, U.S. Correspondence—September 7–13, 1956, Box 9, ACOA Papers, Amistad Research Center; Tom Mboya, "Statement," August 16, 1956, Folder: 27, Kenya—ACOA Programs & Activities, Speakers Bureau, Tom Mboya, American Tour, Press Releases, Statements, 1956, Box 89, ACOA Papers, Amistad Research Center.

20. "World's Youngest Statesman," *Sepia*, n.d., Folder: 10, Kenya—Writings—1951–1960, Box 90, ACOA Papers, Amistad Research Center.

21. Ibid.

22. "Kenya Labor Leader Asks U.S. Cooperation," Folder 22, Box 18, Collection: UAW International Affairs, Reuther '56–'62, Reuther Library, Wayne State University. On the Mau Mau rebellion and the British counterinsurgency campaign, see David Anderson, *Histories of the Hanged: The Dirty War in Kenya and the End of Empire* (New York: W. W. Norton, 2005); Caroline Elkins, *Imperial Reckoning: The Untold Story of Britain's Gulag in Kenya* (New York: Henry Holt, 2005); E. S. Atieno Odhiambo and John Lonsdale, *Mau Mau and Nationhood: Arms, Authority, and Narration* (Athens: Ohio University Press, 2003).

23. Robert L. Tallmon to Tom Mboya, March 3, 1960, Folder 25.6, General Correspondence with Foreign Countries, Correspondence

with USA, vol. 1 (For/1/v. 1), 1960 March–April, Box 25, Mboya Papers, Hoover Institute; for example, Victor Reuther to Walter Reuther, July 18, 1956, Folder 22, Box 18, Collection: UAW International Affairs, Reuther '56–'62, Reuther Library, Wayne State University. V. Reuther suggested that UAW contribute to Mboya's trip by sending a check to the American Committee on Africa. "He is a very impressive person who, I am certain, will one day be the Prime Minister of his country." The UAW provided Mboya with substantial support.

24.   Tom Mboya, *Freedom and After* (Boston: Little, Brown, 1963), 29–31.

25.   "The Facts on Grant to American Students Airlift," August 1960, Folder: Commission on Civil Rights, 1958–1963, Africa 1960–1963, Box 1, Papers of Berl Bernhard, JFK Library (memorandum prepared by Senator John F. Kennedy's office); Tom Mboya to Irving Brown, August 4, 1959, Folder 18.5, Trade Unions, Correspondence with Foreign Organizations, vol. 1 (T/9/v. 1), 1959–1960, Box 18, Tom Mboya Papers, Hoover Institute; David Goldsworthy, *Tom Mboya: The Man Kenya Wanted to Forget* (Nairobi: Heinemann, 1982); Oginga Odinga, *Not Yet Uhuru: The Autobiography of Oginga Odinga* (New York: Hill and Wang, 1967); Babafemi A. Badejo, *Raila Odinga: An Enigma in Kenyan Politics* (Nairobi: Yintab Books, 2006), 53.

26.   Clayton Knowles, "African Leader Asks Democracy," *New York Times,* n.d. (1959), Folder: 25, ACOA Program—African Freedom Day—Press Clippings 1959, Box 40, ACOA Papers, Amistad Research Center.

27.   Goldsworthy, *Tom Mboya*, 106–108; Ralph McGill, "Africa Speaks: Can America Hear?" *Detroit News,* p. 22, December 16, 1958; Robert Coughlan, "The Stormy Future for Africa," *Life Magazine,* pp. 82, 89–90, February 2, 1959; Keith Smith to Tom Mboya, November 18, 1959, Folder 25.4, General Correspondence with Foreign Countries, Correspondence with USA, vol. 1 (For/1/v. 1), 1959 November–December, Box 25, Mboya Papers, Hoover Institute; Keith Smith to Tom Mboya, February 2, 1960, Folder: 25.5, General Correspondence with Foreign Countries, Correspondence with USA, vol. 1 (For/1/v. 1), 1960 January–February, Box 25, Mboya Papers, Hoover Institute; Odd Arne Westad, *The Global Cold War: Third World Interventions and the Making of Our Times* (Cambridge: Cambridge University Press, 2005), 133–134.

28.   Goldsworthy, *Tom Mboya*, 160.

29.   Folder 19, ACOA Program—African Freedom Day—Tom Mboya Publicity 1959, Box 40. ACOA Papers, Amistad Research Center; Collection: UAW International Affairs, Reuther '56–'62, Reuther Library, Wayne State University.

30.   Tom Mboya to Gill Jones, June 23, 1959, Folder 25.2, General
Correspondence with Foreign Countries, Correspondence with USA,
vol. 1 (For/1/v. 1), 1959 June–July, Box 25, Mboya Papers, Hoover
Institute; Tom Mboya to Ralph Helstein, July 17, 1959, Folder 25.2,
General Correspondence with Foreign Countries, Correspondence with
USA, vol. 1 (For/1/v. 1), 1959 June–July, Box 25, Mboya Papers, Hoover
Institute; Leonard Ingalls, "Kenya Curbs Mboya's Activity as Political
Leader of Africans," July 17, 1959, *New York Times*, Folder 7, Box 103,
Collection: UAW International Affairs, '56–'62, Reuther Library, Wayne
State University.

31.   Nicholas Best, *Happy Valley: The Story of the English in Kenya*
(London: Secker & Warburg, 1979), 1–18. "Maasai" has been spelled
differently in English-language sources. The current preferred spelling
is Maasai. Original spelling is retained in quotations and in titles of
sources.

32.   Best, *Happy Valley*, 13; Michael Blundell, *So Rough a Wind*
(London: Weidenfeld and Nicholson, 1964), 21.

33.   Thomas Pakenham, *The Scramble for Africa: White Man's
Conquest of the Dark Continent from 1876 to 1912* (New York: Random
House, 1991); Jeffrey Herbst, *States and Power in Africa: Comparative
Lessons in Authority and Control* (Princeton, NJ: Princeton University
Press, 2000); Bruce Berman and John Lonsdale, *Unhappy Valley:
Conflict in Kenya & Africa, Book One: State & Class* (Athens: Ohio
University Press, 1992), 13.

34.   Berman and Lonsdale, *Unhappy Valley*, 18–19.

35.   Ibid.; Blundell, *So Rough a Wind*, 19–20. Traditions of land tenure
for the Kikuyu tribe are described in Jomo Kenyatta, *Facing Mount
Kenya* (London: Secker & Warburg, 1938), 20–52.

36.   Berman and Londsale, *Unhappy Valley*, 104–114; Yash Ghai and
Dharam Ghai, "The Asian Minorities of East and Central Africa (up to
1971)," Minority Rights Group, Report No. 4 (London, 1971), p. 6.

37.   Blundell, *So Rough a Wind*, 30–31, 34, 65, 83.

38.   Best, *Happy Valley*, 103–104.

39.   Berman and Lonsdale, *Unhappy Valley*, 114.

40.   Ngũgĩ wa Thiong'o, *Weep Not, Child* (Oxford: Heinemann, 1964),
30–32.

41.   Elizabeth Borgwardt, *A New Deal for the World: America's Vision
for Human Rights* (Cambridge, MA: Harvard University Press, 2005),

1–4; John Reader, *Africa: A Biography of the Continent* (New York: Knopf, 1998), 639–640; Nikil Pal Singh, *Black Is a Country: Race and the Unfinished Struggle for Democracy* (Cambridge, MA: Harvard University Press, 2004), 103–104.

42. Reader, *Africa*, 643. On pan-Africanism, see P. Olisanwuche Esedebe, *Pan-Africanism: The Idea and Movement, 1776–1991*, 2nd ed. (Washington, DC: Howard University Press, 1994); Ronald W. Walters, *Pan Africanism in the African Diaspora: An Analysis of Modern Afrocentric Political Movements* (Detroit: Wayne State University Press, 1993).

43. Westad, *The Global Cold War*, 110, 131, 134; Thomas J. Noer, *Cold War and Black Liberation: The United States and White Rule in Africa, 1948–1968* (Columbia: University of Missouri Press, 1985), 2, 17–18; George White Jr., *Holding the Line: Race, Racism, and American Foreign Policy toward Africa, 1953–1961* (Lanham, MD: Rowman and Littlefield, 2005); Ebere Nwaubani, *The United States and Decolonization in West Africa, 1950–1960* (Rochester, NY: University of Rochester Press, 2001); Steven Metz, "American Attitudes toward Decolonization in Africa," *Political Science Quarterly* 99 (Fall 1984) 515–533.

44. Westad, *The Global Cold War*, 131–143; Noer, *Cold War and Black Liberation*, 17, 27, 48–49; Odinga, *Not Yet Uhuru*, 186–192; Blundell, *So Rough a Wind*, 226–227.

45. Blundell, *So Rough a Wind*, 249–250.

46. Dwight D. Eisenhower, "Radio and Television Address to the American People on the Situation in Little Rock," September 24, 1957, *Public Papers of the Presidents of the United States: Dwight D. Eisenhower, 1957* (Washington, DC: U.S. Government Printing Office, 1958), 690–694.

47. Dwight D. Eisenhower, *The White House Years: Waging Peace, 1956–61* (Garden City, NJ: Doubleday, 1965), 162; Dudziak, *Cold War Civil Rights*, 133–151; Tony A. Freyer, *Little Rock on Trial: Cooper v. Aaron and School Desegregation* (Lawrence: University Press of Kansas, 2007).

48. Blundell, *So Rough a Wind*, 249–250; Thomas Borstelmann, *The Cold War and the Color Line: American Race Relations in the Global Arena* (Cambridge, MA: Harvard University Press, 2001); Thomas Borstelmann, *Apartheid's Reluctant Uncle: The United States and Southern Africa in the Early Cold War* (New York: Oxford University Press, 1993).

49. James H. Meriwether, *Proudly We Can Be Africans: Black Americans and Africa, 1935–1961* (Chapel Hill: University of North Carolina Press, 2002), 12, 9–20; James T. Campbell, *Songs of Zion: The African Methodist Episcopal Church in the United States and South Africa* (New York: Oxford University Press, 1995), 64–99; Esedebe, *Pan-Africanism,* 3; David Levering Lewis, *W. E. B. Du Bois: Biography of a Race, 1868–1919* (New York: Henry Holt, 1994), 8–9, 248–251, 574–578; David Levering Lewis, *W. E. B. Du Bois: The Fight for Equality and the American Century, 1919–1963* (New York: Henry Holt, 2000), 29–30, 37, 108–117, 208–211, 530–531, 554; Borstelmann, *Cold War and the Color Line*; Brian Urquhart, *Ralph Bunche: An American Life* (New York: W. W. Norton, 1993), 125–128; Penny Von Eschen, *Race against Empire: Black Americans and Anticolonialism, 1937–1957* (Ithaca, NY: Cornell University Press, 1997), 96–121; Penny M. Von Eschen, *Satchmo Blows Up the World: Jazz Ambassadors Play the Cold War* (Cambridge, MA: Harvard University Press, 2004), 58–91; Mary L. Dudziak, *Cold War Civil Rights: Race and the Image of American Democracy* (Princeton, NJ: Princeton University Press, 2000), 61–63, 250–251; Martin Bauml Duberman, *Paul Robeson* (New York: Knopf, 1988), 382–383; James Baldwin, *The Fire Next Time* (New York: Dial, 1963), 54. See also Paul Gilroy, *The Black Atlantic: Modernity and Double Consciousness* (Cambridge, MA: Harvard University Press, 1993), 17–19, on the transformative impact of travel.

The cold war had an impact on civil rights activists. Civil rights lawyers and others were red-baited in the South, and some organizations, including the NAACP, threw members with communist ties out of the organization. Marshall has been criticized for communicating with FBI director J. Edgar Hoover regarding communist influence in the civil rights movement. Marshall's voluminous FBI file, however, shows that he came to the attention of the FBI in the 1940s due to his outspoken criticism of the Bureau for failing to investigate lynchings. Persistent criticism led the FBI to go to great lengths to respond to Marshall, and the Bureau repaid his interest with steady surveillance of Marshall's civil rights work. The FBI critic eventually came to develop a working relationship with Hoover. On a few occasions, Marshall did pass information on to the FBI director, possibly to insulate himself from harassment or because of his concerns about the role of communists within the movement. This was common, but in light of disclosures about abuses by the Bureau, was unfortunate. Thurgood Marshall,

FBI File, Federal Bureau of Investigation Web page, http://foia.fbi.gov/
foiaindex/marshall.htm. On FBI surveillance of the civil rights
movement, see Kenneth O'Reilly, *Racial Matters: The FBI's Secret File
on Black America, 1960–1972* (New York: Free Press, 1989).

50. Horace Mann Bond, *Education for Freedom: A History of Lincoln
University, Pennsylvania* (Lincoln University, PA: Lincoln University
Press, 1976), 487–550; Roger Goldman with David Gallen, *Thurgood
Marshall: Justice for All* (New York: Carroll & Graf, 1992), 24–25; Levi
A. Nwachuku, "Nnamdi Azikiwe and Lincoln University: An Analysis
of a Symbiotic Relationship," *Lincoln Journal Social and Political
Thought* (Fall 2002), available at http://www.lincoln.edu/history/
journal/azikwe.htm; David McBride, "Africa's Elevation and Changing
Racial Thought at Lincoln University, 1854–1886," *Journal of Negro
History* 62 (October 1977): 363–377; Sibusiso Nkomo, "Strong Ties:
Past and Present," *Lincoln Journal Social and Political Thought*
(Summer 1990): 19–20.

51. Bond, *Education for Freedom*, 487–550; Goldman with Gallen,
Thurgood Marshall, 24–25; Nwachuku, "Nnamdi Azikiwe and Lincoln
University"; McBride, "Africa's Elevation and Changing Racial Thought
at Lincoln University"; Nkomo, "Strong Ties"; Herbert L. Wright to
Gloster Current, January 12, 1953, Folder: Africa—Kenya, 1952–55,
Box A5, Papers of the NAACP, Group II, General Office Files, 1940–55,
LOC. Before Marshall was approached, a committee to support Gatheru
had already retained counsel for him, so an embarrassed Horace Mann
Bond, president of Lincoln, had to withdraw a request for NAACP
legal support. Horace M. Bond to Herbert L. Wright, January 23, 1953,
Folder: Africa—Kenya, 1952–55, Box A5, Papers of the NAACP, Group
II, General Office Files, 1940–55, LOC.

52. Houser, telephone interview by author. Marshall said that two
friends, "one from the Urban League and one from the UAW came
to me with this idea." One of those friends would have been Frank
Montero of the Urban League, an ACOA member. William Scheinman
and Lansdale Christie were involved in funding the trip. Ibid.; Marshall,
"Reminiscences," 446; Tom Mboya to Thomas Emerson, January
1960, Folder: 25.5, General Correspondence with Foreign Countries,
Correspondence with USA, vol. 1 (For/1/v. 1), January–February, Box
25, Tom Mboya Papers, Hoover Institute; Thomas Emerson to Tom
Mboya, January 27, 1960, Folder: 25.5, General Correspondence with
Foreign Countries, Correspondence with USA, vol. 1 (For/1/v. 1),
January–February, Box 25, Tom Mboya Papers, Hoover Institute.

Chapter 2

1. Anonymous to Colonial Secretary Macleod, Blundell, and [illegible], January 1960, Folder: Kenya Constitutional Conference, 1960, Miscellaneous Representations, CO 822/2349, TNA, PRO; Anonymous to Colonial Secretary Macleod, received January 15, 1960, Folder: Kenya Constitutional Conference, 1960, Miscellaneous Representations, CO 822/2349, TNA, PRO.

2. H. S. Wilson, *African Decolonization* (New York: E. Arnold, 1994), 177; Ritchie Ovendale, "Macmillan and the Wind of Change in Africa, 1957–1960," *The Historical Journal* 38 (June 1995): 455–477.

3. Keith Kyle, *The Politics of the Independence of Kenya* (Hampshire: Palgrave Macmillan, 1999), 8–9, 23; Robert L. Tignor, *The Colonial Transformation of Kenya: The Kamba, Kikuyu and Maasai from 1900 to 1939* (Princeton, NJ: Princeton University Press, 1979); David Anderson, *Histories of the Hanged: The Dirty War in Kenya and the End of Empire* (New York: W. W. Norton, 2005), 230–288; E. S. Atieno Odhiambo and John Lonsdale, *Mau Mau and Nationhood: Arms, Authority, and Narration* (Athens: Ohio University Press, 2003), 227–250; Caroline Elkins, *Imperial Reckoning: The Untold Story of Britain's Gulag in Kenya* (New York: Henry Holt, 2005), 31–61.

4. Anderson, *Histories of the Hanged*, 9–63; Elkins, *Imperial Reckoning*, 31–37; Odhiambo and Lonsdale, *Mau Mau and Nationhood*, 19–24.

5. Anderson, *Histories of the Hanged*, 4–5, 326–327; Elkins, *Imperial Reckoning*, 121–153; Carolyn Elkins, "Detention, Rehabilitation and Destruction of Kikuyu Society," in Odhiambo and Lonsdale, *Mau Mau and Nationhood*, 191–226; Joanna Lewis, " 'Daddy Wouldn't Buy Me a Mau Mau': The British Popular Press and Demoralization of Empire," in Odhiambo and Lonsdale, *Mau Mau and Nationhood*, 227–250.

6. Anderson, *Histories of the Hanged*, 63–68; Amconsul Nairobi to Department of State, Despatch no. 337, January 8, 1960, Records of the Department of State, RG 59, Central Decimal File, 1960–63, 745R.00/1–860, National Archives; Nairobi to Secretary of State, Telegram no. 222, January 7, 1960, Records of the Department of State, RG 59, Central Decimal File, 1960–63, 745R.00/1–760, National Archives; B. A. Ogot, "The Decisive Years, 1956–63," in *Decolonization and Independence in Kenya 1940–93*, ed. B. A. Ogot and W. R. Ochieng' (Athens: Ohio University Press, 1995), 48, 52–53.

7. Oginga Odinga, *Not Yet Uhuru: The Autobiography of Oginga Odinga* (New York: Hill and Wang, 1967), 173; Mary L. Dudziak,

"Working toward Democracy: Thurgood Marshall and the Constitution of Kenya," *Duke Law Journal* 56 (December 2006): 721–780.

8. Mrs. Buckley-Mathews to Vera H. Whaler (extract of letter), received January 29, 1960, Folder: Kenya Constitutional Conference, 1960, Miscellaneous Representations, CO 822/2349, TNA, PRO; Nicholas D. Hayne-Upson to Secretary of State for the Colonies, January 13, 1960, Folder: Kenya Constitutional Conference, 1960, Miscellaneous Representations, CO 822/2349, TNA, PRO (with attachments on "A 'Common Sense' Appreciation of the Problem of White Settlement in Kenya"); Marion W. Knowles to Ian Macleod, February 10, 1960, Folder: Kenya Constitutional Conference, 1960, Miscellaneous Representations, CO 822/2349, TNA, PRO; Anderson, *Histories of the Hanged*, 332–333; Elkins, *Imperial Reckoning*, 340–353.

9. "U.S. Negro Leader Arrives in Kenya," *New York Times*, January 11, 1960, p. 5; Thurgood Marshall, "The Reminiscences of Thurgood Marshall," Columbia Oral History Research Office, 1977, reprinted in *Thurgood Marshall: His Speeches, Writings, Arguments, Opinions, and Remembrances*, ed. Mark V. Tushnet (Chicago: Lawrence Hill, 2001), 443; Claude A. Clegg III, *The Price of Liberty: African Americans and the Making of Liberia* (Chapel Hill: University of North Carolina Press, 2004), 53–76; James Campbell, *Middle Passages: African American Journeys to Africa, 1787–2005* (New York: Penguin, 2006), 99–135.

10. Tom Mboya to Thurgood Marshall, March 25, 1960, Folder 25.6, General Correspondence with Foreign Countries, Correspondence with USA, vol. 1 (For/1/v. 1), 1960 March–April, Box 25, Mboya Papers, Hoover Institute. Marshall's work on the Kenyan constitution was funded by a man he thought to be a multimillionaire, but who he later discovered "had less money than I did. Then, I got two and two—and I still suspect it was CIA money, that's all I could—I know it wasn't Commie money, so what else could it be? I don't know." According to George Houser of ACOA, this man was William Scheinman, who became a close American friend of Mboya's. Marshall, "Reminiscences," 446–447; Houser, interview by author. A Freedom of Information Act request filed by the author with the CIA resulted in no records pertaining to Thurgood Marshall.

11. Arturo Escobar, *Encountering Development: The Making and Unmaking of the Third World* (Princeton, NJ: Princeton University Press, 1995), 3–12; Harry S Truman, Inaugural Address, 1949, *Public Papers* 112, 115 (January 20, 1949); James C. N. Paul, "Foreword," in

Law and Development: Facing Complexity in the 21st Century, ed.
John Hatchard and Amanda Perry-Kessaris (London: Cavendish, 2003),
vii–xi; John Henry Merryman, "Comparative Law and Social Change:
On the Origins, Style, Decline and Revival of the Law and Development
Movement," *American Journal of Comparative Law* 25 (Summer 1977):
457, 462–463; John Tamanaha, "The Lessons of Law-and-Development
Studies," *American Journal of International Law* 89 (April 1995): 470;
David M. Trubek and Marc Galanter, "Scholars and Self-Estrangement:
Some Reflections on the Crisis in Law and Development Studies in the
United States," *Wisconsin Law Review* 1974, no. 4 (1974): 1062, 1066;
Yves Dezalay and Bryant G. Garth, *The Internationalization of the Palace
Wars: Lawyers, Economists, and the Contest to Transform Latin American
States* (Chicago: University of Chicago Press, 2002). On development and
the idea of "modernization" in Africa, see James Ferguson, *Expectations
of Modernity: Myths and Meanings of Urban Life on the Zambian
Copperbelt* (Berkeley: University of California Press, 1999).

12.   Richard M. Dalfiume, *Desegregation of the U.S. Armed Forces:
Fighting on Two Fronts, 1939–1953* (Columbia: University of Missouri
Press, 1969), 201; Bernard C. Nalty, *Strength for the Fight: A History of
Black Americans in the Military* (New York: Free Press, 1986), 255–269;
Roger Goldman with David Gallen, *Thurgood Marshall: Justice for
All* (New York: Carroll & Graf, 1992), 112–116; Thurgood Marshall,
"Summary Justice: The Negro GI in Korea," in *Supreme Justice: Speeches
and Writings: Thurgood Marshall*, ed. J. Clay Smith Jr. (Philadelphia:
University of Pennsylvania Press, 2003), 134–141; Mark V. Tushnet,
*Making Civil Rights Law: Thurgood Marshall and the Supreme Court,
1956–1961* (New York: Oxford University Press, 1994), 311–312.

13.   Jack Greenberg, *Crusaders in the Courts: How a Dedicated Band
of Lawyers Fought for the Civil Rights Revolution* (New York: Basic
Books, 1994), 223; e-mail from Jack Greenberg to author, May 13, 2002;
James M. Nabrit III, telephone interview by author, January 22, 2008;
"U.S. Negro Leader Arrives in Kenya," *New York Times*, January 11,
1960, p. 5. Nabrit does not recall whether they discussed the Universal
Declaration of Human Rights. This was "extracurricular" work for the
busy LDF office, so they were unable to spend much time on it.

14.   Marshall, "Reminiscences," 444.

15.   Ibid.; Amconsul Nairobi to Department of State, Despatch no. 349,
January 15, 1960, Records of the Department of State, RG 59, Central
Decimal File, 1960–63, 745R.03/1–1560, National Archives.

16. Marshall, "Reminiscences," 444. The American consul in Kenya described Marshall's exclusion from the meeting slightly differently; however, the consul did not witness these events firsthand: "The Acting District Commissioner refused him permission to enter the meeting, saying that his name was not on the list of persons scheduled for attendance submitted at the time the license was granted for the meeting." Amconsul Nairobi to Department of State, Despatch no. 349, January 15, 1960, Records of the Department of State, RG 59, Central Decimal File, 1960–63, 745R.03/1–1560, National Archives.

17. Marshall, "Reminiscences," 444–445. Marshall loved to tell stories, and it is likely that he massaged this narrative a bit for dramatic effect; however, the underlying facts of his exclusion from the meeting are supported by other sources. See Amconsul Nairobi to Department of State, Despatch no. 349, January 15, 1960, Records of the Department of State, RG 59, Central Decimal File, 1960–63, 745R.03/1–1560, National Archives. On Marshall as a storyteller, see David B. Wilkins, "Justice as Narrative: Some Personal Reflections on a Master Storyteller," *Harvard BlackLetter Law Journal* 6 (Spring 1989): 68–77.

18. Amconsul Nairobi to Department of State, Despatch no. 349, January 15, 1960, Records of the Department of State, RG 59, Central Decimal File, 1960–63, 745R.03/1–1560, National Archives; Berl Bernhard, interview by author, Washington, DC, July 16, 2003.

19. Amconsul Nairobi to Department of State, Despatch no. 349, January 15, 1960.

20. "Negroes' Lawyer on World Stage," *New York Times*, January 22, 1960, p. 2; "U.S. Negro Leader Arrives in Kenya," *New York Times*, January 11, 1960, p. 5; David Goldsworthy, *Tom Mboya: The Man Kenya Wanted to Forget* (Nairobi: Heinemann, 1982), 133.

21. "Thurgood Freezes as Kenyans Feud," *Cleveland Call and Post*, January 30, 1960, p. 1A. Marshall said that prior to his work on the Kenyan constitution he had "helped a little" with the Nigerian constitution. He told an interviewer that he was unable to provide details due to State Department restrictions. Marshall, "Reminiscences," 450–451. There is no information on this in U.S. State Department files pertaining to Nigeria, but this may simply be because Marshall did not travel to Nigeria for this work. Marshall's personal papers from this period are in the papers of the NAACP Legal Defense Fund, which remain closed.

22.   Goldsworthy, *Tom Mboya*, 11–14; Odinga, *Not Yet Uhuru*, 130–133, 200; Marshall, "Reminiscences," 445; Kyle, *Politics of the Independence of Kenya*, 115–118.

23.   Marshall, "Reminiscences," 445; Kyle, *Politics of the Independence of Kenya*, 115–118. The *East African Standard* expected the Africans to submit the following proposals:

> Welcome for common roll elections; one adult, one vote; a demand for nine elected Ministers, including the Chief Minister; single-member constituencies, based geographically; perhaps three Civil Service Ministers for a transitional period; opposition to high qualifications for the franchise as a safeguard for minorities; no franchise on racial grounds; Africans willing to accept responsibility in the Government; reserved seats definitely unsatisfactory; and a national Parliament instead of the Legislative Council.

"Optimism Prevails in London," *East African Standard*, January 25, 1960, p. 1.

24.   Marshall, "Reminiscences," 445; Michael Blundell, *So Rough a Wind: The Kenya Memoirs of Sir Michael Blundell* (London: Weidenfeld and Nicolson, 1964), 248–250, 258, 266.

25.   Amembassy London to Secretary of State, Telegram no. 555, January 13, 1960, Records of the Department of State, RG 59, Central Decimal File, 1960–63, 745R.00/1–1360, National Archives; Amembassy to Secretary of State, Telegram no. 3552, January 18, 1960, Records of the Department of State, Central Decimal File, 1960–63, 745R.00/1–1860, National Archives; Saullers [illegible] to Macleod, January 12, 1960, Folder: Kenya Constitutional Conference, 1960 Miscellaneous Representations, CO 822/2349, TNA, PRO (emphasis in original).

26.   Robert C. Ruark, "Hits Marshall's Role in Kenya Negotiations," *New York World-Telegram*, February 3, 1960; Kempton, "The Diplomat," *New York Post*, January 26, 1960, p. 24.

27.   Department of State to Amembassy London, Telegram no. 5700, January 28, 1960, Records of the Department of State, RG 59, Central Decimal File, 1960–63, 745R.00/1–2860, National Archives; London to Secretary of State, Telegram no. 3782, January 29, 1960, Records of the Department of State, RG 59, Central Decimal File, 1960–63, 745R.00/1–2960, National Archives; London to Secretary of State, Telegram no. 3551; Nairobi to Secretary of State, Telegram no. 262.

28.   Odinga, *Not Yet Uhuru*, 177; Goldsworthy, *Tom Mboya*, 133–136.

29. "Thurgood Freezes as Kenyans Feud," *Cleveland Call and Post*, January 30, 1960, p. 1A.

30. Ibid.

31. London to Secretary of State, Telegram no. 3552, January 18, 1960, Records of the Department of State, RG 59, Central Decimal File, 1960–63, 745R.00/1–1860, National Archives; Record of Kenya Constitutional Conference, 1st plenary session, January 18, 1960, Folder: Kenya Constitutional Conference, 1960, Record of Plenary Meetings, CO 822/2358, TNA, PRO.

32. Record of Kenya Constitutional Conference, 1st plenary session, January 18, 1960; Record of Kenya Constitutional Conference, 2nd plenary session, January 20, 1960, Folder: Kenya Constitutional Conference, 1960, Record of Plenary Meetings, CO 822/2358, TNA, PRO.

33. Record of Kenya Constitutional Conference, 1st plenary session, January 18, 1960; Record of Kenya Constitutional Conference, 2nd plenary session, January 20, 1960; London to Secretary of State, Telegram no. 3551, January 18, 1960, Records of the Department of State, RG 59, Central Decimal File, 1960–63, 745R.00/1–1860, National Archives; Nairobi to Secretary of State, Telegram no. 262, February 2, 1960, Records of the Department of State, RG 59, Central Decimal File, 1960–63, 745R.00/2–260, National Archives. The other committees were on the Council of Ministers and on the franchise and the colonial legislature.

34. "Kikuyu Protest at Second Advisor: Telegram from Loyalists Sent to Mr. Macleod," *East African Standard*, January 25, 1960, p. 5.

35. Ibid.

36. J. G. Amamoo, "London Letter: Kenya's Future," *Ghana Times*, February 2, 1960, p. 8.

37. London to Secretary of State, Telegram no. 3666, January 23, 1960, Records of the Department of State, RG 59, Central Decimal File, 1960–63, 745R.00/1–2360, National Archives; Goldsworthy, *Tom Mboya*, 133–134.

38. London to Secretary of State, Telegram no. 3782, January 29, 1960, Records of the Department of State, RG 59, Central Decimal File, 1960–63, 745R.00/1–2960, National Archives.

39. Greenberg, *Crusaders in the Courts*, 271. On Greensboro, see William H. Chafe, *Civilities and Civil Rights: Greensboro, North*

Carolina, and the Black Struggle for Freedom (New York: Oxford University Press, 1980), 71–101. Events like the sit-ins would generate widespread international media coverage and sympathetic international reaction. On the international impact of the civil rights movement, see Mary L. Dudziak, *Cold War Civil Rights: Race and the Image of American Democracy* (Princeton, NJ: Princeton University Press, 2000).

40.   Clayborne Carson, *In Struggle: SNCC and the Black Awakening of the 1960s*, rev. ed. (Cambridge, MA: Harvard University Press, 1995), 22–23; Wesley C. Hogan, *Many Minds, One Heart: SNCC's Dream for a New America* (Chapel Hill: University of North Carolina Press, 2007), 20–21, 33. Gandhi widely influenced civil rights activists, including Martin Luther King Jr. According to John D'Emilio, it was Bayard Rustin "more than anyone else" who "brought the message and methods of Gandhi to the United States." John D'Emilio, *Lost Prophet: The Life and Times of Bayard Rustin* (New York: Free Press, 2003), 1.

41.   D'Emilio, *Lost Prophet*, 134; Raymond Arsenault, *Freedom Riders: 1961 and the Struggle for Racial Justice* (New York: Oxford University Press, 2006), 36–37.

42.   Juan Williams, *Thurgood Marshall: American Revolutionary* (New York: Times Books, 1998), 286–289; Derrick Bell, "An Epistolary Exploration for a Thurgood Marshall Biography," *Harvard Blackletter Law Journal* 6 (1989): 51; Tushnet, *Making Civil Rights Law*, 310; Constance Baker Motley, *Equal Justice Under Law: An Autobiography* (New York: Farrar, Straus, and Giroux, 1998), 131.

43.   "Meeting with Lew Sargentich," n.d. (handwritten notes), Folder: Marshall, Thurgood—book project, Box 60, Series II, Derrick Bell Papers, NYU Archives.

44.   "Memorandum Report of Lawyers' Conference on Sit-In Demonstrations Held in Washington, D.C. by NAACP Legal Defense and Education Fund, Inc.," circa 1960, Folder: 9, *Louisiana v. Mary Briscoe*, Box 67, Alexander Pierre Tureaud Papers, Amistad Research Center.

45.   Louis H. Pollak, "The Supreme Court and the States: Reflections on *Boynton v. Virginia*," *California Law Review* 49 (1961): 16–18, quoting Transcript of Record, pp. 28–29, *Boynton v. Virginia*, 364 U.S. 454 (1960).

46.   Ibid.; *Henderson v. United States*, 339 U.S. 816 (1950).

47.   Douglas Brinkley, *Rosa Parks* (New York: Penguin, 2000); Sandi Tibbetts Murphy, "'In Those Days We Had to Be Bold': Edna Griffin

and the Des Moines Sit-in" (unpublished paper, University of Iowa College of Law, December 17, 1993); "Activists Keep Alive Memory of Iowa's Civil-Rights Pioneers," *Des Moines Register*, June 21, 1998, http://desmoinesregister.com/extras/civilrights/katz.html; Arsenault, *Freedom Riders*, 22–57.

48.   "Sit Downs Issue Faces Legal Test," *New York Times*, February 29, 1960, p. 18; *Boynton v. Virginia*, 364 U.S. 454 (1960).

49.   Nabrit, interview by author; The Oyez Project, *Boynton v. Virginia*, 364 U.S. 454 (1960), available at http://www.oyez.org/cases/1960–1969/1960/1960_7/ (accessed August 17, 2007); Anthony Lewis, "High Court Hears Restaurant Case," *New York Times*, October 13, 1960; John Lewis with Michael D'Orso, *Walking with the Wind: A Memoir of the Movement* (New York: Simon & Schuster, 1998), 141–143; Arsenault, *Freedom Riders*, 93, 121–122.

50.   Cecilia Marshall, interview by author, July 10, 2007, Washington, DC.

51.   "Kikuyu Protest at Second Advisor: Telegram from Loyalists Sent to Mr. Macleod," *East African Standard*, January 25, 1960, p. 5; James Meriwether, *Proudly We Can Be Africans: Black Americans and Africa, 1935–1961* (Chapel Hill: University of North Carolina Press, 2002), 208–240. On law and social change in South Africa, see Richard Abel, *Politics by Other Means: Law and the Struggle against Apartheid* (New York: Routledge, 1995).

52.   Stephen J. Whitfield, *A Death in the Delta: The Story of Emmett Till* (Baltimore, MD: Johns Hopkins University Press, 1988), 21–23.

53.   Dorothy Beeler, "Race Riot in Columbia, Tennessee, February 25–27, 1946," *Tennessee Historical Quarterly* 39 (Spring 1980): 49–61; Marshall, "Reminiscences," 428; Gail Williams O'Brien, *The Color of the Law: Race, Violence, and Justice in the Post–World War II South* (Chapel Hill: University of North Carolina Press, 1999), 7–55.

54.   Marshall, "Reminiscences," 428–430; Tushnet, *Making Civil Rights Law*, 54–55.

55.   Marshall, "Reminiscences," 428–430; Tushnet, *Making Civil Rights Law*, 54–55.

56.   Jogesh Chadha, *Gandhi* (New York: John Wiley, 1997), 124–126; D'Emilio, *Lost Prophet*, 231; Clayborne Carson, ed., *The Autobiography of Martin Luther King, Jr.* (New York: Warner Books, 1998); Mary King, *Mahatma Gandhi and Martin Luther King, Jr.: The Power of Nonviolent Action* (UNESCO Publishing, 1999).

57. Daniel Branch, "Loyalists, Mau Mau, and Elections in Kenya: The First Triumph of the System, 1957–1958," *Africa Today* 53 (Winter 2006): 27–50; Caroline Elkins, "Detention, Rehabilitation & the Destruction of Kikuyu Society," in *Mau Mau and Nationhood: Arms, Authority, and Narration,* ed. E. S. Atieno Odhiambo and John Lonsdale (Athens: Ohio University Press, 2003), 218–219; Claude Ake, *The Feasibility of Democracy in Africa* (Dakar, Senegal: Council for the Development of Social Science Research in Africa, 2000), 191.

Chapter 3

1. James Yorke, *Lancaster House: London's Greatest Town House* (London: Merrell, 2001).

2. Thurgood Marshall, "The Reminiscences of Thurgood Marshall," Columbia Oral History Research Office, 1977, reprinted in *Thurgood Marshall: His Speeches, Writings, Arguments, Opinions and Remembrances,* ed. Mark V. Tushnet (Chicago: Lawrence Hill, 2001), 445; Record of Kenya Constitutional Conference, 6th plenary session, January 26, 1960, Folder: Kenya Constitutional Conference, 1960, Record of Plenary Meetings, CO 822/2358, TNA, PRO. During 1960 negotiations, the focus was not on the minority rights of smaller tribes in Kenya. This would be front and center during 1962 constitutional negotiations, principally taking the form of a debate over federalism.

3. Record of Kenya Constitutional Conference, 4th plenary session, January 25, 1960, Folder: Kenya Constitutional Conference, 1960, Record of Plenary Meetings, CO 822/2358, TNA, PRO.

4. Ibid.; Record of Kenya Constitutional Conference, 6th plenary session.

5. Record of Kenya Constitutional Conference, 6th plenary session; "Kenya Talks: Capt. Briggs Afraid of African Majority," *Ghana Times,* February 8, 1960, p. 9.

6. Secretary of State for the Colonies to Kenya (O.A.G.), Telegram no. 30, February 15, 1960, Folder: Kenya Constitutional Conference, 1960, Record of Proceedings, CO 822/2354, TNA, PRO.

7. B. A. Ogot, "The Decisive Years," in *Decolonization and Independence in Kenya, 1940–93,* ed. B. A. Ogot and W. R. Ochieng' (London: James Curry, 1995), 61.

8. Secretary of State for the Colonies to Kenya (O.A.G.), Telegram no. 150, February 16, 1960, Folder: Kenya Constitutional Conference, 1960, Record of Proceedings, CO 822/2354, TNA, PRO.

9. Ian Macleod to Prime Minister, P.M. (60) 7, February 17, 1960, Folder: Kenya Constitutional Conference, 1960, Record of Proceedings, CO 822/2354, TNA, PRO; Commonwealth Relations Office to Ottawa and Others, Telegram no. 75, February 16, 1960, Folder: Kenya Constitutional Conference, 1960, Record of Proceedings, CO 822/2354, TNA, PRO; Draft Note for the Prime Minister, Folder: Kenya Constitutional Conference, 1960, Record of Proceedings, CO 822/2354, TNA, PRO; Kenya (Acting Governor) to Secretary of State for the Colonies, Telegram 193, February 17, 1960, CO 822/2356, Folder: Kenya Constitutional Conference 1960, Reactions in Kenya, TNA, PRO; Kenya (Acting Governor) to Secretary of State for the Colonies, Telegram 176, February 12, 1960, CO 822/2356, Folder: Kenya Constitutional Conference 1960, Reactions in Kenya, PRO, U.K.; Secretary of State for the Colonies to Kenya (O.A.G.), Telegram no. 150.

10. Oginga Odinga, *Not Yet Uhuru: The Autobiography of Oginga Odinga* (New York: Hill and Wang, 1967), 179.

11. Marshall, "Reminiscences," 445–446. "Land Tenure and Bill of Rights: Kenya Whites Seek to Perpetuate Evil," *Ghana Times*, February 20, 1960, p. 4.

12. A. W. Brian Simpson, *Human Rights and the End of Empire: Britain and the Genesis of the European Convention* (Oxford: Oxford University Press, 2001), 863–869; "Convention for the Protection of Human Rights and Fundamental Freedoms," November 4, 1950, *Treaty Series: Treaties and International Agreements Registered or Filed and Recorded with the Secretariat of the United Nations* 213, no. 2889 (1955): 221. On ethnic conflict and constitutionalism in Nigeria, see Rotimi T. Suberu, *Federalism and Ethnic Conflict in Nigeria* (Washington, DC: United States Institute of Peace Press, 2001).

13. Mary L. Dudziak, "Working toward Democracy: Thurgood Marshall and the Constitution of Kenya," *Duke Law Journal* 56 (December 2006): 721–780.

14. Proposed Draft Bill of Rights, attachment to J. A. Sankey and T. M. Heiser, Note by the Secretaries, February 2, 1960, Folder: Kenya Constitutional Conference, 1960 Committee on Safeguards, Memoranda, CO 822/2362, TNA, PRO. The *Ghana Times* reported that three papers on a bill of rights were circulated at the conference:

one by Thurgood Marshall, one by Colonial Office Advisor W. J. M. Mackensie, and one based on the Nigerian constitution, and that "another document covering the best features of all three had been prepared by Dr. Marshall and had been accepted in its general terms by all delegates." Lancaster House records, however, reveal only one document circulated by Thurgood Marshall. "Land Tenure and Bill of Rights: Kenya Whites Seek to Perpetuate Evil," *Ghana Times*, February 20, 1960, p. 4.; Proposed Draft Bill of Rights, attachment to J. A. Sankey and T. M. Heiser, Note by the Secretaries, February 2, 1960, Folder: Kenya Constitutional Conference, 1960 Committee on Safeguards, Memoranda, CO 822/2362, TNA, PRO.

15. Kenya (Director of Information) to Secretary of State for the Colonies, Telegram no. 53160, February 6, 1960, Folder: Kenya Constitutional Conference, 1960, Record of Proceedings, CO 822/2354, TNA, PRO.

16. Nairobi to Secretary of State, Airgram no. 60, November 28, 1961, Records of the Department of State, RG 59, Central Decimal File, 1960–63, 745R.03/11–2861, National Archives.

17. Juan Williams, *Thurgood Marshall: American Revolutionary* (New York: Three Rivers Press, 1994), 285; Carol Anderson, *Eyes off the Prize: The United Nations and the African American Struggle for Human Rights, 1944–1955* (Cambridge: Cambridge University Press, 2003), 8–112; Proposed Draft Bill of Rights, attachment to J. A. Sankey and T. M. Heiser, Note by the Secretaries, February 2, 1960, Folder: Kenya Constitutional Conference, 1960 Committee on Safeguards, Memoranda, CO 822/2362, TNA, PRO; Kenya Constitutional Conference, Committee on Safeguards, 1st meeting, February 16, 1960, Folder: Kenya Constitutional Conference, 1960, Committee on Safeguards, Record of Meetings, CO 822/2363, TNA, PRO; Universal Declaration of Human Rights, G.A. Res. 217A, p.75, U.N. GAOR, 3d Session, 1st plenary meeting, U.N. Doc. A/810, December 12, 1948.

Just how Marshall's thinking developed regarding putting international human rights in the Kenya Constitution is unfortunately not reflected in the historical record. Nabrit does not recall whether he and Marshall discussed the Universal Declaration of Human Rights. They simply had little time to spend on it. James M. Nabrit III, telephone interview by author, January 22, 2008. On the Universal Declaration of Human Rights, see Mary Ann Glendon, *A World Made New: Eleanor Roosevelt and the Universal Declaration of Human Rights*

(New York: Random House, 2001); Elizabeth Borgwardt, *A New Deal for the World: America's Vision for Human Rights* (Cambridge, MA: Harvard University Press, 2005).

18. Kenya Constitutional Conference, Committee on Safeguards, 1st meeting February 16, 1960, Folder: Kenya Constitutional Conference, 1960, Committee on Safeguards, Record of Meetings, CO 822/2363, TNA, PRO. Minutes from the meeting summarized Marshall's comments, so some passages may be paraphrases of Marshall, and not all quotes are verbatim.

19. Proposed Draft Bill of Rights; Kenya Constitutional Conference, Committee on Safeguards, 1st meeting, February 16, 1960. Although Marshall's proposal included voting rights protection, he does not appear to have participated directly in debates over the franchise at the conference. The voting rights section of his proposal does not appear to have been a topic of debate. On the right to a "living wage," see MaryBeth Lipp, "Legislators' Obligation to Support a Living Wage: A Comparative Constitutional Vision of Justice," *Southern California Law Review* 75 (January 2002): 475–528.

20. The property rights clause incorporated the idea that a taking could be for public purposes only through a reference to previously existing statutes establishing property rights and obligations. Proposed Draft Bill of Rights; Marshall, "Reminiscences," 446. On courts in East Africa, see Jennifer A. Widner, *Building the Rule of Law: Francis Nyalai and the Road to Judicial Independence in Africa* (New York: W. W. Norton, 2001). On the role of lawyers in contemporary Africa, see *Access to Justice in Africa and Beyond: Making the Rule of Law a Reality*, ed. Penal Reform International and the Bluhm Legal Clinic of the Northwestern University School of Law, (Louisville, CO: National Institute for Trial Advocacy, 2007).

21. Keith Kyle, *The Politics of the Independence of Kenya* (Hampshire: Palgrave Macmillan, 1999), 152–158; Ogot, "Decisive Years," 64.

22. Kenya Constitutional Conference, Committee on Safeguards, 1st meeting, February 16, 1960.

23. Ibid.

24. Secretary of State for the Colonies to Kenya (O.A.G.), Telegram no. 34, February 18, 1960, Folder: Kenya Constitutional Conference, 1960, Record of Proceedings, CO 822/2354, TNA, PRO; Ian Macleod to Prime Minister, February 20, 1960, PREM 11/3030, New Constitutional Arrangements for Kenya, 1957–60, TNA, PRO.

25. Secretary of State for the Colonies to Kenya (O.A.G.), Telegram no. 34, February 18, 1960; Ian Macleod to Prime Minister, February 20; Kenya (Acting Governor) to Secretary of State for the Colonies, Telegram no. 200, February 19, 1960, Folder: Kenya Constitutional Conference, 1960, Record of Proceedings, CO 822/2354, TNA, PRO.

26. The language of the proposal is follows:

PROPERTY RIGHTS
Suggested Formula for Report

[p. 1] In regard to rights in property, the Conference considered that the Bill of Rights should include provision to the effect:

(i) that private rights in property of all kinds should be respected and should not be compulsorily acquired or extinguished without full and fair compensation;

(ii) that any question or dispute as to the property to be acquired or the compensation to be paid therefor should be open to judicial determination by the Courts at the instance of the person from whom the property is to be acquired, and that such judicial determination should be subject to the normal avenues of judicial appeal in civil cases; and

(iii) that compulsory acquisition of property of any kind should be confined to circumstances in which such acquisition is required for the fulfilment of contractual or other legal obligations attaching to the owner of the property or circumstances in which such acquisition is justified in the general public interest.

[p. 2] The Conference did not however consider that compulsory acquisition of private rights in property would be "justified in the general public interest" if the purpose of the acquisition would be to make the property available to another person or persons for his or their private advantage unless the property is after acquisition to be so applied as to be of service to the public outweighing the resultant hardship to the dispossessed owner.

The Conference considered that the provisions in this regard in the Nigerian constitution would provide a convenient model for adaptation and modification to these requirements.

Right Honourable Viscount Kilmuir [to Macleod?], February 19, 1960, Folder: Kenya Constitutional Conference, 1960, Record of Proceedings, CO 822/2354, Record of Proceedings, TNA, PRO.

27. Ibid.

28. Ian Macleod to Prime Minister, February 20, 1960; Michael Blundell, *So Rough a Wind: The Kenya Memoirs of Sir Michael Blundell* (London: Weidenfeld and Nicolson, 1964), 150–151.

29. Ian Macleod to Prime Minister, February 20, 1960.

30. On the involvement of women in African politics and land reform, see Judith M. Abwunza, *Women's Voices, Women's Power: Dialogues of Resistance from East Africa* (Peterborough, Ontario: Broadview Press, 1997); *Women and Land in Africa: Culture, Religion, and Realizing Women's Rights*, ed. L. Muthoni Wanyeki (Cape Town: David Philip, 2003). On the limits of political change in Kenya, see Godwin Rapando Murunga, "A Critical Look at Kenya's Non-transition to Democracy," *Journal of Third World Studies* (Fall 2002), http://findarticles.com/p/articles/mi_qa3821/is_200210/ai_n9109265/pg_2.

31. Claude Ake, *The Feasibility of Democracy in Africa* (Dakar, Senegal: Council for the Development of Social Science Research in Africa, 2000).

32. Cecelia Marshall, interview by author, July 10, 2007, Washington, DC.

33. Johnnie A. Jones, telephone interview by author, June 19, 2007; *Garner v. Louisiana*, 368 U.S. 157 (1961); *Taking a Seat for Justice: The 1960 Baton Rouge Sit-Ins*, documentary film directed by Rachel L. Emanuel, Southern University Law Center.

34. Jones, interview by author.

35. Jevaillier Jefferson, "The Southern University 16: A Tribute to 16 African-American College Students Whose Sacrifices Improved the Lives of All of Us," *Black Collegian Online*, http://www.black-collegian.com/issues/1stsem04/southern16_2004–1st.shtml.

36. Ibid.

37. Kenneth Johnson, telephone interview by author, June 13, 2007.

38. Ibid.; "Negro Students Arrested Here After Sit-Down," *Morning Advocate* (Baton Rouge, LA), March 29, 1960, p. 1, Folder 11–La v. Hoston, Legal Documents, Box 67, Alexander Pierre Tureaud Papers, Amistad Research Center.

39. Jefferson, "Southern University 16"; "Negro Students Arrested Here After Sit-Down."

40. "Long Suggests That Dissatisfied Negroes Leave," Folder 11–La v. Hoston, Legal Documents, Box 67, Alexander Pierre Tureaud Papers, Amistad Research Center; "Negroes Sit Down Here; 3 Whites Held in Georgia," Folder 11–La v. Hoston, Legal Documents, Box 67, Alexander

Pierre Tureaud Papers, Amistad Research Center; Johnson, interview by author.

41. Thurgood Marshall to Friends of the Committee, March 31, 1960, Folder 2/17, Correspondence, 1960, January 4–March 31, Box 2, Ralph Samuel Harlow Papers. Amistad Research Center; Jack Greenberg, *Crusaders in the Courts: Legal Battles of the Civil Rights Movement*, rev. ed. (New York: Twelve Tables Press, 2004), 290–295.

42. Marshall to Friends of the Committee, March 31, 1960; "Memorandum Report of Lawyers' Conference on Sit-In Demonstrations Held in Washington, D.C. by NAACP Legal Defense and Education Fund, Inc.," circa 1960, Folder 8, *Louisiana v. Mary Briscoe*, Box 67, Alexander Pierre Tureaud Papers, Amistad Research Center. On the history of civil rights legislation during these years, see Hugh Davis Graham, *The Civil Rights Era: Origins and Development of National Policy, 1960–1972* (New York: Oxford University Press, 1990).

43. Marshall to Friends of the Committee, March 31, 1960.

44. Marshall to Friends of the Committee, March 31, 1960; Michael Meltsner, interview by author, May 23, 2007, Boston, Massachusetts.

45. Johnson, interview by author; Brief for the Appellants, *State of Louisiana v. Jannette Hoston, et al.*, Louisiana Supreme Court, filed May 9, 1960, Folder 11–La v. Hoston, Legal Documents, Box 67, Alexander Pierre Tureaud Papers, Amistad Research Center.

46. Jefferson, "Southern University 16"; "'Sit-Downers' Found Guilty; Plan Appeals," *Morning Advocate* (Baton Rouge, LA), June 3, 1960, p. 9-A, Folder 11–La v. Hoston, Legal Documents, Box 67, Alexander Pierre Tureaud Papers, Amistad Research Center; Trial transcript, pp. 9–10, *State of Louisiana v. Jannette Hoston, et al.*, 19th Judicial District, Parish of East Baton Rouge, Folder 11–La v. Hoston, Legal Documents,, Box 67, Alexander Pierre Tureaud Papers, Amistad Research Center.

47. Trial transcript, p. 11, *State of Louisiana v. Jannette Hoston*.

48. *Shelley v. Kraemer*, 334 U.S. 1 (1948); Carol Rose, "*Shelley v. Kraemer*," in *Property Stories*, ed. Gerald Korngold and Andrew P. Morriss (New York: Foundation Press, 2004).

49. *Taylor v. Louisiana*, 370 U.S. 154 (1962); *Garner v. Louisiana*, 368 U.S. 157 (1961); Howard Ball, *A Defiant Life: Thurgood Marshall and the Persistence of Racism in America* (New York: Crown, 1998), 181.

50. *Taylor v. Louisiana*, 370 U.S. 154 (1962); *Garner v. Louisiana*, 368 U.S. 157 (1961). After the passage of the Civil Rights Act of 1964, thousands of pending cases were dismissed. In a creative innovation, the Supreme Court ruled in *Hamm v. City of Rock Hill* (1964) that passage of the Act resulted in the "abatement," or annulment, of these cases, because the student's attempts to integrate private businesses were now protected by federal law. According to the Court, after the passage of the Civil Rights Act, the "public policy of our country is to prohibit discrimination in public accommodations," and so there was "no public interest to be served in the further prosecution of the petitioners." "Constitutional Law: Supreme Court Avoids Constitutional Question of State Action in Sit-In Cases by Extending the Doctrine of Abatement," *Duke Law Journal*, 1965, No. 3 (Summer 1965): 640–648; *Hamm v. Rock Hill*, 379 U.S. 306 (1964).

51. Meltsner, interview by author; Johnson, interview by author; *Taking a Seat for Justice*.

52. Marshall, "Reminiscences," 471. King wrote his world-famous "Letter from Birmingham Jail" on the margins of newspapers, smuggled in and out of the jail. Taylor Branch, *Parting the Waters: America in the King Years, 1954–63* (New York: Simon & Schuster, 1998), 737–745; David Garrow, *Bearing the Cross: Martin Luther King, Jr., and the Southern Christian Leadership Conference* (New York: William Morrow, 1986), 231–286; Thomas F. Jackson, *From Civil Rights to Human Rights: Martin Luther King, Jr., and the Struggle for Economic Justice* (Philadelphia: University of Pennsylvania Press, 2007), 158–160. In spite of their differences, Marshall understood King's importance to the movement and the nation. In the spring of 1968, Marshall cancelled a speaking engagement, insisting that a period of national mourning was in order following the assassination of King. Telephone record, Folder: March–April 1968, Box 32, Supreme Court File, Chronological File, Marshall Papers, LOC.

53. Michael D. Davis and Hunter R. Clark, *Thurgood Marshall: Warrior at the Bar, Rebel on the Bench* (New York: Birch Lane Press, 1992), 214–218.

54. London to Secretary of State, Telegram no. 4038, February 16, 1960, Records of the Department of State, RG 59, Central Decimal File, 1960–63, 745R.00/2–1660, National Archives; London to Secretary of State, Telegram no. 4088, February 18, 1960, Records of the Department of State, RG 59, Central Decimal File, 1960–63,

745R.00/2–1860, National Archives; "Kenya Talks Crisis: Macleod Attempts to Break Deadlock," *Ghana Times*, February 22, 1960, p. 9 (quoting *The Times* [London]); "Kenya Conference: Report to Be Placed Before Parliament Today," *Ghana Times*, February 25, 1960, p. 4.

55. Speech by the Secretary of State for the Colonies, Kenya Constitutional Conference, 1960, February 21, 1960, Folder: Kenya Constitutional Conference, 1960, Memoranda, CO822/2357, TNA, PRO.

56. "Africans Win at Kenya Talks," *Ghana Times*, February 15, 1960, p. 9; Editorial, "Kenya Talks," *Ghana Times*, February 18, 1960, p. 2; London to Secretary of State, Telegram no. 4129, February 22, 1960, Records of the Department of State, RG 59, Central Decimal File, 1960–63, 745R.00/2–2260, National Archives; "Kenya African Leaders Appeal for Calm," *Ghana Times*, February 15, 1960, p. 4.

57. Amconsul Nairobi to Department of State, Despatch no. 402, March 1, 1960, Records of the Department of State, RG 59, Central Decimal File, 1960–63, 745R.00/3–160, National Archives; Kyle, *Politics of the Independence of Kenya*, 63, 81–82, 102–07; Amconsul Nairobi to Department of State, Despatch no. 407, March 3, 1960, Records of the Department of State, RG 59, Central Decimal File, 1960–63, 745R.00/3–360, National Archives.

58. Amconsul Nairobi to Department of State, Despatch no. 344 (January 14, 1960), Records of the Department of State, RG 59, Central Decimal File, 1960–63, 745R.00/1–1460, National Archives; Daniel Branch and Nic Cheeseman, "The Politics of Control in Kenya: Understanding the Bureaucratic-Executive State, 1954–73," *Review of African Political Economy*, 33 (2006): 11–31.

59. Ogot, "Decisive Years," 61; Colin Leys, *Underdevelopment in Kenya: The Political Economy of NeoColonialism 1964–1971* (Berkeley: University of California Press, 1975), 55–56, 62; Kyle, *Politics of the Independence of Kenya*, 118; Amconsul Nairobi to Department of State, Despatch no. 344, January 14, 1960, Records of the Department of State, RG 59, Central Decimal File, 1960–63, 745R.00/1–1460, National Archives; Jomo Kenyatta, *Suffering without Bitterness: The Founding of the Kenya Nation* (Nairobi: East African Publishing House, 1968), 147. On the emergence of political parties, see Jennifer A. Widner, *The Rise of a Party-State in Kenya: From "Harambee!" to "Nyayo!"* (Berkeley: University of California Press, 1992), 30–37; David Throup and Charles Hornsby, *Multi-Party Politics in Kenya* (Athens: Ohio University Press, 1998).

The final 1963 Kenya constitutional provisions on property rights are as follows:

> 19. (1) No property of any description shall be compulsorily taken possession of, and no interest in or right over property of any description shall be compulsorily acquired, except where the following conditions are satisfied, that is to say:
>
> > (a) the taking of possession or acquisition is necessary in the interests of defence, public safety, public order, public morality, public health, town and country planning or the development or utilization of property in such a manner as to promote the public benefit; and
> >
> > (b) the necessity therefor is such as to afford reasonable justification for the causing of any hardship that may result to any person having an interest in or right over the property; and
> >
> > (c) provision is made by a law applicable to that taking of possession or acquisition for the prompt payment of full compensation.
>
> (2) Every person having an interest or right in or over property which is compulsorily taken possession of or whose interest in or right over any property is compulsorily acquired shall have a right of direct access to the Supreme Court for:
>
> > (a) the determination of his interest or right, the legality of the taking of possession or acquisition of the property, interest or right, and the amount of any compensation to which he is entitled; and
> >
> > (b) the purpose of obtaining prompt payment of that compensation: Provided that if Parliament so provides in relation to any matter referred to in paragraph (a) of this subsection the right of access shall be by way of appeal (exercisable as of right at the instance of the person having the right or interest in the property) from a tribunal or authority, other than the Supreme Court, having jurisdiction under any law to determine that matter.
>
> (3) The Chief Justice may make rules with respect to the practice and procedure of the Supreme Court or any other tribunal or authority in relation to the jurisdiction conferred on the Supreme Court by subsection (2) of this section or exercisable by the other tribunal or authority for the purposes of that subsection (including rules with respect to the time within which applications or appeals to the Supreme Court or applications to the other tribunal or authority may be brought).

Constitution, Chapter II (1963) (Kenya), http://www.4cskenyatuitakayo.org/downloads/1963Constitution.pdf.

The particular language of these provisions, and of other specific clauses, was hammered out in ongoing negotiations in Kenya between the 1960 conference and subsequent Lancaster House conferences. The Kenya Constitution has been amended several times since 1963, but substantive changes have not been made to these clauses. Compare with Constitution, Chapter V (1998) (Kenya), http://www.4cskenyatuitakayo.org/downloads/The%20Kenyan%20Current%20Constitution.pdf.

60. "Blundell Heckled by Whites in Kenya," *Ghana Times*, February 26, 1960, p.12.

61. Ibid.

62. Ibid.; Nairobi to Secretary of State, Telegram no. 310, February 29, 1960, Records of the Department of State, RG 59, Central Decimal File, 1960–63, 745R.00/2–2960, National Archives.

63. Thurgood Marshall to Tom Mboya, March 15, 1960, Folder 25.6, General Correspondence with Foreign Countries, Correspondence with USA, vol. 1 (For/1/v. 1) 1960 March–April, Box 25, Tom Mboya Papers, Hoover Institute; Tom Mboya to Thurgood Marshall, March 25, 1960, Folder 25.6, General Correspondence with Foreign Countries, Correspondence with USA, vol. 1 (For/1/v. 1) 1960 March–April, Box 25, Tom Mboya Papers, Hoover Institute.

Chapter 4

1. Jeremy Murray-Brown, *Kenyatta* (New York: E. P. Dutton, 1973); Richard L. Revesz, "Thurgood Marshall's Struggle," 68 *New York University Law Review* 237 (May 1993): 237–263; Berl Bernhard, interview by author, Washington, DC, July 16, 2003.

2. Bernhard, interview by author; Mary L. Dudziak, "Working toward Democracy: Thurgood Marshall and the Constitution of Kenya," *Duke Law Journal* 56 (December 2006): 721–780.

3. Bernhard, interview by author.

4. Carl M. Braur, *John F. Kennedy and the Second Reconstruction* (New York: Columbia University Press, 1977), 205–210, 212–213; Harris Wofford, *Of Kennedys and Kings: Making Sense of the Sixties* (New York: Farrar, Straus, and Giroux, 1980), 124; Taylor Branch, *Parting the Waters: America in the King Years, 1954–63* (New York: Simon & Schuster, 1988), 586–587.

5. Branch, *Parting the Waters*, 586–587; Raymond Arsenault, *Freedom Riders: 1961 and the Struggle for Racial Justice* (New York: Oxford University Press, 2006).

6. Diane McWhorter, *Carry Me Home: Birmingham, Alabama, the Climactic Battle of the Civil Rights Revolution* (New York: Simon & Schuster, 2001), 363–374.

7. Mary L. Dudziak, *Cold War Civil Rights: Race and the Image of American Democracy* (Princeton, NJ: Princeton University Press, 2000), 169–178.

8. Ibid.

9. Mark V. Tushnet, *Making Civil Rights Law: Thurgood Marshall and the Supreme Court, 1956–1961* (New York: Oxford University Press, 1994), 313; Juan Williams, *Thurgood Marshall: American Revolutionary* (New York: Times Books, 1998), 290–296.

10. Howard Ball, *A Defiant Life: Thurgood Marshall and the Persistence of Racism in America* (New York: Crown, 1998), 180–183; Williams, *Thurgood Marshall*, 296–303.

11. Ralph Winter, interview by author, New Haven, Connecticut; Simon E. Sobeloff to Thurgood Marshall, September 12, 1962, Folder: "S" Miscellaneous, Box 6, Court of Appeals, General Correspondence, Thurgood Marshall Papers, LOC; Hugo Black to Thurgood Marshall, November 8, 1962, Folder: "B" Miscellaneous, 1961–63, Box 2, U.S. Court of Appeals, General Correspondence, Thurgood Marshall Papers, LOC; Revesz, "Thurgood Marshall's Struggle."

12. Revesz, "Thurgood Marshall's Struggle"; Ball, *A Defiant Life,* 181–183; Thurgood Marshall, FBI File, Federal Bureau of Investigation Web page, http://foia.fbi.gov/foiaindex/marshall.htm.

13. Cecilia Marshall, interview by author, July 10, 2007, Washington, DC; Mark V. Tushnet, *Making Constitutional Law: Thurgood Marshall and the Supreme Court, 1961–1991* (New York: Oxford University Press, 1997), 5, 13; Williams, *Thurgood Marshall*, 298.

14. Thurgood Marshall Jr., interview by author, June 21, 2007, Washington, DC. Thurgood Marshall Jr. was not aware of his father's St. Louis protest but noted that it was uncharacteristic. His father's usual practice would be to stay and try to work things out.

15. George Dugan, "Marshall Quits Church Session," *New York Times*, October 22, 1964; George Dugan, "New Vista Given to Episcopalians," *New York Times*, October 24, 1964; Gardiner H. Shattuck Jr., *Episcopalians and Race: Civil War to Civil Rights* (Lexington: University Press of Kentucky, 2000), 143–144. On religion and the civil rights movement, see David L. Chappell, *A Stone of Hope: Prophetic Religion*

and the Death of Jim Crow (Chapel Hill: University of North Carolina Press, 2004); Jane Dailey, "Sex, Segregation, and the Sacred after *Brown*," *Journal of American History* 91 (June 2004): 119–144.

16. Shattuck, *Episcopalians and Race*, 145.

17. "Civil Disobedience Resolution Fails in Episcopalian Body," *St. Louis Post-Dispatch*, October 21, 1964, p. 3A; Dugan, "Marshall Quits Church Session"; Dugan, "New Vista Given to Episcopalians"; Shattuck, *Episcopalians and Race*, 145. Reverend Gilett's last name is not legible in the available copy of the *St. Louis Post-Dispatch* article. "Gilett" is my best approximation of the spelling of his name.

18. Dugan, "Marshall Quits Church Session"; "Civil Disobedience and Anarchy," *St. Louis Globe-Democrat*, October 23, 1964, p. 12A; Dugan, "New Vista Given to Episcopalians."

19. Dugan, "New Vista Given to Episcopalians."

20. Cecilia Marshall, interview by author; Dugan, "Marshall Quits Church Session."

21. Diamond to Editor, *Time*, March 18, 1965, Papers of Thurgood Marshall, U.S. Court of Appeals, General Correspondence, Box 6, Folder "P" Miscellaneous, LOC.

22. "The Central Points," *Time*, March 19, 1965; Taylor Branch, *At Canaan's Edge: America in the King Years, 1965–68* (New York: Simon & Schuster, 2006), 44–47; Branch, *Parting the Waters*, 889–890; Taylor Branch, *Pillar of Fire: America in the King Years, 1963–65* (New York: Simon & Schuster, 1998), 434–435.

23. Williams, *Thurgood Marshall*, 316.

24. John Fabian Witt, *Patriots and Cosmopolitans: Hidden Histories of American Law* (Cambridge, MA: Harvard University Press, 2007), 85–154. See also Claude A. Clegg III, *The Price of Liberty: African Americans and the Making of Liberia* (Chapel Hill: University of North Carolina Press, 2004).

25. Chana Kai Lee, *For Freedom's Sake: The Life of Fannie Lou Hamer* (Champaign: University of Illinois Press, 1999), 103–107; Kay Mills, *This Little Light of Mine: The Life of Fannie Lou Hamer* (New York: Plume, 1994), 135–139; Dudziak, *Cold War Civil Rights*, 221–226; Kevin K. Gaines, *American Africans in Ghana: Black Expatriates and the Civil Rights Era* (Chapel Hill: University of North Carolina Press, 2006), 111.

26. Derrick Bell, *And We Are Not Saved: The Elusive Quest for Racial Justice* (New York: Basic Books, 1987). For an exploration of the

longstanding interest of African Americans in international and foreign law, see Henry J. Richardson III, *The Origins of African-American Interests in International Law* (Durham, NC: Carolina Academic Press, 2008). On African Americans and foreign affairs, see Brenda Gayle Plummer, *Rising Wind: Black Americans and U.S. Foreign Affairs, 1935–1960* (Chapel Hill: University of North Carolina Press, 1999); *The African American Voice in U.S. Foreign Policy since World War II*, ed. Michael L. Krenn (New York: Garland, 1999).

27. "Welcome for Famed U.S. Judge," *Daily Nation* (Nairobi), July 11, 1963, p. 1; John Dumonga, "They Call Him...Mr. Civil Rights," *Daily Nation* (Nairobi), July 11, 1963, p. 13.

28. Branch, *Parting the Waters*, 786; McWhorter, *Carry Me Home*, 228–235; Bernhard, interview by author; Schedule of Appointments for Thurgood Marshall and Berl Bernhard, (not dated), Folder: Africa Trip, 1963, Box 1, Papers of Thurgood Marshall, U.S. Court of Appeals, General Correspondence, LOC; "Welcome for Famed U.S. Judge," *Daily Nation*. On the international reaction to Birmingham, see Dudziak, *Cold War Civil Rights*, 169–175.

29. On U.S. propaganda on race, see Dudziak, *Cold War Civil Rights*, 47–56; Penny Von Eschen, *Satchmo Blows Up the World: Jazz Ambassadors Play the Cold War* (Cambridge, MA: Harvard University Press, 2004), 58–61.

30. "Fighting Back (1957–62)," *Eyes on the Prize: America's Civil Rights Years*, PBS, VHS, directed by Judith Vecchione (1986; Alexandria, VA) (transcript online at http://www.pbs.org/wgbh/amex/eyesontheprize/about/pt_102.html); "Winds of Change... 'Take Time,'" *Daily Nation* (Nairobi), July 12, 1963, p. 20.

31. The classic example of this way of characterizing race in America at midcentury is "The Negro in American Life" (undated, circa 1950), folder 503, box 112, series 2, Chester Bowles Papers, Manuscripts and Archives, Yale University. See Dudziak, *Cold War Civil Rights*, 49–56.

32. Thurgood Marshall, Voice of America transcript, p. 4, March 15, 1961, Folder: United States Information Agency, Box 11, U.S. Court of Appeals, Administrative File, Sept. Term 1961, Thurgood Marshall Papers, LOC; Memorandum of Telephone Conversation, n.d., Folder: Africa Trip, 1963, Box 1, U.S. Court of Appeals, General Correspondence, Thurgood Marshall Papers, LOC (regarding June 1963 briefing); Thurgood Marshall to Laurence C. Vass, August 19, 1963, Folder: Africa Trip, 1963, Box 1, U.S. Court of Appeals, General

Correspondence, Thurgood Marshall Papers, LOC; Schedule of
Appointments for The Honorable Thurgood Marshall…and Mr. Berl
Bernhard, Folder: Africa Trip, 1963, Box 1, U.S. Court of Appeals,
General Correspondence, Thurgood Marshall Papers, LOC.

33. Schedule of Appointments for Thurgood Marshall and Berl Bernhard,
Papers of Thurgood Marshall; Berl Bernhard, interview by author.

Studies of Kenyan politics during this period more traditionally focus
on tribalism and the problem of land, especially land rights of white
settlers and of forest fighters once they returned from seclusion. See, for
example, Gary Wasserman, *Politics of Decolonization: Kenya Europeans
and the Land Issue, 1960–1965* (Cambridge: Cambridge University
Press, 1976); B. A. Ogot and W. R. Ochieng', eds., *Decolonization and
Independence in Kenya, 1940–93* (London: James Curry, 1995). These
issues were of great importance in Kenya, but new scholarship also
emphasizes tensions within groups. Daniel Branch, "Loyalism during
the Mau Mau Rebellion in Kenya, 1952–60" (PhD diss., Oxford, 2005).
The status of Asians cuts through Kenyan history and was an important
issue as independence neared, even if some accounts of the Kenyan
independence story do not emphasize it.

34. Berl Bernhard, telephone conversation with author, January 12,
2007; Bernhard, interview by author.

The historical record is unfortunately unclear on one detail: when
Marshall and Kenyatta first met. It is clear from a variety of sources
that they did not meet in 1960 in Kenya. Marshall's next trip to Africa
for independence ceremonies in Sierra Leone was in April 1961, when
Kenyatta was still in detention, so they would not have met in Sierra Leone
or elsewhere in Africa at that time. There is no other record of travel by
Marshall to Africa, travel by Kenyatta to the United States, or travel by
both to another location at the same time, from 1960 until Marshall's trip
to Kenya in July 1963. In oral history interviews and archival sources,
Marshall did not leave a record about this first meeting. Friends, family,
and colleagues have memories of Marshall talking about Kenyatta, but
not of their first meeting. The Legal Defense Fund's papers are, most
unfortunately, still closed to researchers, but Marshall left the LDF in
October 1961, one month after Kenyatta's release, so those papers are
unlikely to contain the answer to this puzzle. Berl Bernhard was present
when Marshall and Kenyatta greeted each other in Kenya in July 1963,
and the greeting was so warm that he remembers it as a greeting of friends
who already knew each other. Because of this, it is possible that there was
an occasion when the two came together before that date. But it is

also the case that Kenyatta and Marshall would have known and admired each other *by reputation*. Kenyatta's importance to Kenya was well known to Marshall, and Kenyatta would have been well informed about Marshall's assistance to his colleagues, especially since his organization mentioned Marshall as a possible advisor for 1962 constitutional talks. It is most likely that the warm greeting in July 1963 was between two people who had been hearing about each other for some time and had greatly looked forward to finally meeting in person.

35. "We'll Lose No Time," *Daily Nation* (Nairobi), January 5, 1963, p. 1; Amconsul Nairobi to Department of State, January 9, 1963, Airgram A-449, 745R.00/1–963, RG 59, Central Decimal File, 1960–63, National Archives; Keith Kyle, *The Politics of the Independence of Kenya* (Hampshire: Palgrave Macmillan, 1999); "Kenyatta Gives an Assurance to Settlers," *Daily Nation* (Nairobi), January 7, 1963, p. 1; Jeremy Murray-Brown, *Kenyatta* (New York: E. P. Dutton, 1972), 368.

36. Chanan Singh, "The Republican Constitution of Kenya: Historical Background and Analysis," *International and Comparative Law Quarterly* 14 (July 1965): 946–967; Kenya Independence Constitution (1963), Chapter I: Citizenship.

37. Memorandum, Committee on Safeguards, Kenya Constitutional Conference, 1960, February 2, 1960, The National Archives of the United Kingdom, TNA, PRO; Kenya Constitutional Conference, 1960, Committee on Safeguards, Record of a Meeting held in the Music Room, Lancaster House, London, S.W.1, on Tuesday, February 16, 1960, at 11.15 A.M., Folder: CO 822/2363, Kenya Constitutional Conference, 1960, Committee on Safeguards, Record of Meetings, TNA, PRO.

38. Wasserman, *Politics of Decolonization*, 119.

39. Donald Rothchild, *Racial Bargaining in Independent Kenya: A Study of Minorities and Decolonization* (London: Oxford University Press, 1973), 326–334. The middle status of Kenyan Asians was reflected in their income levels. The average annual per capita earnings in Kenya in 1960 were 75 pounds sterling for Africans, 480 for Asians, and 1,300 for Europeans. Agehananda Bharati, *The Asians in East Africa: Jayhind and Uhuru* (Chicago: Nelson-Hall, 1972), 105. They were in the middle in population as well. In 1962, there were an estimated 8,365,942 Africans, 176,613 Asians, and 55,759 Europeans; 34,048 were listed as Arabs, and 3,901 as "Other." The majority, nearly 62 percent, of Asians in Kenya had been born in the colony. Dana April Seidenberg, *Uhuru and the Kenya Indians: The Role of a Minority Community in Kenya*

Politics, 1939–1963 (New Delhi: Vikas Publishing House, 1983), 173, 177.

40. Yash Ghai and Dharam P. Ghai, "The Asian Minorities of East and Central Africa (Up to 1971)," Minority Rights Group, Report No. 4 (London, 1971), p. 6.

41. Ibid., 13–14.

42. George Delf, *Asians in East Africa* (London: Oxford University Press, 1963), vii. Although 1962 immigration regulations were enacted in part in an effort to limit black and Asian immigration, Ian R. G. Spencer argues that over the long term, the statute laid the basis for "the making of multi-racial Britain." Ian R. G. Spencer, *British Immigration Policy Since 1939: The Making of Multi-Racial Britain* (London: Routledge, 1997), 129, 154.

43. Yogesh Chadha, *Gandhi: A Life* (New York: John Wiley, 1998), 114, 218; J. M. Nazareth, *Brown Man, Black Country: A Peep into Kenya's Freedom Struggle* (New Delhi: Tidings Publications, 1981), 96–97; Mahmood Mamdani, *From Citizen to Refugee: Uganda Asians Come to Britain* (London: Francis Pinter, 1973), 13–14, 17. Mamdani writes about Uganda, where tension over the role of Asians peaked with Idi Amin's expulsion of Asians from the country in 1972. Such extreme anti-Asian policy was never adopted in Kenya. The earlier histories of Asian settlement in both countries, however, bore similarities.

44. Dharam P. Ghai and Yash P. Ghai, "Asians in East Africa: Problems and Prospects," *Journal of Modern African Studies*, 3 (May 1965): 35.

45. Seidenberg, *Uhuru and the Kenya Indians*, 164.

46. Ibid., 161, quoting *East African Standard*, March 25, 1960, p. 2.

47. Ogot and Ochieng', *Decolonization and Independence in Kenya*, 48–79; Jennifer Widner, *The Rise of the Party-State in Kenya: From "Harambee!" to "Nyayo!"* (Berkeley: University of California Press, 1992), 30–34.

48. "I Don't Give a Damn, Says Keen," *Daily Nation* (Nairobi), February 16, 1963; "I'm Only After the Fence-Sitters—Keen," *Daily Nation* (Nairobi), February 22, 1963.

49. N. S. Toofan, "The Asians and the Land," *Daily Nation* (Nairobi), March 29, 1963, p. 6.

50. "Inquiry into Threats," *Daily Nation* (Nairobi), February 25, 1963; "Asians Join Up—Keen," *Daily Nation* (Nairobi), February 25, 1963, p. 1.

51. "Kampala Picket to Stay on 'Till Asian Quits," *Daily Nation* (Nairobi), March 20, 1963, p. 2.

52. "Mboya Assurance to Asians," *Daily Nation* (Nairobi), April 18, 1963, p. 5.

53. "Kenyatta Welcomes Asians," *Daily Nation* (Nairobi), May 3, 1963, p. 20; "KANU Leader's Assurance to Non-Africans," *Daily Nation* (Nairobi), May 6, 1963; "Intimidation of Asians Denied," *Daily Nation,* May 7, 1963, p. 4. See also Ogot and Ochieng', *Decolonization and Independence in Kenya,* 75–76.

54. Jomo Kenyatta, *Suffering without Bitterness: The Founding of the Kenya Nation* (Nairobi: East African Publishing House, 1969), 149, 168, 211 (quoting *Kenya Weekly News,* 1961); Murray-Brown, *Kenyatta,* 368; Ogot & Ochieng', *Decolonization and Independence in Kenya,* 83–85; Widner, *Rise of the Party-State,* 53–55.

55. Bernhard, interview by author (emphasis in original).

56. Ibid. (emphasis in original).

57. Ibid. (emphasis in original).

58. Ibid. The sharpest critics were not in the Kenyan government. Instead, when speaking at a high school, they got "some really blunt questions."

59. Gaines, *American Africans in Ghana,* 111–118, 132. On Pauli Murray, see Glenda Elizabeth Gilmore, *Defying Dixie: The Radical Roots of Civil Rights, 1919–1950* (New York: W. W. Norton, 2008); Paul L. Edenfield, "The American Heartbreak: A Biographical Sketch of Pauli Murray" (2000), Women's Legal History Biography Project, Stanford Law School, http://womenslegalhistory.stanford.edu/papers/MurrayP-Edenfield00.pdf.

60. Bernhard, interview by author.

61. Ibid.; Thurgood Marshall, "The Reminiscences of Thurgood Marshall," Columbia Oral History Research Office, 1977, reprinted in *Thurgood Marshall: His Speeches, Writings, Arguments, Opinions, and Remembrances,* ed. Mark V. Tushnet (Chicago: Lawrence Hill, 2001), 444–448; Williams, *Thurgood Marshall,* 307–309.

62. Mr. Crockett to G. Mennen Williams, October 11, 1963, RG 59, Bureau of African Affairs, Office of Eastern and Southern African Affairs, Country Files, 1951–1965, Box 1, Folder: POL—Political Affairs & Rel. Kenya, Independence—Ceremonial & Social Affairs, National Archives; Kyle, *Politics of the Independence of Kenya,* 199; Mougo Nyaggah, "Asians in East Africa: The Case of Kenya," *Journal of African Studies* 1 (1974): 204–233; Donald Rothchild, "Kenya's Minorities and the African Crisis over Citizenship," *Race* 9 (April 1968):

421–437; Robert M. Maxom, "Social and Cultural Changes," in Ogot and Ochieng', *Decolonization and Independence in Kenya*, 110–147; Marshall, "Reminiscences," 447; Donald Rothchild, *Racial Bargaining in Independent Kenya: A Study of Minorities and Decolonization* (London: Oxford University Press, 1973), 316–335. On Asians in Uganda, see Mahmood Mamdani, *From Citizen to Refugee; Expulsion of a Minority: Essays on Ugandan Asians*, ed. Michael Twaddle (London: The Athone Press, 1975).

63. For an exploration of creating political space for constitutionalism to work, see Jennifer A. Widner, *Building the Rule of Law: Francis Nyalali and the Road to Judicial Independence in Africa* (New York: W. W. Norton, 2001), discussing Tanzanian chief justice Francis Nyalali's efforts to create a political constituency supportive of judicial review in Tanzania. On contemporary constitutional politics in Kenya, see Makau Mutua, *Kenya's Quest for Democracy: Taming Leviathan* (Boulder: Lynne Rienner, 2008).

The conventional argument about constitutionalism in sub-Saharan Africa is that the region is characterized by "constitutions without constitutionalism." H. W. O. Okoth-Ogendo, "Constitutions without Constitutionalism: Reflections on an African Political Paradox," in *Constitutionalism and Democracy: Transitions in the Contemporary World*, ed. Douglas Greenberg, Stanley N. Katz, Steven C. Wheatley, and Melanie Beth Oliviero (New York: Oxford University Press, 1993). H. Kwasi Prempeh critiques Okoth-Ogendo and argues that previous scholarship has focused too heavily on the role of judicial review. "Marbury in Africa: Judicial Review and the Challenge of Constitutionalism in Contemporary Africa," *Tulane Law Review* 80 (March 2006): 1239–1324. In "Working toward Democracy," I argue that constitutionalism functioned in Kenya during the independence era not by leading to the creation of an American-style iconic constitution but by creating a peaceful arena for conflict during a difficult political transition. Constitutions and constitutional politics can have an important impact during distinct historical moments, even when the result is not an iconic document that is thought to constrain politics from that day forward.

64. Bernhard, interview by author; Marshall, "Reminiscences," 447–448.

65. Bernhard, interview by author.

66. G. Mennen Williams, Arrival Statement at Nairobi, Kenya, December 7, 1963, Folder: African Trip: December 5–15, 1963, Box 17-N, Non-Gubernatorial Papers, Papers of G. Mennen Williams, Bentley Historical Library; Dudziak, *Cold War Civil Rights*, 200, 205–207.

67. Dudziak, *Cold War Civil Rights*, 200, 205–207.

68.   G. Mennen Williams, Arrival Statement at Nairobi, Kenya, December 7, 1963.

Chapter 5

1.   "Hough Riots," Ohio Historical Society Web site, http://www
.ohiohistorycentral.org/entry.php?rec=1597 (this site is based on primary
sources at the Ohio Historical Society); Kerner Commission, *Report of the
National Advisory Commission on Civil Disorders* (Washington, DC: U.S.
Government Printing Office, 1968); Taylor Branch, *At Canaan's Edge:
America in the King Years, 1965–68* (New York: Simon & Schuster, 2006).

2.   California Governor's Commission on Watts, McCone Commission
Report, December 2, 1965 (Los Angeles: Kimtex Corp., 1965), 11A;
Mark Baldassare, ed., *The Los Angeles Riots: Lessons for the Urban
Future* (Boulder, CO: Westview Press, 1994); Gerald Horne, *Fire This
Time: The Watts Uprising and the 1960s* (Charlottesville: University
Press of Virginia, 1995), 53–115.

3.   Michael W. Flamm, *Law and Order: Street Crime, Civil Unrest,
and the Crisis of Liberalism in the 1960s* (New York: Columbia
University Press, 2005), 61–66.

4.   Thurgood Marshall to Lyndon B. Johnson, January 14, 1966,
Folder: White House, 1965–67, Box 28, Papers of Thurgood Marshall,
U.S. Solicitor General File, LOC; 61–66; Mark V. Tushnet, *Making
Constitutional Law: Thurgood Marshall and the Supreme Court, 1961–
1991* (New York: Oxford University Press, 1997), 18–20; Juan Williams,
Thurgood Marshall: American Revolutionary (New York: Times Books,
1998), 317–325.

5.   Wallace Terry to Richard M. Clurman, November 25, 1966,
U.S. Solicitor General File, Box 28, Folder: General Correspondence,
1966–67, LOC.

6.   Peniel E. Joseph, *Waiting 'Til the Midnight Hour: A Narrative
History of Black Power in America* (New York: Henry Holt, 2006),
141–142. According to Harold Cruse, Adam Clayton Powell originated
the slogan "Black Power" at a Chicago rally in May 1965 and then
elaborated on it in a Howard University commencement speech in May
1966. Harold Cruse, *The Crisis of the Negro Intellectual* (New York:
William Morrow, 1967), 545. On Meredith, see Branch, *At Canaan's
Edge*, 475–476. On the internationalism of Black Power and the African
American left, see Nikhil Pal Singh, *Black Is a Country: Race and*

the Unfinished Struggle for Democracy (Cambridge, MA: Harvard University Press, 2004), 186–193.

7. Joseph, *Waiting 'Til the Midnight Hour*, 141–142.

8. Ibid., 144.

9. Cruse, *Crisis of the Negro Intellectual*, 544, 555, 565; Peniel E. Joseph, "Rethinking the Crisis of the Negro Intellectual: Harold Cruse, Black Nationalism and the Black Power Movement," in *Harold Cruse's The Crisis of the Negro Intellectual Reconsidered*, ed. Jerry Watts (New York: Routledge, 2004), 242. In spite of Cruse's critique, his book *The Crisis of the Negro Intellectual* became, in Joseph's words, "the unofficial bible of black nationalists." Joseph, "Rethinking the Crisis of the Negro Intellectual."

10. Joseph, *Waiting 'Til the Midnight Hour*, 146; Robert L. Allen, *Black Awakening in Capitalist America: An Analytic History* (New York: Doubleday, 1969), 55.

11. "Alphas Take Stand on 'Black Power,'" August 26, 1966, *St. Louis Argus*, p. 4A. On Alpha Phi Alpha, see Charles H. Wesley, *The History of Alpha Phi Alpha: A Development in College Life*, 12th ed. (Chicago: Foundation, 1979); Herman "Skip" Mason, *The Talented Tenth: The Founders and Presidents of Alpha*, 2nd ed. (Jonesboro, AR: FOUR-G, 1999). On black fraternal organizations and civil rights, see Theda Skocpol, Ariane Liazos, and Marshall Ganz, *What a Mighty Power We Can Be: African American Fraternal Groups and the Struggle for Racial Equality* (Princeton, NJ: Princeton University Press, 2006).

12. "Marshall Tells Negro Group to Take Over Job in Ghettos," *St. Louis Post-Dispatch*, August 16, 1966, p. 14A; *Dred Scott v. Sandford*, 19 How. 393 (1857); Don E. Ferenbacher, *The Dred Scott Case: Its Significance in American Law and Politics* (New York: Oxford University Press, 1978); Paul Finkelman, *Dred Scott v. Sandford: A Brief History with Documents* (Boston: Bedford Books, 1997); Mark Graber, *Dred Scott and the Problem of Constitutional Evil* (Cambridge, UK: Cambridge University Press, 2006).

13. Al Delugach, "Marshall Lashes Out at Race Riots," *St. Louis Globe-Democrat*, August 17, 1966, p. 10A.

14. "Marshall Tells Negro Group to Take Over Job in Ghettos," *St. Louis Post-Dispatch*. (Insert in quote in original.)

15. Timothy Tyson, *Radio Free Dixie: Robert F. Williams and the Roots of Black Power* (Chapel Hill: University of North Carolina Press,

1999), 298; *Independent Lens: Negroes with Guns: Robert Williams and Black Power,* PBS Web site: http://www.pbs.org/independentlens/ negroeswithguns/rob.html (quote is from 1959); Lance Hill, *The Deacons for Defense: Armed Resistance and the Civil Rights Movement,* (Chapel Hill: University of North Carolina Press, 2004), 45; William Van Deburg, *New Day in Babylon: The Black Power Movement and American Culture* (Chicago: University of Chicago Press, 1992), 22–23.

16. Thurgood Marshall, "The Gestapo in Detroit" (1943), in *Supreme Justice: Speeches and Writings: Thurgood Marshall,* ed. J. Clay Smith (Philadelphia: University of Pennsylvania Press, 2003), 9–10.

17. Thurgood Marshall, FBI File, Federal Bureau of Investigation Web page, http://foia.fbi.gov/foiaindex/marshall.htm.

18. McCone Commission Report, 15A-29A; Horne, *Fire This Time,* 343. See also Thomas J. Sugrue, *Origins of the Urban Crisis: Race and Inequality in Postwar Detroit* (Princeton, NJ: Princeton University Press, 1996), 260–261.

19. "Marshall Warns Negro Militants," *New York Times,* May 6, 1969, p. 32; ABC Evening News for Monday, May 05, 1969, Headline: Campus Unrest / Marshall, Vanderbilt Television News Archive, http:// tvnews.vanderbilt.edu/diglib-fulldisplay.pl?SID=20080127435150146& code=tvn&RC=5508&Row=21; NBC Evening News for Monday, May 05, 1969, Headline: Campus Unrest / Marshall, Vanderbilt Television News Archive, http://tvnews.vanderbilt.edu/diglib-fulldisplay.pl?SID= 20080127435150146&code=tvn&RC=445888&Row=23.

20. "Marshall Warns Negro Militants," *New York Times.*

21. Joseph, *Waiting 'Til the Midnight Hour,* 132–173; Taylor Branch, *At Canaan's Edge: America in the King Years, 1965–68* (New York: Simon & Schuster, 2006), 532–533.

22. "Address of Solicitor General Thurgood Marshall," *To Secure These Rights,* June 1, 1966, 52–53. Marshall repeated these words in his address in 1987 on the bicentennial of the U.S. Constitution. Thurgood Marshall, "Reflections on the Bicentennial of the United States Constitution," in *Thurgood Marshall: His Speeches, Writings, Arguments, Opinions, and Remembrances,* ed. Mark V. Tushnet (Chicago: Lawrence Hill, 2001), 284.

23. Jeremy Murray-Brown, *Kenyatta* (New York: E. P. Dutton, 1973), 372–374.

24. Ibid., 374–375; Benjamin Read to McGeorge Bundy, November 11, 1964, Folder: National Security File, Special Head of State

Correspondence File, Kenya—Kenyatta Correspondence, National
Security File, Special Head of State Correspondence, Box 32, LBJ
Library; Central Intelligence Agency, "Special Report: Leftist Activity
in Kenya," July 31, 1974, Folder: Kenya, vol. 1, 11/63–11/68, Box 91,
National Security File, Country File, LBJ Library.

25. Jomo Kenyatta to Lyndon B. Johnson, May 8, 1965, Folder:
National Security File, Special Head of State Correspondence File,
Kenya, Special Head of State Correspondence, 7/1/66–1/20/69, Box
32, National Security File, LBJ Library; Jomo Kenyatta to Lyndon
B. Johnson, May 27, 1965, Folder: National Security File, Special
Head of State Correspondence File, Kenya, Special Head of State
Correspondence, 7/1/66–1/20/69, Box 32, National Security File,
LBJ Library. On Selma, see Taylor Branch, *Pillar of Fire: America in
the King Years, 1963–65* (New York: Simon & Schuster, 1998),
560–568.

26. Lyndon B. Johnson to Jomo Kenyatta, June 7, 1966, Folder:
National Security File, Special Head of State Correspondence File,
Kenya, 7/1/66–1/20/69, Box 32, National Security File, Special Head
of State Correspondence, LBJ Library; Murray-Brown, *Kenyatta*, 377;
Donald Rothchild, *Racial Bargaining in Independent Kenya: A Study of
Minorities and Decolonization* (London: Oxford University Press, 1973),
316–335.

27. Murray-Brown, *Kenyatta*, 376.

28. Odinga Oginga, *Not Yet Uhuru: The Autobiography of Oginga
Odinga* (New York: Hill and Wang, 1967), 155; David W. Throup and
Charles Hornsby, *Multi-Party Politics in Kenya* (Oxford: James Curry,
1998), 13–15.

29. SecState to AmEmbassy Nairobi, Telegram 790, January 1968,
Folder: Kenya, vol. I, Cables [1 of 2], 11/63–11/68, Box 91, National
Security File, Country File, Kenya, LBJ Library; AmEmbassy Nairobi
to White House, Telegram 4231, January 1968, Folder: Kenya, vol. I,
Cables [1 of 2], 11/63–11/68, Box 91, National Security File, Country
File, Kenya, LBJ Library.

30. Joseph, *Waiting 'Til the Midnight Hour*, 216–218, 240, 258–260,
283–293; Ron Walters, *Pan Africanism in the Modern Diaspora:
An Analysis of Modern Afrocentric Political Movements* (Detroit:
Wayne State University Press, 1997), 67–68; Cedric Johnson,
*Revolutionaries to Race Leaders: Black Power and the Making of
African American Politics* (Minneapolis: University of Minnesota Press,
2007); William Van Deburg, *New Day in Babylon: The Black Power*

Movement and American Culture (Chicago: University of Chicago Press, 1992), 192–247.

31. Kevin K. Gaines, *African Americans in Ghana: Black Expatriates and the Civil Rights Era* (Chapel Hill: University of North Carolina Press, 2006), 234–243; Kenneth Ingham, *Obote: A Political Biography* (London: Routledge, 1994); James Meriwether, *Proudly We Can Be Africans: Black Americans and Africa, 1935–1961* (Chapel Hill: University of North Carolina Press, 2002), 241–245.

32. David Goldsworthy, *Tom Mboya: The Man Kenya Wanted to Forget* (Nairobi: Heineman, 1982), 274–275.

33. "Tom Mboya under Fire in Harlem," *Pittsburgh Courier*, April 5, 1969, p. 2. On Mboya's political fortunes, see Goldsworthy, *Tom Mboya*, 267–274.

34. "Mboya in Harlem," *Chicago Defender*, March 31, 1969; "Mboya under Fire," *Pittsburgh Courier*; Tom Mboya, "Africa and the Black American: An African Viewpoint" (manuscript), 1969, pp. 1–2, Folder 30.2, Public Affairs, Press Statements, vol. 7 (PS/7), Box 30, Mboya Papers, Hoover Institute.

35. "Mboya under Fire," *Pittsburgh Courier*; "Mboya in Harlem," *Chicago Defender*.

36. Mboya, "Africa and the Black American," 10–11.

37. Ibid., 3–4; Tom Mboya to John A. Morsell, May 23, 1969, Folder 30.1, Public Affairs, Press Statements, vol. 6 (PS/6), Box 30, Mboya Papers, Hoover Institute.

38. Mboya, "Africa and the Black American," 7–14.

39. Ibid., 16. Rustin himself addressed the attack on Mboya in a letter to the editor of the *New York Times*. Bayard Rustin, "Blacks and Africa," March 31, 1969 (Letter to the Editor, *New York Times*), Folder 30.1, Public Affairs, Press Statements, vol. 6 (PS/6), Box 30, Mboya Papers, Hoover Institute.

40. Tom Mboya to John A. Morsell, May 23, 1969, Folder 30.1, Public Affairs, Press Statements, vol. 6 (PS/6), Box 30, Mboya Papers, Hoover Institute (quoting Martin Luther King Jr., *Where Do We Go from Here: Chaos or Community?* (New York: Harper and Row, 1967).

41. Ibid.

42. Tom Mboya to H.E. D. T. arap Moi and J. Osogo, April 1, 1969, Folder 26.2, General Correspondence with Foreign Countries,

Correspondence with USA, vol. 3 (FOR/1/v. 3), Box 26, Mboya Papers, Hoover Institute.

43. Goldsworthy, *Tom Mboya*, 280 (quoting *East African Standard*, July 7, 1969).

44. Ibid., 281–282.

45. Ibid., 284–285.

46. Berl Bernhard, interview by author, July 16, 2003, Washington, DC. On Marshall's speculation about Moi and how that reflects on political intrigue in Kenya, I am grateful for suggestions and advice from David Anderson and others attending my lecture at the Rothmere Institute, Oxford University, 2007. On Kenya under Moi's presidency, see B. A. Ogot, "The Politics of Populism," in *Decolonization and Independence in Kenya, 1940–98*, ed. B. A. Ogot and W. R. Ochieng' (London: James Curry, 1995), 191–213.

47. Robert L. Allen, *Black Awakening in Capitalist America* (New York: Doubleday, 1969), 108.

48. *Walker v. City of Birmingham*, 388 U.S. 307 (1967). While incarcerated, King wrote his influential "Letter from Birmingham Jail." Taylor Branch, *Parting the Waters: America in the King Years, 1954–63* (New York: Simon & Schuster, 1988), 727, 738–740.

49. *Walker*, 388 U.S. at 320–321.

50. *Walker*, 388 U.S. at 347 (Brennan, J., dissenting).

51. *Walker*, 388 U.S. 307; U.S. Senate, Supreme Court Nominations, present–1789, http://www.senate.gov/pagelayout/reference/nominations/Nominations.htm; David Alistair Yalof, *Pursuit of Justices: Presidential Politics and the Selection of Supreme Court Nominees* (Chicago: University of Chicago Press, 1999), 86–90. On *Walker* and Marshall's confirmation, see Stephen L. Carter, "The Confirmation Mess, Revisited," *Northwestern University Law Review* 84 (Spring/Summer 1990): 962–975.

52. "Dr. King's Conviction," *Washington Evening Star*, June 14, 1967, reprinted in *Supreme Court's Opinion in Martin Luther King Contempt-of-Court Case*, 90th Cong., 1st Sess., *Congressional Record*, vol. 113, pt. 12 (June 15, 1967): 16057. See also "Dr. King's Conviction," *Washington Evening Star*, June 14, 1967, reprinted in *Nomination of Thurgood Marshall to Be Associate Justice of the U.S. Supreme Court*, 90th Cong., 1st Sess., *Congressional Record*, vol. 113, pt. 18 (August 30, 1967):

24614–24615; *Nomination of Thurgood Marshall to Be Associate Justice of the U.S. Supreme Court* (remarks of Sen. Ervin), 90th Cong., 1st Sess., *Congressional Record*, vol. 113, pt. 18 (August 30, 1967): 24589; Clayton Fritchey, "Marshall Appointment to Court Greeted Quietly," *Washington Evening Star*, June 23, 1967, reprinted in *Nomination of Thurgood Marshall to Be Associate Justice of the U.S. Supreme Court*, 90th Cong., 1st Sess., *Congressional Record*, vol. 113, pt. 18 (August 30, 1967): 24616; James J. Kirkpatrick, "Marshall's Appointment Upsets Court Balance," *Washington Evening Star*, June 18, 1967, reprinted in *Nomination of Thurgood Marshall to Be Associate Justice of the U.S. Supreme Court*, 90th Cong., 1st Sess., *Congressional Record*, vol. 113, pt. 18 (August 30, 1967): 24616. Kirkpatrick predicted that Marshall would be "a more congenial Fortas, a less truculent Goldberg, a more disarming Brennan. He said, "The appointment is a great tribute to Marshall's skill and industry.... No critic would wish to take away from the heartwarming success story that came to its climax Tuesday. All the same, in any conservative view of the workings of the court, the nomination...was bad news." Kirkpatrick, "Marshall's Appointment Upsets Court Balance."

53. *The Communist Associations of Thurgood Marshall*, 90th Cong., 1st Sess., *Congressional Record*, vol. 113, pt. 12 (June 15, 1967): 15967. Rarick included in the record details of what he considered to be Marshall's "Communist front" activities.

54. *Nomination of Thurgood Marshall to Be Associate Justice of the U.S. Supreme Court* (remarks of Sen. Holland), 90th Cong., 1st Sess., *Congressional Record*, vol. 113, pt. 18 (August 30, 1967): 24636; *Nomination of Thurgood Marshall to Be Associate Justice of the U.S. Supreme Court* (remarks of Sen. Byrd), 90th Cong., 1st Sess., *Congressional Record*, vol. 113, pt. 18 (August 30, 1967): 24656; Yalof, *Pursuit of Justices*, 89. On the importance of "law and order" to the turn in American politics in the late 1960s, see Flamm, *Law and Order*, 40–45.

Ironically Ramsey Clark, who became attorney general in 1967, predicted to the president that Marshall would be very liberal on civil rights, but "on crime and other cases, he reflects the older generation's attitude." According to David Yalof, President Johnson appointed Clark to be attorney general in order to open up a seat for Marshall on the Court. Out of concern about conflict of interest, when Clark's nomination was announced, his father, Supreme Court Justice Tom

Clark, immediately announced his retirement. Yalof, *Pursuit of Justice*, 88–89.

55. *Thurgood Marshall—President Johnson's Excellent Choice for the Supreme Court,* 90th Cong., 1st Sess., *Congressional Record,* vol. 113, pt. 13 (June 27, 1967): 17506; *Nomination of Thurgood Marshall to Be Associate Justice of the U.S. Supreme Court* (remarks of Sen. Kucel), 90th Cong., 1st Sess., *Congressional Record,* vol. 113, pt. 18 (August 30, 1967): 24647. See, for example, *Nomination of Thurgood Marshall to Be Associate Justice of the U.S. Supreme Court* (remarks of Sen. Hart), 90th Cong., 1st Sess., *Congressional Record,* vol. 113, pt. 18 (August 30, 1967): 24639 (suggesting that Marshall was not nominated because of his race). The *Washington Evening Star* echoed the progress rhetoric, suggesting that it was "a measure of our national progress toward maturity, and cause for modest gratification" that Marshall's nomination was not a source of great controversy, and instead "has produced scarcely a ripple of excitement." "Mr. Marshall's Nomination," *Washington Evening Star,* June 15, 1967, reprinted in *Nomination of Thurgood Marshall to the U.S. Supreme Court,* 90th Cong., 1st Sess., *Congressional Record,* vol. 113, pt. 12 (June 16, 1967): 16138.

56. Thurgood Marshall, "Remembering Lyndon Johnson and the Civil Rights Struggle" (oral history interview, Lyndon Baines Johnson Library, 1969), reprinted in *Thurgood Marshall, Supreme Justice: Speeches and Writings,* ed. J. Clay Smith (Philadelphia: University of Pennsylvania Press, 2003), 197; Yalof, *Pursuit of Justices,* 86–90

57. *Thurgood Marshall to the Supreme Court—A Historic Appointment* (remarks of Sen. Mansfield), 90th Cong., 1st Sess., *Congressional Record,* vol. 113, pt. 18 (August 30, 1967): 24657.

58. Cecilia Marshall, interview by author; Thomas F. Jackson, *From Civil Rights to Human Rights: Martin Luther King, Jr., and the Struggle for Economic Justice* (Philadelphia: University of Pennsylvania Press, 2007), 312.

59. Amembassy Nairobi to SecState WashDC, April 6, 1968, Telegram no. 206, Appointments File [Diary Backup], April 4–11, 1968, Death of Martin Luther King and Riots in Major Cities IV [State Department Telegrams], Box 96, The President's Appointment File [Diary Backup], LBJ Library; Amconsul Kaduna to SecState WashDC, April 6, 1968, Telegram no. 416, Appointments File [Diary Backup], April 4–11, 1968, Death of Martin Luther King and Riots in Major Cities IV, [State

Department Telegrams], Box 96, The President's Appointment File [Diary Backup], LBJ Library.

60. Lyndon Baines Johnson, "Address to the Nation upon Proclaiming a Day of Mourning," April 5, 1968, Papers of the President: Lyndon Baines Johnson, John T. Woolley and Gerhard Peters, *The American Presidency Project* (Santa Barbara, CA: University of California), Gerhard Peters (database), http://www.presidency.ucsb.edu/ws/?pid=28783; Press Conference #1196-A, At the White House with George Christiansen, April 5, 1968, Box 95, The President's Appointment File [Diary Backup], LBJ Library.

61. Amembassy Nairobi to SecState WashDC, April 6, 1968, Telegram no. 206.

Epilogue

1. Thomas J. Sugrue, *Origins of the Urban Crisis: Race and Inequality in Postwar Detroit* (Princeton, NJ: Princeton University Press, 1966), 267–268; William Julius Wilson, *When Work Disappears: The World of the New Urban Poor* (New York: Knopf, 1966), 29–30; Douglas G. Massey and Nancy Denton, *American Apartheid: Segregation and the Making of the Underclass* (Cambridge, MA: Harvard University Press, 1993), 160.

2. *Swann v. Charlotte-Mecklenburg Board of Education*, 402 U.S. 1 (1971); Davison M. Douglas, *Reading, Writing, and Race: The Desegregation of the Charlotte Schools* (Chapel Hill: University of North Carolina Press, 1995); *Milliken v. Bradley*, 418 U.S. 717 (1974). The *Milliken* case was handled by the NAACP, not the NAACP Legal Defense Fund.

3. *Milliken*, 418 U.S. at 741.

4. Ibid., 744–745.

5. Warren Weaver Jr., "Court Puts a Stone Wall before the School Bus," *New York Times*, July 28, 1974; William Safire, *Before the Fall: An Inside View of the Pre-Watergate White House* (New York: Doubleday, 1975), 485; Robert Reingold, "Impact of the Ruling," *New York Times*, July 26, 1974; Warren Weaver Jr., "Decision by 5 to 4: Curb on Detroit Area Busing Stirs Bitter Marshall Dissent," *New York Times*, July 26, 1974, p. 17; Lawrence M. Friedman, *American Law in the Twentieth Century* (New Haven, CT: Yale University Press, 2002), 296.

6. Weaver, "Decision by 5 to 4," 1.

7. Dissent, Read in Court by Justice Marshall, Nos. 73–434, 73–435, and 73–346 [*sic*], *Milliken v. Bradley,* July 25, 1974, Folder: 73–434 *Milliken v. Bradley,* 73–435, *Allen Park Pub. Schools v. Bradley* (1 of 2), Box 131, Papers of Thurgood Marshall, Supreme Court Papers, Case File, OT 1973, Opinions, Appellate, LOC.

8. *San Antonio Independent School District v. Rodriguez,* 411 U.S. 1 (1973); William Coleman, interview by author, May 18, 2004, Washington, DC; William Taylor, interview by author, May 18, 2004, Washington, DC. On the Court's trajectory, see Mark V. Tushnet, *A Court Divided: The Rehnquist Court and the Future of Constitutional Law* (New York: W. W. Norton, 2005); David M. O'Brien, *Storm Center: The Supreme Court in American Politics,* 7th ed. (New York: W. W. Norton, 2005).

9. Robert Reinhold, "Impact of the Ruling," *New York Times,* July 26, 1974; Derrick Bell to Thurgood Marshall, October 2, 1969, Folder: Correspondence, 1958–May 1993; Correspondence, 1950s–1969; Series I, Derrick Bell Paper, NYU Archive; Derrick A. Bell Jr., "Serving Two Masters: Integration Ideals and Client Interests in School Desegregation Litigation," *Yale Law Journal* 85 (March 1976): 470–516. See also Nathaniel R. Jones, "School Desegregation Litigation," *Yale Law Journal* 85 (December 1976): 378–382; Derrick A. Bell Jr., "School Desegregation: Author's Reply," *Yale Law Journal* 86 (December 1976): 382–384. See also *The Derrick Bell Reader,* ed. Richard Delgado and Jean Stefancic (New York: New York University Press, 2005).

On views of African American parents, see Tomiko Brown-Nagin, "Race as Identity Caricature: A Local Legal History Lesson in the Salience of Intraracial Conflict," *University of Pennsylvania Law Review* 151 (June 2003): 1913–1976; Mark V. Tushnet, *The NAACP's Legal Strategy against Segregated Education, 1925–1950* (Chapel Hill: University of North Carolina Press, 1987), 139–140.

10. David Alistair Yalof, *Pursuit of Justices: Presidential Politics and the Selection of Supreme Court Nominees* (Chicago: University of Chicago Press, 1999), 90–96; Laura Kalman, *Abe Fortas* (New Haven: Yale University Press), 327, 331–332; Bruce Allen Murphy, *Fortas: The Rise and Ruin of a Supreme Court Justice* (New York: William Morrow, 1988), 283, 286–287.

11. Yalof, *Pursuit of Justices,* 90–132; Mark Kurlansky, *1968: The Year That Rocked the World* (New York: Ballantine Books, 2003).

12. Kerner Commission, *Report of the National Advisory Commission on Civil Disorders* (Washington: U.S. Government Printing Office,

1968). See also Sugrue, *Origins of the Urban Crisis*, 266; William Julius Wilson, *The Truly Disadvantaged: The Inner City, the Underclass and Public Policy* (Chicago: University of Chicago Press, 1987), 46–49; Massey and Denton, *American Apartheid*, 16.

13. *Report of the National Advisory Commission on Civil Disorders*, 7.

14. John Hope Franklin, telephone interview by author, June 1, 2007; John Hope Franklin, *Mirror to America: The Autobiography of John Hope Franklin* (New York: Farrar, Straus, and Giroux, 2005), 156–160; *Regents of the University of California v. Bakke*, 438 U.S. 265 (1978).

15. *Bakke*, 438 U.S. 387–402.

16. Franklin, interview by author; Thurgood Marshall, "Reflections on the Bicentennial of the United States Constitution," *Harvard Law Review* 101 (1987): 1–5.

17. Marshall, "Reflections on the Bicentennial of the United States Constitution."

18. Thurgood Marshall, "The Reminiscences of Thurgood Marshall," Columbia Oral History Research Office, 1977, reprinted in *Thurgood Marshall: His Speeches, Writings, Arguments, Opinions and Remembrances*, ed. Mark V. Tushnet (Chicago: Lawrence Hill, 2001), 446.

19. Thurgood Marshall Jr., interview by author, June 21, 2007, Washington, DC.

20. Thurgood Marshall, "Civil Rights Enforcement and the Supreme Court's Docket, Remarks at the Second Circuit Judicial Conference," September 8, 1978, in Tushnet, *Thurgood Marshall*, 174.

21. B. A. Ogot, "The Politics of Populism," in *Decolonization and Independence in Kenya, 1940–98*, ed. B. A. Ogot and W. R. Ochieng' (London: James Curry, 1995), 193, 198; Margaretta wa Gacheru, "Ngũgĩ wa Thiong'o Still Bitter over His Detention," interview, 1979, in *Ngũgĩ wa Thiong'o Speaks: Interviews with the Kenyan Writer*, ed. Richard Sander and Bernth Lindfors (Oxford: James Currey, 2006), 91; Ngũgĩ wa Thiong'o, *Detained: A Writer's Prison Diary* (Oxford: Heinemann Educational Books, 1981), 3.27, Appendix.

22. Ngũgĩ, *Detained*, ix, 5–6; Ngũgĩ wa Thiong'o, *Devil on the Cross* (Oxford: Heinemann Educational Books, 1982).

23. Berl Bernhard, interview by author, July 16, 2003, Washington, DC; Photograph by Franz Jantzen, *Collection of the Supreme Court of the United States*, March 19, 1993.

ACKNOWLEDGMENTS

The research for this book took me across three continents, and so I have accumulated three continents' worth of debts. This manuscript could not have been written without generous support from a number of places. The work began at the Law and Public Affairs Program in the Woodrow Wilson School at Princeton University, then under the directorship of Chris Eisgruber, with a semester's leave. As an Americanist writing about Africa, I needed to retool, and Jeffrey Herbst kindly allowed me to audit his course on African Development and Security. Later, I had a glorious month to write at the Rockefeller Study and Conference Center in Bellagio, Italy. Essential research funding came in the form of a Zumberge Award from the University of Southern California, and a Moody Grant from the Lyndon Baines Johnson Foundation. For support from USC Law School, I thank deans Matthew Spitzer, Edward McCaffery, and Robert Rasmussen. An indispensable final year of writing was made possible by a fellowship from the American Council of Learned Societies. I placed the finishing touches on the manuscript at the Institute for Advanced Study at Princeton, while also supported by a fellowship from the Guggenheim Foundation.

Several friends and colleagues of Thurgood Marshall, and others who played a part in his story, met with me or allowed me to interview them on the telephone. Without their help, this narrative would have been incomplete. I thank Berl Bernhard, William Coleman, John Hope Franklin, George Houser, Kenneth Jackson, John A. Jones, Michael Meltsner, the late Constance Baker Motley, James M. Nabrit III, William Taylor, and Ralph Winter. I am especially grateful to Mrs. Cecilia Marshall and Thurgood Marshall Jr., who were very generous with their time. Special thanks to Mrs. Marshall for permission to publish Thurgood Marshall's Draft Bill of Rights as an appendix to this book. Others who answered queries, large and small, gave me wise advice, and helped in other ways are David Anderson, Hunter Clark, Drew Days, Rachel Emannuel, Kevin Gaines, Elizabeth Garrett, Mark Graber, Jack Greenberg, Dennis Hutchinson, Makau Mutua, Henry Richardson, Dan Rodgers, Harry Scheiber, Margo Schlanger, and Mark Tushnet. For assistance in Kenya, I am grateful to the wonderful and resourceful Leah Kimathi.

Behind any work of history is usually a small army of archivists and librarians. All of the archivists and librarians I encountered while working on this book have been resourceful and patient, and some made crucial interventions: finding the unfindable book or suggesting a source that I hadn't thought of. I thank the staffs of Manuscripts and Archives Division, Library of Congress, Washington, DC; the National Archives and Records Service, College Park, Maryland; the National Archives of the United Kingdom, Kew, England; the Kenya National Archives; the Amistad Research Center in New Orleans, Louisiana; the Hoover Institute Library and Archive, Stanford, California; the John F. Kennedy Library, Boston, Massachusetts; the Lyndon Baines Johnson Library, Austin, Texas; the New York University Archives; and the Bentley Historical Library, Ann Arbor, Michigan. Special thanks to the LBJ Library for promptly handling my requests to review classified documents, enabling the release of newly declassified material in time. At the Walter P. Reuther

Library, Wayne State University, William LeFevre kindly provided me with materials from the Walter Reuther collection. Thanks also to Gary Faires at Lancaster House and to the staff at the Old Courthouse, St. Louis, Missouri. Thank you to Jennifer Carpenter of the Supreme Court of the United States, Curator's Office, who provided me with copies of photographs and to photographer Franz Jantzen for filling in the details. Marcia Tucker of the Historical Studies–Social Science Library, Institute for Advanced Study, was an indispensable resource during final editing. I thank every member of the library staff at the University of Southern California Law School, including Hazel Lord, Diana Jaque, Paul Moorman, Anahit Petrosyan, Renee Rastorfer, and Jessica Wimer. Leonard Wilson and other members of the USC IT staff solved computer mysteries so that I could continue my work.

There are no words to describe Susan Davis, my USC assistant. Never phased by a deadline or by long-distance requests, whether from Princeton, Bellagio or Nairobi, it is hard to imagine this project staying on track without her. I thank my students at USC and Harvard law schools, especially those who took my course Constitutional Politics in Africa, and my research assistants. Over the years, many students have helped with research, including Meredith Edelman, Joelle Epstein, Daniel Gillespie, Rocio Herrera, David Newman, Femi Oguntalo, Michael Okayo, Naseem Sagati, Zach Smith, Heather Weisser, and Winston Lin. Thanks to Washington University students Nick Nilce and Jamil Birdling for help with St. Louis sources.

I have benefited from many opportunities to speak about this project. I thank those who attended workshops and lectures for their questions, comments, and criticism, at University of California, Los Angeles, Law School and Department of Political Science; University of Chicago, Department of History; Columbia Law School; Cornell Law School; Drake Law School; Duke Law

School; George Washington Law School; Harvard Law School; University of Michigan Law School; New York University Law School; Northeastern Law School; Princeton University, Law and Public Affairs Program; Rockefeller Foundation Study and Conference Center, Bellagio; Rothermere American Institute, University of Oxford; Rutgers University Law School, Camden; Stanford Law School; USC Law School; Washington University Law School, St. Louis; William Mitchell College of Law; and the Department of History, Vanderbilt University. Special thanks to the editors of the *Duke Law Journal*, who hosted me in Durham as their annual speaker and published my first piece on this topic, "Working Toward Democracy: Thurgood Marshall and the Constitution of Kenya," *Duke Law Journal* 56 (December 2006).

Mark Tushnet, Thurgood Marshall's most insightful biographer, Linda Kerber, and Elaine Tyler May have offered indispensable support and endless inspiration. A number of colleagues and friends have offered the generous gift of their time. Rick Abel, Devon Carbado, Susan Carruthers, Ron Garet, Lani Guinier, Stanley Katz, Kevin Kruse, Ken Mack, Michael Meltsner, Martha Minow, Tiffany Patterson, A. W. Brian Simpson, Matthew Stephenson, and David Wilkins gave especially helpful comments on earlier papers. Margaret Burnham's skepticism about this project when acting as a commentator at a workshop was a gift. I am indebted to Diane Amann, James Campbell, Gary Gerstle, Peniel Joseph, Heather Schafroth, and Mark Tushnet who read all or parts of the book manuscript, offering valuable feedback and needed perspective. Extremely helpful and detailed comments from James Meriwether were facilitated by current political unrest in Kenya. In the country on a Fulbright, his university's closure gave him time for a close read of the manuscript. My editor at Oxford University Press, Tim Bent, gave his careful attention to every sentence. My literary agent, Sandra Dykstra, helped me focus the narrative. Thanks also to Dayne Poshusta and Christine Dahlin at Oxford, who shepherded the book through production. All errors, of course, are mine alone.

My greatest debt is to my family. My daughter, Alicia, who will be seventeen years old when this book is in print, spent half of her sixth grade year with me in Princeton, and tolerated other disruptions and absences. Alicia taught me the value of instant messaging during a summer when I was away for research in England. As the work on this project came to a close, in exchange for tickets to a rock concert, she proved to be a much better proofreader than her mother. My partner, the relentlessly supportive Bill Aitkenhead, provided more than the customary encouragement of a companion. When I wasn't sure how to pull together the resources for a leave to finish the book, Bill had a solution: I should move in with him! Little did he know that my entourage included not only a teenager, two cats, and a dog, but also more books and files than any home could comfortably accommodate. Then Bill found me the perfect birthday gift: a little office in the square in Sharon, Massachusetts, so I would have a quiet place to write. Even more important, he read every word, over and over. Needless to say, along the way he earned much more than his rightful spot on the dedication page.

INDEX

Page numbers in bold indicate photographs.